CIPS STUDY MATTERS

D0587294

ADVANCED DIPLOMA IN PROCUREMENT AND SUPPLY

COURSE BOOK

Sustainability in supply chains

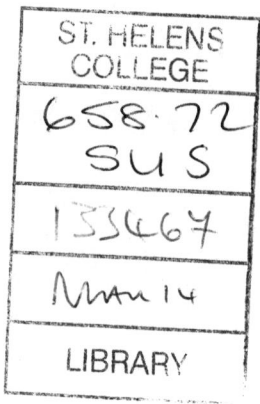

Printed and distributed by:

The Chartered Institute of Purchasing & Supply, Easton House, Easton on the Hill, Stamford, Lincolnshire PE9 3NZ
Tel: +44 (0) 1780 756 777
Fax: +44 (0) 1780 751 610
Email: info@cips.org
Website: www.cips.org

First edition December 2012

Contents

Preface

Welcome to your new Study Pack, consisting of two elements.

- A **Course Book** (the current volume). This provides detailed coverage of all topics specified in the unit content.
- A small-format volume of **Revision Notes.** Use your Revision Notes in the weeks leading up to your exam.

For a full explanation of how to use your new Study Pack, turn now to page xi. And good luck in your exams!

A note on style

Throughout your Study Packs you will find that we use the masculine form of personal pronouns. This convention is adopted purely for the sake of stylistic convenience – we just don't like saying 'he/she' all the time. Please don't think this reflects any kind of bias or prejudice.

December 2012

The Unit Content

The unit content is reproduced below, together with reference to the chapter in this Course Book where each topic is covered.

Unit purpose and aims

On completion of this unit, candidates will be able to understand approaches to help achieve sustainability.

This unit explores the concept and initiatives in sustainability which includes aspects of corporate social responsibility. It includes the impact on communities and society, environmental aspects of sourcing, ethical trading and working standards. The alignment of sustainable goals within supply chains has both global and local dimensions and is a developing area for organisational commitment, procedures, systems and practices.

Learning outcomes, assessment criteria and indicative content

Chapter

1.0 Understand the impact of sustainability in supply chains

1.1 Critically assess the main implications of sustainability in supply chains

• Definitions of aspects of sustainability such as corporate social responsibility, responsible procurement and environmental purchasing	1
• The reasons for the focus on sustainability	1
• The risks and rewards of sustainability	1
• The development of sustainable procurement policies	1

1.2 Critically assess the main drivers of globalisation in supply chains

• Use of STEEPLE analysis to explain the drivers of globalisation	2
• Competitive advantage through global sourcing	2
• Globalisation and low cost country sourcing	2

1.3 Critically assess the main cultural and social issues in supply chains

• Language and cultural barriers	2
• Labour standards and forced working	2
• Wages and social security payments	2
• Inequalities of workers	2
• Health and safety standards	2

1.4 Explain the potential conflicts that may arise between the needs of stakeholders in supply chains

• The profit motive and the search for low cost sourcing	2
• Demand management and the need for urgent orders	2
• Short-term commercial gains versus long-term availability of supplies	2

How to Use Your Study Pack

Organising your study

'Organising' is the key word: unless you are a very exceptional student, you will find a haphazard approach is insufficient, particularly if you are having to combine study with the demands of a full-time job.

A good starting point is to timetable your studies, in broad terms, between now and the date of the examination. How many subjects are you attempting? How many chapters are there in the Course Book for each subject? Now do the sums: how many days/weeks do you have for each chapter to be studied?

Remember:

- Not every week can be regarded as a study week – you may be going on holiday, for example, or there may be weeks when the demands of your job are particularly heavy. If these can be foreseen, you should allow for them in your timetabling.
- You also need a period leading up to the exam in which you will revise and practise what you have learned.

Once you have done the calculations, make a week-by-week timetable for yourself for each paper, allowing for study and revision of the entire unit content between now and the date of the exams.

Getting started

Aim to find a quiet and undisturbed location for your study, and plan as far as possible to use the same period each day. Getting into a routine helps avoid wasting time. Make sure you have all the materials you need before you begin – keep interruptions to a minimum.

Using the Course Book

You should refer to the Course Book to the extent that you need it.

- If you are a newcomer to the subject, you will probably need to read through the Course Book quite thoroughly. This will be the case for most students.
- If some areas are already familiar to you – either through earlier studies or through your practical work experience – you may choose to skip sections of the Course Book.

The content of the Course Book

This Course Book has been designed to give detailed coverage of every topic in the unit content. As you will see from pages vii–ix, each topic mentioned in the unit content is dealt with in a chapter of the Course Book. For the most part the order of the Course Book follows the order of the unit content closely, though departures from this principle have occasionally been made in the interest of a logical learning order.

Each chapter begins with a reference to the assessment criteria and indicative content to be covered in the chapter. Each chapter is divided into sections, listed in the introduction to the chapter, and for the most part being actual captions from the unit content.

All of this enables you to monitor your progress through the unit content very easily and provides reassurance that you are tackling every subject that is examinable.

Each chapter contains the following features.

- Introduction, setting out the main topics to be covered
- Clear coverage of each topic in a concise and approachable format
- A chapter summary
- Self-test questions

The study phase

For each chapter you should begin by glancing at the main headings (listed at the start of the chapter). Then read fairly rapidly through the body of the text to absorb the main points. If it's there in the text, you can be sure it's there for a reason, so try not to skip unless the topic is one you are familiar with already.

Then return to the beginning of the chapter to start a more careful reading. You may want to take brief notes as you go along, but bear in mind that you already have your Revision Notes – there is no point in duplicating what you can find there.

Test your recall and understanding of the material by attempting the self-test questions. These are accompanied by cross-references to paragraphs where you can check your answers and refresh your memory.

The revision phase

Your approach to revision should be methodical and you should aim to tackle each main area of the unit content in turn. Read carefully through your Revision Notes. Check back to your Course Book if there are areas where you cannot recall the subject matter clearly. Then do some question practice. The CIPS website contains many past exam questions. You should aim to identify those that are suitable for the unit you are studying.

Additional reading

Your Course Book provides you with the key information needed for each module but CIPS strongly advocates reading as widely as possible to augment and reinforce your understanding. CIPS produces an official reading list of books, which can be downloaded from the bookshop area of the CIPS website.

To help you, we have identified one essential textbook for each subject. We recommend you read this for additional information. The essential textbook for this unit is *The Sustainable Procurement Guide: Procuring Sustainably Using BS 8903* by Cathy Berry.

CHAPTER 1

Introduction to Sustainability

Assessment criteria and indicative content

 Critically assess the main implications of sustainability in supply chains

- Definitions of aspects of sustainability such as corporate social responsibility, responsible procurement and environmental purchasing
- The reasons for the focus on sustainability
- The risks and rewards of sustainability
- The development of sustainable procurement policies

Section headings

1 The background to sustainability
2 Aspects of sustainability
3 Drivers for sustainability
4 Risks and rewards of sustainability
5 Developing and implementing sustainable procurement policy

Introduction

This first section of the syllabus sets the context for your study of sustainability with an overview of the main implications of sustainability for supply chains.

In this chapter we start by defining sustainability and the related concepts of sustainable development and sustainable procurement. We then go on to define the three main 'aspects' commonly identified with sustainability: the economic context, the environmental context (the focus of 'environmental purchasing') and the social context (the focus of 'responsible procurement'). We also consider the related concepts of the Triple Bottom Line (Profit, Planet and People) and corporate social responsibility (or CSR).

We look at some of the main drivers for sustainability: factors in the internal and external environments of organisations that have brought heightened focus on sustainability issues.

We present the business case for sustainability: considering both its rewards and benefits for organisations (and their supply chains and secondary stakeholders) and its risks and costs.

Finally, we look in overview at some of the main processes and factors in successfully developing and implementing corporate sustainable procurement policies.

1   The background to sustainability

The emerging concept of sustainability

1.1   'Sustainability' basically means the ability of an activity to be maintained (sustained or 'kept up') at a similar level into the future. More specifically, in the present context, it means ensuring that actions taken today do not limit or jeopardise our plans or quality of life in the future. The British Standards Institution's *Sustainable Procurement Guide* (BIP 2203) defines it as taking 'a longer-term view when making decisions, to ensure that meeting our own needs does not compromise the needs of others both today and for future generations.'

1.2   The concept of sustainability arguably first emerged into mainstream discourse in 1972, during the United Nations Conference on the Human Environment. At a time when serious environmental concerns were beginning to be raised in relation to industrial development and practices (on issues such as deforestation, pollution and the use of toxic pesticides, for example), conference delegates debated which was more important: economic development or environmental protection? A series of high-profile environmental disasters (such as the Exxon Valdez oil spill and the Chernobyl nuclear reactor explosion) subsequently raised the public and political profile of environmental issues.

1.3   At the same time, issues of social justice also became a matter of widespread concern, with a particular focus on the apartheid (racial segregation) policies of South Africa, which attracted popular activism and economic sanctions. Public bodies, in particular, were urged to be 'socially responsible' and 'ethical' in their investments, in order to bring financial pressure to bear on companies to recognise issues such as human rights, worker rights and equal opportunity.

1.4   Through its discussions, the UN had recognised that economic development and environmental protection were inextricably linked – and potentially, mutually reinforcing. Economic development would be required to raise living and working conditions, and to support investment in environmental conservation and viable technologies. At the same time, any attempt to improve human wellbeing that threatened the environment was doomed to failure in the long run – because the depletion of resources, the degradation of environments and the pollution of air and water (for example) would impact on the wellbeing and development potential of future generations.

1.5   The UN therefore appointed a think-tank, under the chairmanship of Gro Harlem Brundtland, to come up with strategies to enable continuing economic development without threatening the environment. The Brundtland Commission focused on the need to develop a stable relationship between human activity and the natural world, which would not reduce the prospects of future generations to enjoy a quality of life at least as good as that of the present generation. The Brundtland Commission's report, *Our Common Future,* was published in 1987, and contained a general definition of **sustainable development** which is still widely used:

'Development that meets the needs of the present without compromising the ability of future generations to meet their own needs.'

1.6   These ideas were refined by the 1992 Rio Declaration on Environment and Development, in which social justice and human rights issues (such as peace, poverty, child labour, the role of women and the plight of indigenous peoples) were explicitly added to the mix.

1.7   This three-dimensional (economic-environmental-social) view of sustainability subsequently became widely adopted, and in 1997, the term 'triple bottom line' (TBL) was coined by John Elkington to highlight the need for nations and organisations to measure their performance in all three areas.

1.8   In recent years, these three dimensions have formed a framework for a range of issues broadly related to business ethics and corporate social responsibility, including corporate governance, fair trade, labour relations, diversity, transparency – and an increasing number of existing and emerging environmental concerns: climate change, renewable energy, pollution, genetic modification and so on. They have been variously expressed as:

- Profit (economic performance), People (social sustainability) and Planet (environmental sustainability)
- Economics, Environment and Equity (social justice)
- Resources (the wise use and management of economic and natural resources) and Respect (for people and other living things).

Sustainable development

1.9 'Development' is a shorthand term for a range of social, economic, industrial and technological activity, with the broad aim of bettering conditions for human life. Sustainable development is therefore development activity that can be sustained, or kept up, over the long term; that does not undermine or put at risk the conditions and resources required to preserve wellbeing into future.

1.10 According to the Brundtland Commission, for development to be sustainable, it must satisfy the following criteria.

- *Long-term decision-making*. Sustainable development requires the use of a long-term horizon for decision making, in which society pursues long-term aspirations (and recognises the long-term impacts and consequences of its actions), rather than making short-term, reactive responses to problems.
- *Interdependence*. As outlined above, sustainable development recognises the interdependence of economic, environmental, and social wellbeing. It promotes actions designed to expand economic opportunity, improve environmental quality and increase social wellbeing.
- *Participation and transparency*. Sustainable development depends on decision-making that is inclusive, participatory, and transparent. It recognises the importance of process in decision-making and implementation, including the consultation and involvement of stakeholders.
- *Equity*. Sustainable development promotes equity between generations and among different groups in society, aiming to reduce disparities in access to the benefits (and sharing of the risks and costs) of development.
- *Proactive prevention*. Sustainable development is anticipatory: it promotes efforts to prevent problems and minimise risks as the first course of action.

1.11 You should already be able to see how the basic principles of sustainable development apply directly to the activity of business organisations – and other social stakeholders, such as governments, regulatory bodies, academic and scientific institutions and public interest groups (NGOs).

1.12 William Blackburn (*The Sustainability Handbook*) argues that the aim of sustainability or sustainable development from an organisation's perspective is 'long-term wellbeing, for society as a whole, as well as for itself.' Note that this emphasises the place of economic performance within the concerns of sustainability: the continuing financial viability of organisations supports human and social wellbeing, by creating and maintaining employment, and stimulating investment. Meanwhile, human and social wellbeing supports organisational survival, by maintaining the flow of skilled and willing labour, consumer spending and investment. We will return to this idea as we make the business case for sustainability.

Sustainable consumption and production (SCP)

1.13 Economic systems depend on two basic processes: demand (arising from the consumption of goods and services) and supply (arising from the production of goods and services). For an industrialised society to be sustainable, it must therefore seek to attain the economic, environmental and social sustainability of both consumption (or demand-side processes) and production (or supply-side processes). 'Sustainable consumption and production' (SCP) is a term used to describe this aspect of sustainable development.

1.14 The term **production** can be used to describe a wide range of activities undertaken in the process of transforming raw materials, resources and other inputs into goods and services, including: product and service design; procurement and supply; logistics; resource consumption; extraction, processing, manufacturing, assembly or service delivery; waste management; technology management; facilities management; human resource management; outsourcing and offshoring of production; and so on.

1.15 Each of these activities has the potential to create negative environmental and social impacts. Some examples of key sustainability concerns include the need to:

- Minimise environmental pollution, damage and degradation from industrial activity
- Manage waste products (often referred to as the 3Rs: reduction, re-use, recycling) from production, packaging and end-of-life products
- Reduce greenhouse gas (GHG) emissions, or reduce the 'carbon footprint' of organisational activity
- Minimise the use of non-renewable materials and resources, and develop design specifications using renewable, recyclable, clean or sustainably produced materials
- Design products which are environmentally-friendly in their materials, production processes, consumption and end-of-life disposal
- Design or adapt production processes to be environmentally 'clean', resource-efficient and safe for workers
- Minimise negative impacts on communities and social amenities from business activity (eg traffic congestion, noise, dirt, loss of employment)
- Ensure the ethical and responsible treatment of labour, supply chains and communities (eg labour conditions, health and safety standards, fair trading, and stakeholder participation in development)
- Build and manage sustainable production capacity, through education, training, environmental management systems, monitoring and reporting and so on.

1.16 Sustainable **consumption** is closely linked to sustainable production.

- Producers are themselves consumers of labour, materials, components, products and services: sustainable production implies the sustainable procurement and use of these resources. 'Improving production efficiencies means using less resources; this saves money and boosts competitiveness. Organisations also need to be concerned about how and where things are made to ensure that neither the environment nor the communities producing their goods and services are being exploited, therefore ensuring the reputation of the organisation is not put at risk.' (BSI *Sustainable Procurement Guide*)
- Sustainable consumption imposes a responsibility on producers to think beyond the sustainability of their own inputs and processes, to how their *outputs* will be used, maintained and disposed of – so that sustainable production actively supports sustainable consumption (eg by supporting recycling and safe end-of-life disposal).
- It is a key strand of the strategy of governments and pressure groups (and corporations already committed to sustainability) to educate and motivate *consumers* to engage in sustainable consumption, in order to create a demand-side stimulus for sustainable production. As we will see later, some of the main pressures for corporate sustainability come from increasing consumer demand for sustainable brands, the reputational capital available from developing them – and the reputational risk of *not* developing them!

1.17 A wide variety of published and online guidance is now available for consumers, to help them make 'green' and ethical choices and lifestyle changes. In addition, product labelling, international standards certification, and product endorsement by pressure groups provide consumers with information on the sustainability of particular products and brands.

1.18 Examples of sustainable consumption which can be applied by organisations (as well as individual consumers) include the following.

- Buying energy efficient equipment and appliances (eg as identified by certified energy efficiency rating systems) and reducing energy consumption (eg by raising awareness and switching off appliances not in use)
- Reducing unnecessary transport mileage, fuel usage and carbon emissions (eg using public transport or cycling, buying fuel-efficient and clean-fuel vehicles, telecommuting, reducing unnecessary air travel)
- Re-using and recycling, and purchasing re-usable, recyclable and biodegradable products, and products with recyclable (and ideally, less) packaging. (Waste plastic bags are a major environmental problem, for example, and many countries now impose taxes, fines or outright bans on their use.)
- Purchasing local, seasonal materials and produce (to minimise transport miles, a major contributor to GHG emissions)
- Carbon 'offsetting': compensating for domestic or corporate carbon emissions, if they cannot be reduced, by purchasing 'offsets' (or 'carbon credits') on the carbon credit market, or independently investing in renewable energy, energy efficiency, reforestation and other carbon-reducing projects. (This is generally regarded as a last resort.)
- Buying ethically sourced and produced goods (eg cosmetics not tested on animals, and certified Fair Trade products which guarantee the ethical treatment of labour and suppliers). This is a major trend, with increasing consumer demand for Fair Trade cotton, coffee, tea and chocolate brands, among others: we will discuss it in detail in Chapter 3.
- Using local, small and diverse suppliers where possible (to support communities and equal opportunity, and to reduce transport miles)
- Consuming less. This is a controversial area, since – understandably from the point of view of producers – would-be sustainable consumers are more often urged to buy more environmentally friendly or ethical products than actually to buy less 'stuff' altogether... Nevertheless, consumption may be reduced without jeopardising the economic sustainability of producers: for example, by placing a premium on durability, 'less-goes-further' and so on.

Sustainable procurement

1.19 As we will see in the next section of this chapter, various terms are used to discuss this topic, including responsible procurement, ethical procurement and environmental procurement (or 'green' procurement). The term 'sustainable procurement', however, emphasises the full spectrum of economic, environmental and social criteria.

1.20 Many bodies (including CIPS) have adopted the definition of sustainable procurement used by the UK Sustainable Procurement Task Force (*Procuring the Future*).

'A process whereby organisations meet their needs for goods, services, works and utilities in a way that achieves value for money on a whole-life basis in terms of generating benefits not only to the organisation, but also to society and the economy, whilst minimising damage to the environment.'

1.21 Sustainable procurement is therefore an approach that takes economic, environmental and social sustainability into account when making purchasing decisions. It's about looking at what purchased items are made of, where they come from, how they are made and by whom, how they are procured, how they will be used – and whether they are in fact necessary. Here are some questions to ask.

- Does procurement meet the present needs of the organisation and its stakeholders, without compromising the ability to continue to do so in future – eg by depleting resources or undermining trading or employment relationships?
- Does procurement protect or enhance the economic security of the organisation (by adding value, controlling costs, securing supply continuity and so on), without negative environmental or social impacts?
- Does procurement comply with the organisation's corporate social responsibility values, and

international standards, in regard to ethical issues such as environmental protection, poverty eradication, international equity in the distribution of resources, labour conditions and human rights?

1.22 The British Standards Institution *Sustainable Procurement Guide* argues that, for buyers:

'Purchasing goods, works and services, efficiently, with minimum risk and at the best possible value, remain central elements of the job. However, buyers must now also consider "value" in a broader way. They must also consider the additional risks (and opportunities), including the ethical, social and environmental impacts of what they buy. This goes even further. Buyers must also consider the impacts on the supply chain of *how* they buy and operate. Shortening lead times and purchase prices may seem like a good business strategy, but not at the expense of labour standards further down the supply chain or the risk to your reputation due to worker exploitation.'

1.23 The Guide suggests four main aims for sustainable procurement.

- To minimise negative impacts of goods, works or services (eg on health and wellbeing, communities or the environment) across their lifecycle and through the supply chain
- To minimise demand for non-renewable resources (eg by reducing purchases, purchasing recycled products or using resource-efficient processes)
- To ensure that fair contract prices and terms are applied and respected, *at least* meeting minimum ethical, human rights and employment standards
- To promote diversity and equality throughout the supply chain. Supply chains should aim to reflect the diversity and demographics of the societies that they touch and should provide opportunities for small and medium-sized businesses (SMEs) and voluntary sector organisations. Sustainable procurement should also support training and skills development. In summary, sustainable procurement should attempt to minimise negative outcomes and promote positive outcomes for the economy, environment and society.

1.24 Table 1.1 summarises some of procurement's potential value-adding contributions in each area of sustainability.

Table 1.1 *Potential for procurement to add value through sustainability*

Profit: adding economic value	Securing value for money Effective investment appraisal and capital purchasing Cost management and budgetary control Added value (through sourcing efficiencies, supplier involvement, quality improvement) Ethical trading to support the long-term financial viability of suppliers and supply markets (including sustainable pricing, ethical tendering and negotiation, payment on time)
Planet: adding environmental value	Input to design and specification of green products and services Sourcing of green materials and resources Green sourcing, including selection, management and development of suppliers with environmental capability and commitment Reducing the waste of resources throughout the sourcing cycle Managing logistics (including reverse logistics) to minimise waste, pollution, GHG emissions and environmental impacts (and to support re-use, recycling and safe disposal)
People: adding social value	Encouraging diversity in the purchasing team and among suppliers Monitoring supplier practices to ensure observance of human rights and labour standards (eg re slavery, child labour, conditions of work, health and safety, equal opportunity) Input to health and safety of products and services (design, specification, supplier quality management) Fair and ethical trading (fair pricing, ethical use of power, ethical business practices) Local and small-business sourcing

2 Aspects of sustainability

2.1 Sustainable procurement (the phrase generally used by CIPS) goes by many different names, according to the aspects prioritised: 'green procurement', 'environmental procurement', 'affirmative procurement', 'responsible procurement', 'socially responsible procurement' – and so on.

2.2 Some definitions clearly focus primarily on environmental concerns, although social aspects are gaining prominence in the business-focused literature, particularly because of growing awareness of the reputational risk faced by organisations which ignore issues such as child labour or enforced labour, and workforce or supplier exploitation in their supply chains. In addition, global financial crisis has renewed the former emphasis on economic and financial viability concerns: maintaining profitability to support corporate survival and employment, while avoiding transferring economic stress and risk to vulnerable supply chains (as an issue both of ethics or social responsibility *and* supply security).

Corporate social responsibility (CSR)

2.3 The CIPS Practice Guide on CSR states that: 'It is an increasingly popular view that it is no longer acceptable that an organisation continues to operate in isolation without considerations of its environment and its stakeholders.' There is increasing demand from Non Governmental Organisations (NGOs), stakeholder activists and consumers for organisations to be accountable for their impacts on their stakeholders. There has also been a broad recognition by organisations that such accountability is not only increasingly required to secure their legitimacy and 'licence to operate', but that it can be turned to the positive benefit of the organisation in many ways.

2.4 The term 'corporate social responsibility' is generally used to describe a wide range of obligations that an organisation may feel it has towards its secondary stakeholders, or the society in which it operates. The European Commission defines CSR as 'the concept whereby companies integrate social and environmental concerns in their business operations and in their interaction with their stakeholders on a voluntary basis.'

2.5 One CIPS examiner has written that: 'CSR means the commitment to systematic consideration of the environmental, social and cultural aspects of an organisation's operations. This includes the key issues of sustainability, human rights, labour and community relations, and supplier and customer relations beyond legal obligations. The objective [is] to create long-term business value and contribute to improving the social conditions of the people affected by our operations.'

2.6 The term 'corporate social responsibility' is often used interchangeably with 'sustainability' (although sustainability adds a distinctive focus on the wellbeing of future generations), and covers the same broad range of economic, social and environmental issues. CIPS recognises ten key CSR issues, which are most relevant to supply chains: environmental responsibility, human rights, equal opportunities, diversity, corporate governance, sustainability, impact on society, ethics and ethical trading, biodiversity, and community involvement.

2.7 We will discuss some of these issues (as 'sustainability' issues) in Chapter 2. The key point about CSR, in this context, is that for many corporations, it has already begun to establish a cultural and strategic platform for the development of sustainable procurement. Sustainable procurement policies will often be prompted by, and aligned with, corporate-level CSR policies.

EXAMPLE: MARKS & SPENCER'S 'PLAN A'

According to a 2006 survey commissioned by UK retailer Marks & Spencer, 90% of consumers think retailers should ensure their products are manufactured in a fair and humane way – and 31% said these considerations had actively influenced a purchase decision. In 2007, M & S launched a cutting-edge corporate social responsibility programme called 'Plan A' (so called because

'There is no Plan B'), built on five 'pillars' of CSR, reflecting a spectrum of sustainability commitments.

- **Climate change:** eg reducing energy-related CO2 emissions from stores and offices; supporting farmers who are investing in small-scale renewable energy production; piloting 'eco-stores'; monitoring the carbon footprint of the food business; and encouraging consumers in more eco-friendly washing of clothing products.
- **Waste:** eg engaging customers in reducing plastic bag usage and recycling clothing; reducing packaging; increasing use of recycled materials; improving recycling of construction waste and coat hangers. (The target is to send zero waste to landfill.)
- **Sustainable raw materials:** eg promoting animal welfare in fashion and food production; increasing use of Fair Trade and organic cotton and recycled polyester; increasing sales of organic food.
- **Fair partner:** eg extended use of Fair Trade certified products; supporting local farmers; raising money in the community for charitable projects; updating commitments on labour standards and working with overseas suppliers to help them identify and share best practice.
- **Health:** eg removing artificial colourings and flavourings from 99% of food products; reducing salt levels and introducing front-of-pack Food Standards Agency 'traffic lights' to identify salt levels; and training employees as 'healthy eating assistants'.

Note how M & S is involving stakeholders, including employees, suppliers and customers (using 'pledges' of commitment to each of the five pillars) in Plan A. The programme therefore addresses sustainable production, procurement (upstream activity involving the supply chain) and consumption (downstream activity involving consumers).

2.8 From a CIPS perspective, CSR implicitly requires sustainable procurement. 'In the midst of the ongoing debate on how best to achieve good social and environmental performance, supply chains are becoming a defining factor. Few could have missed the furore that has erupted over unethical practices within global supply chains, such as child labour and exploitation of migrant workers, for example. However, while the supply chain does bring risks, it also brings opportunities: for example, organisations are working with suppliers to identify new energy sources, new power sources for vehicles and an increasing emphasis on minimal environmental footprints. These changes shake out markets and create opportunities in the supply chain.'

2.9 For our present purposes, therefore, it is sufficient to note that CSR is a significant driver and enabler of sustainable procurement policies and initiatives in the marketplace as a whole – and within a given organisation.

Environmental purchasing

2.10 As one of the early drivers of the sustainability agenda, 'green' or environmental procurement was once seen as a standalone issue, embracing themes such as the following.

- Mitigating overexploitation of, or damage to, scarce and non-renewable resources (eg by ensuring that inputs are bought from certified sustainable sources, and ensuring that processes are non-polluting and resource-efficient)
- Addressing climate change (eg by reducing carbon emissions arising from logistics and manufacture throughout the supply chain)
- Minimising waste (eg by challenging demand, increasing the use of recycled materials, reducing packaging, and designing products for disassembly, re-use, recycling or safe disposal at the end of life)
- Implementing supplier selection, development and management processes to ensure that supply chains have adequate (and continually increasing) capability to comply with environmental standards
- Acting as the interface between suppliers and product development and design departments, to encourage knowledge-sharing, research and innovation for 'greener' product specifications and more collaborative processes
- Developing and presenting the business case for 'green' inputs, purchases and processes, through techniques such as whole life costing and value definition, and sustainability risk assessment.

2.11 However, environmental purchasing is now generally regarded as part of a wider sustainable procurement approach. 'Environmentally friendly' products and supply chains are increasingly demanded by consumers, shareholders and investors, employees and pressure groups – as well as being the focus of legislation and government policy (eg in areas such as the disposal of electronic and electrical waste, and the reduction of carbon emissions).

2.12 The British Standards Institution notes that: 'the scope of green procurement is broad, and can vary from buying stationery from recycled sources to procuring buildings with green roofs that enhance the biodiversity of the area, add insulation to reduce heating in the winter and reduce the need for cooling in summer through the evaporative cooling effect of plants (which also absorb carbon).' We will discuss a range of 'green' issues for procurement in Chapter 2.

Responsible procurement

2.13 The term 'responsible procurement' is sometimes used to describe 'procurement practices that combine commercial considerations with social, labour and environmental performance' (Responsible Purchasing Initiative, *Taking the Lead*): in other words, it may be synonymous with 'sustainable procurement'.

2.14 However, terms such as 'responsible procurement' (along with 'social responsibility' and 'corporate citizenship') may also be used to refer more specifically to the *social* dimension of sustainability, addressing issues such as labour relations and working conditions, community involvement, social inclusion and diversity, social justice, fair trading, ethical conduct, the responsible use of market power, and human rights – especially in developing country supply markets.

- *Developed countries* are industrialised countries, generally characterised by high levels of industrialisation, technological development, educational attainment, health standards and personal incomes.
- *Developing countries* are those countries in the process of industrialisation, with low or middle national income (as defined by the World Bank), and typically with lower levels of technological development and educational attainment and lower living standards. Such countries are found in parts of Africa, Asia, Eastern Europe and South America.

2.15 Responsible procurement may thus be seen as a component of sustainable procurement (Responsible Purchasing Initiative, *Win/Win: Achieving Sustainable Procurement with the Developing World*). 'Responsible purchasing, in the context of buying from developing countries, refers... to purchasing processes which result in improvements to the lives of workers and farmers in developing countries who contribute to supply chains, achieving at least minimum working conditions as defined by the International Labour Organization.'

2.16 The Responsible Purchasing Initiative consultation document *Buying Matters* similarly focuses on the responsibilities purchasing organisations may be perceived to have towards globalised supply chains. 'Purchasing can have a huge impact on suppliers, especially in developing countries... Millions of people in developing countries depend on international buyers for their livelihoods. Many companies recognise the responsibility this gives them, and have taken steps to stop exploitative practices in their supply chains.... If companies take specific steps to purchase in a responsible way, working conditions could be improved, workers' rights respected, small [producers'] rights to a livelihood could be realised and environmental damage and costs could be reduced.'

2.17 Aspects of responsible procurement highlighted by the *Buying Matters* report are summarised in Table 1.2. We will discuss these issues in more detail in Chapter 2.

Table 1.2 *Elements of responsible purchasing*

ELEMENT	AIM
Good relationships with suppliers	Buyers aim for long-term, stable, trust-based, risk-sharing relationships
Clear, timely communication	Suppliers know the terms of trade which govern the relationship; receive clear communications about buyer expectations; and are able to feed back on their own needs, in a two-way relationship
Sustainable prices	Prices paid should allow both supplier and buyer to benefit from the relationship and should enable those further along the chain to also benefit from a price which adequately covers the costs of production
Clear lead-times and payments	Suppliers should have clear, consistent and transparent payment terms and a comprehensive order timetable, including when final specification details for the order will be placed and when delivery is expected.
Respect for human and labour rights in the supply chain	Buyers and suppliers understand and work towards minimum human and labour rights standards. Buyers give preference to suppliers who demonstrate improving social and environmental conditions. Buyers manage their own practices to enable suppliers to observe these standards.
Support for small-scale producers and homeworkers	The percentage of products bought from smallholders, homeworkers, democratic co-operatives and disadvantaged areas does not unintentionally change.

2.18 As recently as a couple of decades ago, corporate social responsibility was generally focused on basic issues such as the health and safety of an organisation's own workforce and first-tier suppliers. However, the British Standards Institution argues that an organisation's social procurement responsibilities can extend to all the individuals and communities involved in, or affected by, the operations of its supply chains. 'We operate in an increasingly globalised market; supply chains can be long and complex and organisations are recognising that they must take adequate measures to ensure socially responsible business practices throughout these.' *(BSI Sustainable Procurement Guide)*

2.19 *Taking the Lead* emphasises that 'it is [up to] the purchasing organisation to select and develop the social, labour and environmental standards they expect of their supply base. As a minimum, a purchasing organisation would be expected to source from suppliers meeting the law of the country of production, as well as enabling the achievement of minimum internationally agreed labour standards, as set out by the International Labour Organization.'

EXAMPLE: IKEA GROUP

'Low prices are the cornerstone of the IKEA vision and our business idea – but not at any price. The IKEA vision is to create a better everyday life for our customers, co-workers and the people who produce our products. Consequently, low prices at IKEA must not be achieved at the expense of people or the environment. That is a condition for doing good business.'

The group's corporate social responsibility statement (*People and the Environment*) covers commitments to:

- Product safety (for the environment and human health)
- Economy in the use of resources (minimising use of materials, designing for disassembly)
- Sourcing wood from sustainably managed forests, and cotton from sustainable sources; and partnering with the World Wildlife Fund in advocacy and supplier support for sustainable management
- Serving and selling certified Fair Trade coffee
- Using long-term supplier relationships and supplier development programmes to ensure that products are 'manufactured under acceptable working conditions by suppliers who take responsibility for the environment'
- A code of conduct (The IKEA Way on purchasing home furnishing products: IWAY) which specifies the minimum requirements placed on suppliers and describes what they can expect in return. IWAY requirements include: compliance with national legislation; no forced or child labour; no discrimination; payment of at least the minimum wage and

compensation for overtime; a safe and healthy working environment; and responsibility for waste, emissions and the handling of chemicals.

- **The IKEA Social Initiative, partnering with Unicef and Save the Children to support children in developing countries (including the abolition of child labour)**
- **Working to reduce carbon emissions from its operations: optimising packaging solutions; transporting goods with the least possible environmental impact; cutting electricity consumption and reducing reliance on fossil fuels; partnering with WWF to create a casebook of best practice for suppliers.**

The economic context

2.20 We will be looking in detail at the environmental and social issues in global supply chains, in Chapter 2. However, it may be worth drawing attention briefly to the importance of the *economic* perspective on sustainable procurement. The economic aspect of sustainability:

- Requires a sound 'business case' for sustainability, recognising that continuing financial viability and stability is the foundation of all other sustainability efforts
- Encourages the use of more resource-efficient goods, services and processes
- Encourages purchasers to evaluate cost performance and value over the whole life of a contract (rather than focusing on up-front costs or price)
- Encourages purchasers to pursue the elimination of wastes throughout the supply chain (while recognising the pressures, vulnerabilities and potential sustainability issues created by excessively lean supply)
- Recognises the need to drive job creation, develop new markets and support innovation (eg by creating markets for recycled products)
- Recognises that sustainable markets and supply chains are essential for long-term growth, and that these are supported by responsible supply chain practices that ensure fair wages, working conditions and contract terms.

3 Drivers for sustainability

3.1 We have already suggested some of the main reasons for the increasing focus on sustainability, in terms of factors such as: growing awareness of the potential negative impacts of international supply chains; growing political, public and activist pressure for greater corporate responsibility and accountability; and growing awareness of the operational, financial and reputational risks of unsustainable business practices.

3.2 It may be helpful to distinguish between two different types of support factors for sustainability.

- *Drivers* are forces which create pressure to develop and implement sustainable procurement strategies (eg by creating opportunities or threats which must be addressed)
- *Enablers* are 'ecological' or support factors which create conditions favourable to the effective and efficient introduction, implementation and acceptance of sustainable procurement strategies.

3.3 Drivers *impel* action for sustainable procurement, which enablers serve to *facilitate*. So, for example, factors such as resource scarcity, legislation, reputational risk and opportunity, and stakeholder pressure are likely to drive organisational measures for sustainability. Factors such as innovation capabilities, established risk management processes, a sustainability-educated management, the availability of sustainable resources and the development of industry-wide sustainability standards are likely to support such measures.

Reasons for the focus on sustainability

3.4 John Elkington (*Cannibals with Forks: Triple Bottom Line of 21ˢᵗ Century Business, 1999)* suggested a number of key drivers for sustainability.

- *Values.* There has been a global shift in societal values towards environmental and social concerns, raising governmental, public and pressure group vigilance in regard to the impacts of global business.
- *Markets.* With increased global competition, growing numbers of companies are finding themselves challenged by customers and financial markets, regarding their sustainability credentials.
- *Transparency.* Information on companies' sustainability plans and activities is increasingly demanded by governments, regulators, investors and consumers.
- *Lifecycle technology.* Stakeholder expectations now span whole business processes, supply chains and product lifecycles. Sustainability must be managed not just in product design and manufacture, but through supply, finance, usage, reverse logistics, end-of-life disposal and so on.
- *Partnerships.* There is an increasing degree of collaboration in sustainability initiatives, including industry alliances (for best practice sharing and standard setting) and partnerships with public and third-sector organisations (such as Greenpeace or Traidcraft), which are able to provide information, guidance, accountability, resources and credibility.
- *Corporate governance.* In the USA the Sarbanes-Oxley Act and in the UK The Stock Exchange Combined Code have reflected public demand for sounder governance of corporations. What is a business for? Who should have a say in how it is run? What is the appropriate balance between the interests of shareholders and other stakeholders?

3.5 The Responsible Purchasing Initiative report *Taking the Lead* emphasises that procurement is particularly 'in the spotlight'. 'Trading relationships and the behaviour of buying organisations influence the flow and allocation of economic resources and have a very significant impact, whether direct or indirect, on poverty, social and environmental conditions and the development of country economies... Purchasing professionals are directly responsible for the selection of their suppliers and whether the relationships they develop with these suppliers result in exploitation, or in the improvement of social, labour and environmental conditions to agreed standards.'

3.6 Other important reasons for the focus on sustainability may be broadly classified as in Table 1.3.

Table 1.3 *Some general drivers for the focus on sustainability*

Values and awareness	Increasing transparency and visibility (eg through global media and the internet and social and environmental activism) has raised awareness of the fact that vulnerable suppliers are open to exploitation, especially in global supply chains, and that the environmental impact of production and consumption is no longer sustainable. Societal attitudes and values create media, public, labour and consumer focus on sustainability.
Accountability	Increasing external scrutiny, and investor and consumer expectations, are shaping the political and corporate agenda. Sustainability is an issue of corporate governance and accountability.
Stakeholder pressures	Both internal stakeholders (such as employees) and external stakeholders (including suppliers, customers, regulatory bodies, pressure groups and host communities) have expectations and concerns in regard to sustainability issues. Addressing these effectively is essential to protect reputation, maintain dialogue, secure co-operation (or minimise resistance) and attract and retain resources (including stakeholder skills and knowledge).
Resource scarcity	The depletion of scarce and non-renewable resources, and resulting rising commodity and energy costs, creating strong pressures for sustainability. Resource issues include fossil fuel depletion, water management, deforestation and loss of biodiversity.
Financial pressures	Despite the perception that sustainability imposes extra costs, it can deliver cost savings eg through: improved resource efficiency; reduced accidents and stoppages; challenging unnecessary demand and over-specification; collaborative supply chain waste reduction; reduced end-of-life disposal costs; and securing the long-term health of the supply chain (maintaining competitiveness and security of supply). Sustainable products may also bear a price premium among committed consumers.

Continued . . .

Marketing and competitive pressures	Competitive advantage and market share can be enhanced by: meeting market demand for sustainable goods, works and services; enhancing corporate image, reputation and brand; differentiating the organisation from competitors; attracting and retaining high-quality staff, suppliers and industry allies; stimulating supply chain innovation; and keeping up with competitors who are doing any or all of these things. Conversely, of course, there may be a loss of market demand for unsustainable products and services.
Risk	All organisations must proactively identify their key business risks and vulnerabilities, and ensure that processes and controls are in place to address them. 'The key question is to what extent buying organisations, particularly in an increasingly globalised marketplace, are exposing themselves to risk by not understanding their impact and inadvertently accentuating inequality or damaging fragile social, economic and environmental resources' (Taking the Lead). Sustainable procurement is a form of risk management, aimed at managing supply chain risks including security of supply, price volatility, moral and compliance risks, financial liabilities – and, crucially, corporate brand and reputational risk.
Government policy, law and regulation	Law and regulation is an important driver for sustainability – particularly for organisations which are lagging behind good practice. Governments may set agendas, targets (eg for reductions in carbon emissions) and standards, with incentives and penalties (eg 'polluter pays' taxes). The public sector also exercises leadership as a buyer, supplier, employer and promoter of best practice sharing.
Frameworks and initiatives	Industry and professional codes of practice, and global initiatives and frameworks (eg the Kyoto Protocol, Fair Trade certification, and International Standards) raise the profile of sustainability issues and increase stakeholder expectations.

Internal drivers and enablers of sustainability

3.7 So far, we have mainly considered drivers for the sustainability agenda among businesses in general. In addition, a number of internal factors may drive – or restrain – the changes required to embed sustainable procurement in a particular organisation.

- The corporate mission, vision and objectives, including sustainability values and aspirations – supported by strategic alignment: enabling the flow-down of sustainability to procurement objectives
- Existing CSR and/or corporate citizenship objectives and policies
- Senior management visionaries, champions and supporters of sustainability – supported by communication programmes to secure the 'buy-in' of internal stakeholders
- Accountability and performance management mechanisms, making rewards contingent on sustainability progressive
- Robust risk management processes, and the recognition of business, reputational and supply risks arising from non-sustainability
- Internal stakeholder demand (or support) for sustainability (eg the need to attract and retain quality managers, employees, investors and supply chain partners)
- The availability of resources (labour, skills, finance), capacity and capabilities (eg in innovation, supply chain management or reverse logistics) to implement sustainable procurement
- The formulation of a robust business case for sustainability – supported by positive added-value seeking through sustainability (in areas such as enhanced reputation; brand strength and sales revenue; cost reduction and eco-efficiencies; enhanced supply chain innovation and efficiency; and reduced regulatory burden)

Drivers emerging and changing over time

3.8 It is worth noting that an organisation will not simply respond to a 'package' of drivers operating at a given time. External factors constantly emerge and shift in priority, with technological developments, social changes, new information and so on. Internal drivers will depend on the changing information and priorities of management. Organisations will develop and readjust their sustainability priorities over time.

3.9 Peter Senge (*The Necessary Revolution*) argues that organisations subject to the same environmental drivers may respond in different ways, at different paces and with different motives. 'As with every trend, for all the early adopters, there are the laggards who wait to see how the prevailing winds are blowing before jumping in. Many people wonder who is just paying lip service and avoiding the hard work of integrating sustainable practices into the fabric of their business. But you've got to start somewhere. Wal-Mart CEO Lee Scott openly admitted that the company's early conservation efforts were part of a campaign to clean up its sullied image. Once organisations make this commitment, however, customers and employees will hold them to it.'

3.10 Senge suggests that organisations start in one of five stages along the path to full integration of sustainability into their strategy and purpose, and that different sets of drivers may emerge to move them to each new stage: Figure 1.1.

Figure 1.1 *Five stages and emerging drivers (adapted from Senge)*

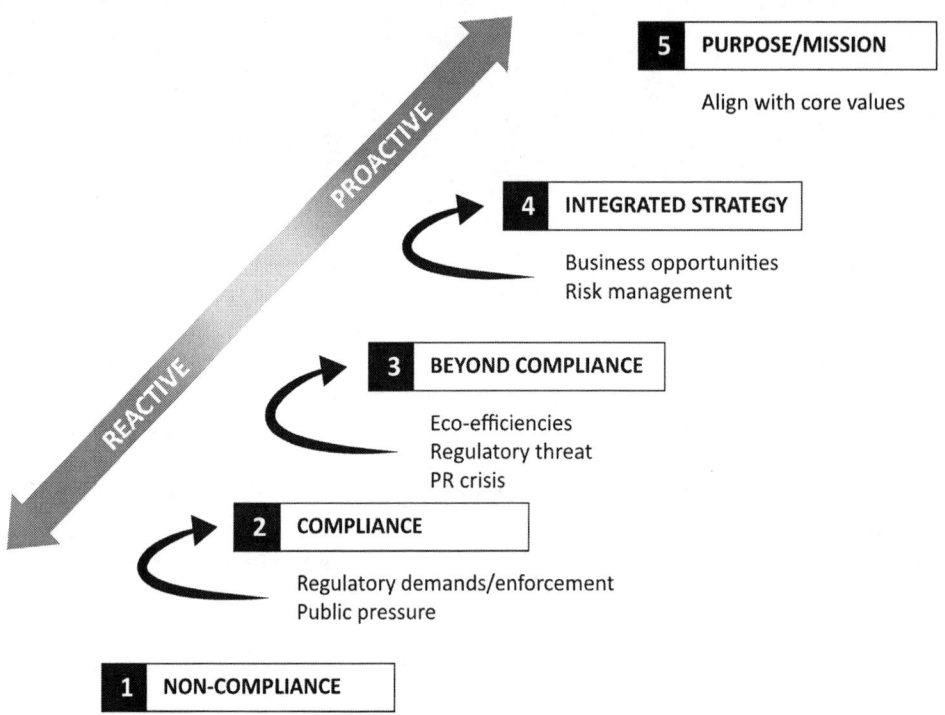

3.11 The key 'driver shifts' in this model can be outlined as follows.

- Organisations may get stuck in the non-compliance or compliance stage, where the drivers for sustainability often involve reacting to external pressures: NGO activism, or enforcement notices from a regulator or employment tribunal, say. 'As this is a very expensive way to change, executives often assume that making the leap beyond compliance will cost even more, and so they miss the benefits and substantial savings of a proactive approach.'
- Momentum for change starts to build when organisations see the cost-effectiveness of going beyond compliance with minimum legal requirements. 'This can become a self-reinforcing snowball, as the re-investment of initial savings leads to more and more gains including an improvement in reputation and brand value.'
- The move to Stage 4 often occurs when organisations discover that broader business opportunities are available – if the sustainability factors are integrated more thoroughly into business strategy, investment and decision-making processes. At this point, sustainability is driven increasingly by senior management, rather than the corporate communications or stakeholder management function. It 'directly impacts internal capital and budget allocations, supply chains, the pursuit of major new markets, core operations and R & D.'
- Some sustainability-leading organisations skip straight to Stage 5: either seeing the opportunities in sustainability from the outset (eg The Body Shop), or recognising the harm they have been doing and shifting direction (eg BP or Nike). The shift to Stage 5 can also occur as part of a natural progression

from Stage 4, 'as leaders learn from their experience of launching new initiatives and getting positive feedback from their employees. They discover for themselves that enormous additional energy can be unleashed by taking steps to align their purpose and mission with the core values their people hold.'

3.12 Sustainability drivers thus operate via a kind of domino or snowball effect. 'As proactive companies make strategic moves in their industries and markets, customers, suppliers, investors and competitors sit up and take notice. These leaders change the game for everyone else by raising the expectations of customers, the public, NGOs and governments alike... Once companies enter Stage 4 or 5, they step into the role of influencing not just their own future but the futures of others in the larger systems in which they operate.'

4 Risks and rewards of sustainability

The business case for sustainable procurement

4.1 Milton Friedman and Elaine Sternberg famously took the view that 'the social responsibility of business is profit maximisation': to give a return on shareholders' investment. Spending funds on objectives not related to shareholder expectations, they argued, is simply irresponsible: regard for shareholder wealth is a healthy discipline for management, providing accountability for corporate governance. The public interest is, in any case, already served by profit maximisation, because the State levies taxes on profits. Meanwhile, healthy corporations increase standards of living through employment, wages and investment in communities and infrastructure: the so-called 'trickle down' effect.

4.2 'Consequently,' argued Friedman, 'the only justification for social responsibility is enlightened self-interest' on the part of business organisations. So how does sustainable procurement serve the interest of the firm, or the supply chain as a whole?

4.3 Different organisations, sectors and industries will have different drivers for sustainability in different areas of their activity. However, a number of general arguments may be advanced for sustainable procurement policies and practices: see Table 1.4.

Table 1.4 *Potential benefits of sustainable procurement*

Compliance	Law and regulation impose certain social and environmental responsibilities on organisations (eg in relation to workplace health and safety, employment protection, consumer rights and environmental care). There are reputational, financial and operational penalties for failure to comply (eg 'polluter pays' taxes, closure notices, law suits and so on).
Reputational benefits and reputational risk management	Voluntary measures and standards accreditation on sustainability may enhance corporate image and reputation, enabling the organisation to attract and retain quality suppliers, employees and investors. The risk of reputational damage extends to 'responsibility by association' in supply chains: buying organisations are increasingly held responsible for unsustainable behaviour by their suppliers.
Brand proposition, differentiation and competitive advantage	Sustainable product design, and sustainably sourced inputs, can create a differentiated and competitive brand proposition, which is increasingly valued by consumers. Examples include the sustainability strategies adopted by The Body Shop and Marks & Spencer. High-profile listings and awards now recognise and promote responsible brands (eg the Medinge Group's Brands with a Conscience: http://www.medinge.org).
Workforce and supply base commitment	Above-statutory provisions for the treatment of employees and suppliers (and more general sustainability credentials) may be necessary to attract, retain and motivate them to provide quality service and commitment – particularly in competition with other employers and purchasers.
Supply continuity	Support for the financial viability and sustainable practices of suppliers protects the ongoing security of supply, which might otherwise be put at risk. (The squeezing of supplier profit margins, for example, may risk supplier failure, corner-cutting on quality, refusal to supply and so on.)

Continued . . .

Minimisation of failure costs	Significant costs may be incurred to rectify failures: eg environmental clean-up, fines, compensation claims and so on – as well as the cost of lost sales, disruption to supply or production while problems are sorted out, loss of employee morale etc. As in quality management, prevention costs are potentially less than failure costs...
Cost management and efficiency	A retained emphasis on economic performance, and particularly, a whole life costing approach (encouraged by the lifecycle focus of sustainability), can contribute to cost management and profitability.
	The environment-friendly focus on resource-efficiency and the reduction or elimination of waste products and processes can lead to measurable efficiencies and cost savings. Videoconferencing, for example, is both 'green' (avoiding travel) and a cost-reducing approach to meetings.
Improvement and innovation	Sustainable procurement initiatives often require increased supply chain communication, and investment in problem-solving and innovation. This may open up new avenues for performance improvement, cost reduction, enhanced collaboration, supplier development and product and service innovation, with flow-on benefits.
Shareholder value	In terms of shareholder returns, the companies listed in the Dow Jones Sustainability Group Index (DJSI) have been shown to outperform the general Dow Jones Index over time.

4.4 The CIPS *Buying Matters* report (focusing on social sustainability in sourcing from developing countries) sums up the business case for responsible purchasing as follows.

- *Sustainable businesses need good long-term suppliers:* purchasers' ability to deliver for their company depends on the continued viability and efficiency of their suppliers – which in turn depends on practices such as fair pricing, enabling suppliers to operate efficiently, and to provide for their workers' welfare (minimising high worker turnover, poor productivity, quality problems and the risk of supplier failure).
- *Unfair sourcing increases reputational risk:* consumers are increasingly concerned about who has made their products and how they were produced – and there is significant reputational risk in being associated with a supplier with a poor human rights record (as companies such as Nike – and, more recently, Apple, have found).

4.5 Of course, business also needs to remember the 'enlightened' (or value-based) part of the 'enlightened self-interest' equation!

- Wider stakeholder needs – even where they impose extra burdens and costs on the organisation – cannot be dismissed: businesses also need to maintain their 'licence to operate', in the form of goodwill and co-operation from customers, suppliers, workers and the general public.
- Profit maximisation and performance improvement does not, by itself, always imply (or lead to) sustainable behaviour – as recurring examples of economic, environmental and human exploitation show.
- Economic prosperity does not invariably 'trickle down'. 'Economic success and the transfer of wealth through increasingly global supply chains bring no guarantee that its ultimate distribution will be fair and equitable, or that it will impact positively on those in greatest need.' (Responsible Purchasing Initiative, *Taking the Lead*)
- Proactive moves in the area of sustainability and ethics – even where they do not directly promote economic value for the firm – can lead to business benefits in the long term. As a strong guiding value, they can enhance culture, morale and unity of direction. They can motivate employees to explore and innovate for further sustainability projects – which may be more economically attractive. And so on.

4.6 Blackburn *(The Sustainability Handbook)* illustrates what he calls the 'Show-Me-The-Money' business case for sustainability: see Figure 1.2.

Figure 1.2 *How sustainability benefits can be argued to help determine business value*

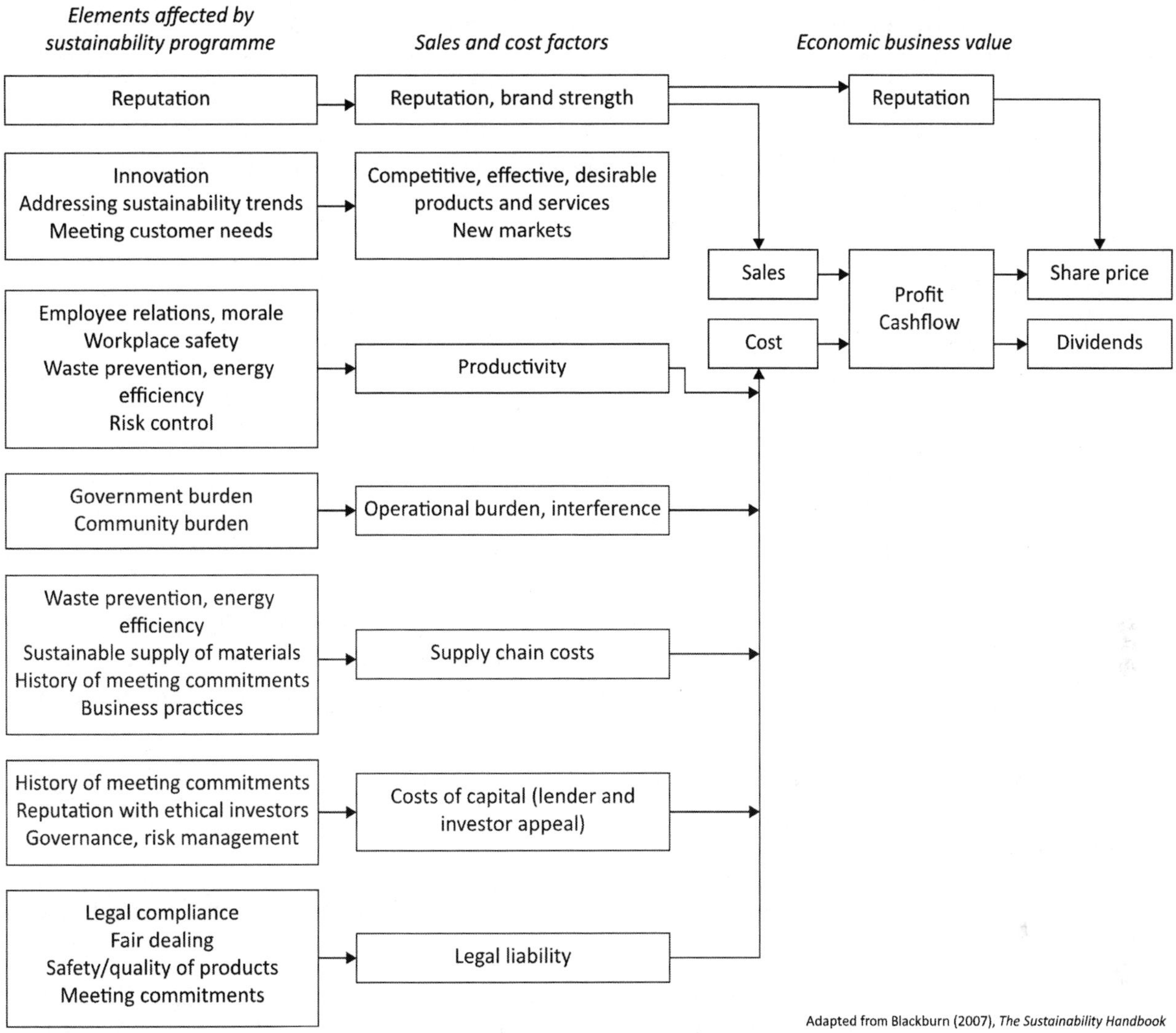

Elements affected by sustainability programme — *Sales and cost factors* — *Economic business value*

Reputation → Reputation, brand strength → Reputation

Innovation / Addressing sustainability trends / Meeting customer needs → Competitive, effective, desirable products and services / New markets

Employee relations, morale / Workplace safety / Waste prevention, energy efficiency / Risk control → Productivity

Government burden / Community burden → Operational burden, interference

Waste prevention, energy efficiency / Sustainable supply of materials / History of meeting commitments / Business practices → Supply chain costs

History of meeting commitments / Reputation with ethical investors / Governance, risk management → Costs of capital (lender and investor appeal)

Legal compliance / Fair dealing / Safety/quality of products / Meeting commitments → Legal liability

Sales / Cost → Profit Cashflow → Share price / Dividends

Adapted from Blackburn (2007), *The Sustainability Handbook*

Conflicts and trade-offs in sustainability

4.7 At the same time, it is recognised that in some key areas there will be conflicts, compromises and trade-offs between business objectives and sustainability objectives.

- Social and environmental responsibility may conflict with economic performance. One classic example would be procurement's desire to reduce sourcing costs by global sourcing from low-cost countries – which might at the same time damage domestic supply markets, risk the use of suppliers with lower labour and human rights standards (or increase the costs of supplier monitoring and development), and increase GHG emissions through supply transport.
- Cost is generally perceived as an issue for sustainable procurement, particularly where targets require short-term cost reductions or maintenance (rather than long-term return on investment over the life of the purchase). Alternative energy, green and fair-trade products often cost more in the early stages of their market development (creating a conflict between lowest achievable price and ethical considerations). Sustainability policies on supplier diversity, small business and local sourcing may likewise impact adversely on cost performance in the short term.
- Pressures for quality and compliance (suggesting sourcing from developed countries) may conflict with cost and sustainable development considerations (suggesting sourcing from developing countries, which may lack standards and infrastructure, but offer low-cost labour).

- Common national and international standards for sustainability, quality and environmental management systems and corporate ethics are key enablers of sustainable procurement and supply – but at the same time, their effect is to lift general practice in an industry or sector: increasing competition and eroding the differentiating competitive edge available from sustainability leadership.

- A pre-occupation with sustainability objectives, in the initial phase of development and implementation, may represent a significant short-term investment in benefits which will take a long time to accrue (and deliver demonstrable shareholder value). It may also represent a disruption to business continuity, as processes and structures are realigned.

4.8 It is also worth noting that there are some counter-arguments to sustainability, and specifically to a 'triple bottom line' (TBL) focus for businesses on Profit, People and Planet.

- Specialisation promotes efficiency, knowledge management, development and (in international trade) comparative advantage. Companies need to focus on their distinctive, value-adding competencies.

- Concern for environmental and social issues is a luxury for corporations in less affluent economies. The need to survive inevitably takes precedence over global, long-term concerns.

- Nationalism – the view that you look after your own citizens first – may get in the way of consensus on sustainability (which is seen as a global issue).

- Sustained economic downturn or recession inevitably refocuses businesses on economic indicators, in the interests of survival.

- Application, in monetary-based economic systems, is a major weakness of TBL, according to *The Challenge of TBL: A Responsibility to Whom?* (Fred Robin). It is difficult to make a genuine business case for TBL, when the costs of sustainability improvements are tangible – and their value is difficult to measure.

4.9 We will examine such conflicts and trade-offs further in Chapter 2.

Risks and rewards in sustainability

4.10 In one sense, we might see 'risk' as the opposite side of the coin to 'reward' in sustainability. As we have just noted, for example:

- There may be financial risks in focusing on long-term value, equity and sustainability over short-term cost considerations – particularly in volatile economic conditions, or for cashflow dependent businesses such as small and medium-sized enterprises (SMEs). The RPI report *Taking the Lead*, for example, was published in 2007, at a time when, in the European Union, 'growth has been positive for 59 successive quarters... corporate profitability is at an all-time high': commitments made to supply chains and stakeholders in such conditions may well have come under severe pressure from the 2008–2009 Global Financial Crisis and the ongoing European sovereign debt crisis...

- There may be a range of operational risks arising from sustainability policies. The BSI *Sustainable Procurement Guide* uses the example of a global construction contractor operating a scheme to employ ex-offenders: this involves an element of risk for the company. (The Guide goes on to note, however, that the risk is generally balanced with the benefits of recruiting loyal workers, reducing the cost of labour turnover – in addition to the benefits for society and the individuals concerned.)

- Reputational risk may actually be *increased* by an organisation's positioning itself publically as a sustainability leader: raising stakeholder and public expectations which may not always be met. A notable example is the reputational damage caused by revelations of exploitative labour practices in the supply chain for Oxfam's 'Make Poverty History' wristbands...

4.11 In another sense, however, 'risks and rewards' can be seen as complementary *drivers* for sustainability. *Taking the Lead* identifies various risk- and reward-based driving forces for sustainable procurement: Table 1.5.

Table 1.5 *Risk- and reward-based components of the business case for action on sustainability*

RISK DRIVERS	REWARD DRIVERS
Loss of control and failure to deliver: Greater supply chain complexity increases the need for clearer accountabilities and secure execution, particularly when working globally or through intermediate suppliers. Poorly selected suppliers may not deliver products or services on time and to correct specification.	*Competitive advantage:* The supply chain is a key source of value creation, and supply management a critical enabler. Good procurement works across the supply chain to align resources behind key business imperatives: a source of competitive advantage.
Increased vulnerability: The legislative, regulatory and consumer environment is tightening and competitive pressure is building. A considered and pro-active stance will make your organisation less vulnerable and reduce the possibility of knee jerk reactions to events you do not control.	*Commitment:* People and suppliers make choices about who they prefer to work for and how much commitment they give. Responsible buying practices create an opportunity to attract and retain the best and most committed suppliers and staff, leading to business savings and innovation.
Loss of stakeholder trust: Consumers and other stakeholders are becoming more demanding, not only expecting your organisation to 'say what it does' but also to 'do what it says'. Losing trust by not following words with actions can happen in minutes but a reputation may take years to rebuild. Trust is the most important asset you have.	*Responsible trading relationships:* Secure the benefits of trade, particularly with developing countries, safe in the knowledge that your organisation is acting responsibly and making the most positive impact it can with its money to many people's lives. Equally, staff appreciate working for a company that 'cares'.

Source: Taking the Lead

5 Developing and implementing sustainable procurement policy

5.1 Sustainable procurement policy may be developed for the public sector at a national and local government level – as in the UK, for example, through the Sustainable Procurement Action Plan. This will be discussed in Chapter 3, where we consider various sustainability initiatives and standards.

5.2 However, as we will see in Chapter 4, one of the critical success factors for implementing sustainable procurement in organisations is to formulate, communicate and enforce effective corporate sustainable procurement policies, in alignment with corporate strategy for sustainability and CSR.

5.3 Corporate and functional strategies are implemented via the development of policies, which communicate the requirements of the strategy for stakeholders. A policy is a 'body of principles, expressed or implied, laid down to direct an enterprise towards its objectives and guide executives in decision making' (Lysons & Farrington, *Purchasing & Supply Management*). Policies are generally set at a senior level, so that they have the force of direct authority: they must be adhered to by all people, in all activities to which they apply.

5.4 The **corporate social responsibility (CSR) policy** of an organisation will have a strong influence on the subordinate policies and programmes established for sustainable procurement. If an organisation has a strong CSR policy in place, with environmental and social sustainability targets clearly articulated, this will require and support the development and implementation of sustainable procurement. If only vague lip service is paid to CSR at the policy level, it will be less easy to secure meaningful commitment and resources for sustainable procurement programmes.

5.5 A 2007 study of CSR across many countries (Vaughn *et al*) found that CSR policies tend to be focused on environmental rather than social aspects. Environmental issues are more established, and arguably more readily measurable and more readily manageable with purely technical solutions. The added emphasis on social and labour issues, which is gaining ground, requires a more ethical and relational approach, which is particularly suited to the concerns of sustainable procurement and ethical sourcing.

5.6 **Sourcing policies** will also be instrumental in directing sustainable procurement, in areas such as: the use of local or global sourcing; preference given to small or diverse suppliers; sustainability criteria used in sourcing decisions; the monitoring and management of supply chain compliance; and so on. We will discuss these measures in detail in later chapters.

5.7   **Human resource development policy** in the organisation may also be important in supporting sustainability, by helping to determine:

- Managerial and workforce understanding of, and commitment to, sustainability values and issues, and the managerial and technical skills available to implement sustainable procurement (eg specification development, fair price negotiation and whole life costing)
- Learning, knowledge and best practice sharing and retention within the organisation (eg through succession planning or mentoring), so that knowledge and practice for sustainable procurement grows and is maintained over time
- The extent to which employees are empowered and resourced to contribute meaningfully to sustainable procurement initiatives
- The extent to which employees are treated ethically and sustainably, with support for diversity, equality of opportunity and a fair and responsible legal (and psychological) contract.

Sustainable procurement policy

5.8   A sustainable procurement policy will align with and support the organisation's commitment to procure all goods, services and works in a sustainable manner. The aims are to integrate sustainability into all procurement activities, to ensure systems are in place to support and develop the policy, and to develop mechanisms for measuring and reporting on performance.

5.9   The broad objectives of a sustainable procurement policy may include the following.

- To support and demonstrate an organisation-wide commitment to sustainability issues throughout the organisation
- To promote sustainability issues throughout the supply network
- To comply with sustainability legislation, regulation and standards
- To define the potential contribution of procurement to sustainable product innovation, development and production
- To ensure that sustainability factors are considered in making all purchasing decisions
- To define how procurement will support and comply with organisational CSR policies in its dealings and relationships with suppliers and other stakeholders.

5.10   A simple sustainable procurement policy document may include the following elements.

- *Introduction:* definition of sustainable procurement; the business need and business case; identified drivers and priority issues; its place within wider organisational CSR and sustainability objectives and strategy
- *Core guiding principles:* what the policy is trying to achieve; how it links with the values of the organisation; beliefs, assumptions, values and commitments by which the organisation defines sustainable procurement; what the organisation expects from its buyers; what the organisation expects from its suppliers, contractors and other supply partners, as part of their contribution to sustainability
- *Objectives and targets:* how progress and performance will be defined and measured.

5.11   More detailed strategic, tactical and operational plans may then be drawn up, setting out: how the policy will be implemented, and action plans with timescales, milestones and targets for meeting specific objectives.

EXAMPLE: CAPGEMINI CONSULTING

To support our sustainability goals, we will be working on initiatives to:

- **reduce our energy consumption**
- **reduce travel**
- **minimise packaging and returns**
- **use more recycled products or products with a high recycled content**
- **minimise logistics activity and wasted journeys**
- **optimise our end-to-end processes We will also ensure our supplier and product selection procedures take into account whole life costs including sustainability impacts.**

We expect suppliers to:

- **document and report on their sustainability performance**
- **where necessary, set performance targets for themselves and their upstream supply chain and work to meet them**
- **agree to identify and correct any activities of immediate concern or risk which fall below the principles set out in our sustainable procurement policy**
- **work with CapGemini in the spirit of continuous improvement**
- **commit to reviewing their compliance with the CapGemini sustainability requirements periodically while continuing to deliver robust goods and services. Suppliers must notify us immediately if there are any negative changes to their compliance with the requirements**

Developing a sustainability operating system

5.12   Blackburn *(The Sustainability Handbook)* puts forward a model of a **sustainability operating system** (SOS), which may be a helpful framework for thinking about the development and implementation of sustainable procurement policies and programmes: Figure 1.3.

Figure 1.3 *Basic elements in a sustainability operating system*

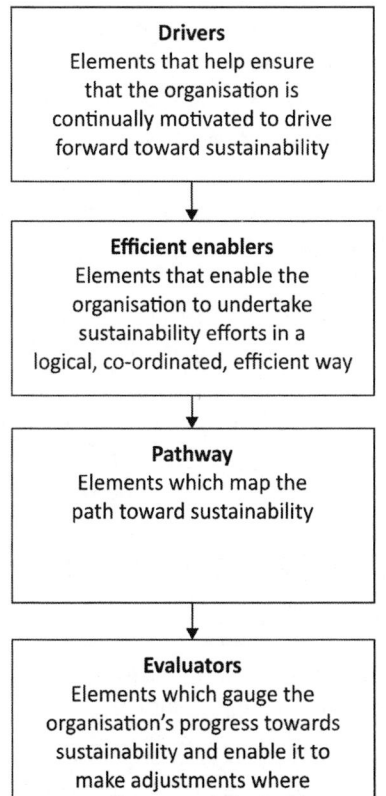

Drivers
Elements that help ensure that the organisation is continually motivated to drive forward toward sustainability

- A champion or leader
- An approach for 'selling' stakeholders on sustainability (securing 'buy-in')
- Accountability mechanisms

Efficient enablers
Elements that enable the organisation to undertake sustainability efforts in a logical, co-ordinated, efficient way

- Organisational structure (sustainability teams, communication)
- Deployment and integration (deploying the idea across values, processes, procedures)

Pathway
Elements which map the path toward sustainability

- Vision, values and policy (sustainability objectives)
- Operating system standards (road-map for pursuing sustainability policy)
- Strategic planning for aligned priorities (prioritising actions towards sustainability)

Evaluators
Elements which gauge the organisation's progress towards sustainability and enable it to make adjustments where performance falls short

- Indicators and goals (picture of the destination)
- Measuring and reporting progress (picture of progress)
- Stakeholder engagement and feedback (reality, perception and credibility check)

A framework for policy development

5.13 A simple general process for policy development may be outlined as follows.

- *Define the vision* for sustainable procurement, and its fit within corporate sustainability and CSR strategies (if any).
- *Identify and prioritise key issues and core processes* as the initial focus of sustainable procurement policy, with reference to: the corporate mission, vision and strategies, critical success factors for the business (and procurement function), and existing and emerging sustainability issues and trends.
- *Identify and define opportunities for improvement in priority areas*, on the basis of risk assessment, benchmarking, supply chain and portfolio analysis and gap analysis (eg benchmarking against industry or international standards). These prioritisation processes will be discussed in detail in Chapter 8.
- *Assess available resources for improvement*, including information systems, management systems, budgetary constraints and the strengths, needs and capabilities of human resources (talent management review) to pursue sustainable procurement objectives.
- *Identify key principles* of sustainable procurement, setting out the procurement function's key values and commitments in relation to economic, social and environmental sustainability in its own activities – and perhaps also its expectations of internal and external supply chain partners. These may be formulated in consultation with key internal and external stakeholders. They will also need to be reviewed for consistency with corporate sustainability and CSR statements.
- *Identify measurable objectives and targets* for achieving improvement in identified priority areas, with realistic timescales and budget estimates, and built-in provisions for progress measurement and review. Objectives and targets will need to be reviewed for consistency with corporate sustainability and business strategies. Their feasibility will need to be assessed, in consultation with management representatives and other stakeholders responsible for their achievement. Budget proposals will need to be approved by fund holders.
- *Identify roles and responsibilities* in the communication, implementation, operation, monitoring and review of the policy.
- *Engage in consultation on the draft policy*, as required, and *gain authorisation* for a final version.
- *Resource the policy*. Staff and supplier training, communication, tools and resources, deployment and operation guidelines, procedure manuals, codes of practice and other measures may need to be planned and developed to support effective deployment of the policy.
- *Document, launch, deploy and integrate the policy*. At a certain point, the policy will 'go live' (or be 'rolled out') and adherence and ongoing management will become part of the responsibility of employees, suppliers and contractors.
- *Establish processes for ongoing management and review* of the policy's acceptance by stakeholders, progress in implementation, effectiveness in achieving its goals, and continuing relevance (in the face of emerging sustainability issues and stakeholder feedback).

Stakeholder consultation and involvement

5.14 A sustainable procurement policy must be robust, feasible and supported by key stakeholders in its implementation: standing up to scrutiny from a wide range of interested parties and taking account of their particular needs, viewpoints and contributions. There is a strong argument for using a multi-disciplinary project team in the development of a sustainable procurement policy. However, other mechanisms may also be used, such as: briefing and consultation meetings; circulation of draft policy documents; and one-to-one presentation of proposals to key stakeholders.

5.15 Procurement will have a particularly important role in consulting with suppliers. It will be helpful to know: what kind of treatment, communication and relationship suppliers define as ethical and sustainable; whether sustainability commitments will be feasible using available suppliers (and at what cost); whether the organisation's expectations of suppliers are perceived as equitable, reasonable and feasible by suppliers; and whether key suppliers will be willing to continue to supply the organisation under those policy requirements.

5.16 One of the key points about consultation at the policy stage is that, as we will see in Chapter 2, different stakeholder groups may well have divergent or conflicting objectives and interests – which will create problems for subsequent buy-in and implementation if not openly addressed. Some suppliers who lack sustainable capabilities may lose out on contracts under the new policy – and this will be an important sustainability consideration in itself (eg if the policy penalises small, local or diverse suppliers).

5.17 In addition, stakeholders may have legitimate concerns on grounds of feasibility, which offer useful input to the decision-making process. They may also raise alternative priorities and ideas, which may helpfully change the organisation's thinking on policy issues. Consultation and involvement can thus contribute to the quality of policy development decisions – as well as to their 'acceptability' and stakeholder buy-in.

Obtaining stakeholder engagement and commitment

5.18 A sustainable procurement policy will need to be supported and signed off at the highest level of management, in order to have legitimate authority over the activities and resource decisions of all relevant functions and business units. It will also need to have the 'buy-in' – acceptance, ownership and commitment – of a range of internal and connected stakeholders (including suppliers) who will be affected by its deployment.

5.19 Blackburn pithily argues that: 'the organisation isn't going anywhere near sustainability unless someone explains why it should.' A strong business case will have to be made – whether to top management, internal stakeholders or supply partners – by the following means.

- Offering a clear definition of sustainability and sustainable procurement
- Linking the drive towards sustainable procurement with core business values, objectives and critical success factors
- Presenting the business case for sustainable procurement, giving concrete examples of risks and rewards
- Highlighting key sustainability issues and trends that are most relevant to the organisation's procurement, and identifying the threats (or opportunities) they represent
- Using the language stakeholders will find most persuasive. For senior management, for example, this will be the language of business: 'enterprise risk and opportunity', 'protecting assets and investments', 'strengthening brands', 'building credibility with key constituents', and so on.

Identifying sustainable priorities

5.20 The first step in developing an effective sustainable procurement policy will be to prioritise sustainability issues, supply categories and action areas. This may be done using techniques such as the following (discussed further in Chapter 8).

- Review of legal and regulatory requirements and applicable standards
- Environmental, purchasing and/or sustainability audit: identifying current and emerging issues, resources and capabilities
- Spend analysis: identifying major spend categories (eg as a proportion of total spend, or over a certain threshold of value)
- Supply chain mapping: identifying points of sustainability risk in the end-to-end supply chain
- Portfolio analysis: eg classifying purchases, categories or contracts according to their importance, sustainability risk, scope for improvement
- Gap analysis: comparing current performance to standards, plans and aspirations, to identify gaps or shortfalls
- Risk and impact assessments: analysing the likelihood and consequences of risk events related to sustainability

- SWOT analysis: assessing internal strengths and weaknesses, and external opportunities and threats relating to sustainability
- Benchmarking exercises: assessment of the organisation's sustainable procurement policies and practices against sector or industry leaders, key competitors or national/international standards.

5.21 Issues will be high priority if:

- They are important to the organisation's business success, in terms of both risks and opportunities
- They are identified critical success factors for procurement
- They are identified as high priority by senior management and corporate CSR and sustainability policy
- They have high public visibility (creating strong external pressure on the organisation to address the issue, or high reputational risk)
- They indicate a significant shortfall in performance, capability or management processes, which might expose the organisation to significant risk
- They offer potential for 'leverage': being relatively easily and cost-effectively addressed, but offering relatively high benefits and returns.

Setting targets and objectives

5.22 Once the key areas of focus for the policy have been identified, the policy development team can articulate specific objectives and targets, expressing exactly what the policy is designed to achieve – and how progress and performance will be measured. We will explore these aspects in detail, in the context of supplier performance measurement, in Chapter 7.

Allocating responsibilities for sustainable procurement

5.23 The sustainability policy or related deployment guidelines should clearly allocate responsibilities (and accountabilities) for implementation – and for the ongoing management of the policy. The important thing is to ensure that there is:

- Clear allocation of responsibility of all key activities and issues
- With no overlaps or gaps
- Matched to the capability, authority and resources of the individuals or teams concerned
- Without creating a separate 'layer' of responsibility or accountability which might frustrate or distract people. Sustainability may initially require 'special attention' – but the aim is to integrate it as fully and swiftly as possible into 'business as usual' for the procurement function and its stakeholders.

5.24 Meanwhile, all members of the procurement team have the general responsibility of implementing and adhering to the sustainability policy in all areas of procurement activity: incorporating principles and practices into specifications, terms of trade, supplier contracts, contract reviews, supplier selection and appraisal criteria, supplier development programmes and so on (as discussed in Chapters 5–7).

Ten practical steps to a sustainable procurement programme

5.25 At an entirely practical level, the *Supply Management Sustainable Procurement Supplement* offered the following helpful checklist for setting up a sustainable procurement programme (Ambridge, 'Power to change', 21 June 2007).

Now

- Find out if there's any support from the top to implement sustainability – will there be budget, time and resources allocated to it?
- Think about what you can measure before you start and map what you currently do, so you have a baseline (eg what percentage of your materials budget goes on environmentally friendly products?)

Next week

- Study your company's objectives to see what procurement can do to support them regarding CSR, and begin writing a business plan

Next month

- Break down how procurement could make a difference in each of the three areas: social, economic and environmental
- Start communicating with internal customers and suppliers to help them understand what you're trying to do and why – and seek their ideas
- Tackle small environmental projects, such as recycling paper

Next three months

- Work out what you want suppliers to do and communicate this to them
- Devise a tool to measure progress against your objectives

Next year

- Measure again after a year to see what progress you have made. This will encourage you to improve and to realise what you have learned so far.

EXAMPLE: VIRGIN GROUP

Particular sustainability challenges are faced by travel and airline businesses, owing to their inevitable promotion of high carbon footprints. The Virgin Group makes an interesting (and typically accessible) case study in CSR and sustainability in this context, with a focus on what Virgin call 'People and Planet'. For example:

Virgin's people and planet promise: tourism

Virgin will work towards offering holiday destinations where tourists and locals benefit today and tomorrow in a lower carbon and sustainable way.

What we think we should focus on:

- Ensuring the adoption of appropriate certification for hotel procurement and hotel operations, editing out all non-certified hotels
- Engaging with our peers to understand what we can do to protect against the overdevelopment of key commercial destinations
- Having active involvement in the plethora of sustainability and tourism debates and promoting these key issues to our customers and opinion formers

Some of our plans to achieve this are:

- Endeavouring to procure from hotels that are appropriately certified on sustainability criteria
- Increasing the number of responsible tourism products in our holiday ranges
- Working collaboratively with other tour operators and bodies – taking a significant role in contributing to the development of sustainable tourism in key destinations
- Encouraging, rewarding and supporting our suppliers to be more sustainable

---

Chapter summary

- Sustainability means the ability of an activity to be maintained at current levels. In recent decades, there has been an increasing business focus on sustainable development, consumption, production and procurement.
- There is an increasing demand from NGOs, stakeholder activists and consumers for organisations to be accountable for the wider impacts of their actions on stakeholders. This has led to a concept of corporate social responsibility.
- There are many drivers for the new focus on sustainability arising both from the external environment and from within firms.
- Friedman and Sternberg argued against the concept of CSR, but most authorities now accept that there is a strong business case in favour of CSR and sustainability.
- Procurement professionals have an important role in this area. Framing a policy for sustainable procurement is increasingly regarded as an important strategic activity.

Self-test questions

Numbers in brackets refer to the paragraphs where you can check your answers.

1   What criteria for sustainable development were identified by the Brundtland Commission? (1.10)

2   Give examples of sustainable consumption that may be applied by organisations. (1.18)

3   List some of the key themes in sustainable procurement. (2.10)

4   List some elements of responsible purchasing. (Table 1.2)

5   List some internal drivers of sustainability. (3.7)

6   Explain the five stages in Senge's model of increasing sustainability awareness. (Figure 1.1)

7   List some potential benefits of sustainable procurement. (Table 1.4)

8   Describe the counter-arguments to sustainability. (4.8)

9   What are the objectives of a sustainable procurement policy? (5.9)

10   What are the stages in developing a policy for sustainable procurement? (5.13)

CHAPTER 2

Sustainability Issues in Supply Chains

Assessment criteria and indicative content

1.2 Critically assess the main drivers of globalisation in supply chains

- Use of STEEPLE analysis to explain the drivers of globalisation
- Competitive advantage through global sourcing
- Globalisation and low cost country sourcing

1.3 Critically assess the main cultural and social issues in supply chains

- Language and cultural barriers
- Labour standards and forced working
- Wages and social security payments
- Inequalities of workers
- Health and safety standards

1.4 Explain the conflicts that may arise between the needs of stakeholders in supply chains

- The profit motive and the search for low cost sourcing
- Demand management and the need for urgent orders
- Short-term commercial gains versus long-term availability of supplies

Section headings

1. Globalisation and supply chains
2. Overview of sustainability issues
3. Cultural and social issues
4. Environmental issues
5. Stakeholder conflicts and trade-offs

Introduction

The syllabus reflects the primary focus of responsible purchasing on the *social* issues arising from *globalisation* of supply: in particular, where buyers in developed countries purchase from (or outsource to) suppliers in developing countries. Developed-country buyers have significant economic power to ameliorate poverty, inequality and poor labour standards in global supply chains – or to perpetuate them. We therefore start by looking at the drivers for *globalisation*, what corporations seek to gain from it, and the associated sustainability risks.

We then go on to explore the main ethical, cultural and social issues that arise in supply chains, both globally and domestically. The syllabus does not explicitly mention environmental issues, but this is an important element in the wider sustainability agenda, so we also highlight some of the main current and emerging environmental issues impacting on global supply chains.

Finally, we acknowledge the potentially conflicting interests of stakeholders in supply chains. We focus on areas in which the interests of corporate shareholders, buyers and suppliers may diverge: acknowledging the need for trade-offs in managing sustainability – and exploring the potential for 'win-win' outcomes.

1   Globalisation and supply chains

Defining globalisation

1.1   Globalisation may be defined as 'the increasing integration of internationally dispersed economic activity' (David Boddy, *Management: An Introduction*)

1.2   This integration may involve the **globalisation of markets.** It has been argued that with worldwide access to media, travel and communications, there has been a convergence of consumer needs and wants: major brands (such as Coca Cola or McDonald's) can be sold worldwide, without much modification for particular geographic markets. This potentially opens up new markets for goods (enabling corporations to move beyond intense competition in mature or saturated domestic markets, prolonging product lifecycles) and offers economies of scale (through higher-volume markets and cost efficiencies learned through wider experience). However, these advantages have proved hard to grasp for some brands, which have failed to gain market share against locally produced brands which cater to specific national and regional cultures, tastes and conditions.

1.3   There has also been a **globalisation of supply**, as developments in transport and information and communication technology (ICT), and the potential for low-cost supply have encouraged the global sourcing of products and commodities. Strictly speaking, global sourcing is not the same as international procurement. International procurement is about buying from abroad, or importing. Global sourcing has a more strategic flavour: it involves the development of an international supply network, from which the company's sourcing requirements can be met flexibly, competitively and in a co-ordinated way. In both cases, there has been continual growth. Global sourcing is now common in industries such as electronic goods, clothing, footwear and toy manufacture, for example, as well as agricultural produce such as chocolate, tea and bananas.)

1.4   A parallel development has been the **globalisation of production**. The differential in labour costs between developed and developing economies has stimulated the growth of offshoring, as developed countries have outsourced the production of finished goods and components, and the delivery of services, to countries such as Taiwan, China, South Korea and India. The media is full of examples of companies offshoring their administrative work, telephone enquires and IT programming (eg most major banks) and product assembly (eg Hitachi, Compaq, Mattel).

1.5   It is also possible to talk about the **globalisation of finance**, with facilities for the movement of finance across borders, through foreign direct investment in developing markets, and an increase in joint ventures and multinational corporations. Indeed, with the establishment of trading blocs and regulators such as the World Trade Organization, it can be argued that there is increasing integration of national economies in world trade.

1.6   We will focus on the globalisation of sourcing and supply chains, as crucial issues for sustainability and responsible procurement. The Responsible Purchasing Initiative report *Taking the Lead* argues that it is largely 'the increase of global sourcing opportunities' that has 'brought the current gaps in [responsible] procurement practice more to the foreground... If the procurement profession is to seize the new opportunities... as well as avoid the risks of globalisation, it must take a wider, more responsible look around.'

The STEEPLE model

1.7 The STEEPLE model (sometimes identified as the PEST or PESTLE model) is a popular tool of environmental analysis, which specifies a number of categories under which the main external factors impacting on organisations can be analysed. These factors are: Socio-cultural, Technological, Environmental, Economic, Political, Legal and Ethical.

1.8 The STEEPLE model is useful for carrying out any kind of external environmental analysis, and can be used, for example, to identify and categorise sustainability issues, trends and risks – to support sustainable procurement planning and decision-making. The model is also used to highlight external factors for further analysis, assessment and measurement, using tools such as SWOT (Strengths, Weaknesses, Opportunities and Threats) analysis.

1.9 However, the syllabus mentions STEEPLE specifically as a methodology for *explaining the drivers for globalisation* in supply chains: we will therefore apply it in this context. 'Drivers', or driving forces, are factors which favour or impel change (in contrast to 'restraining' forces, which work against change*)*. Explaining the 'drivers for globalisation' essentially means explaining why there has been a growing trend towards globalisation.

1.10 Some of the main drivers for globalisation in supply chains (that is, globalisation of supply or production) are summarised, using STEEPLE analysis, in Table 2.1.

Table 2.1 *Drivers for globalised supply chains, using STEEPLE analysis*

FACTOR	EXAMPLES
Socio-cultural factors	• Global communication, marketing and travel creates a 'convergence' of needs and cultural values between cultures. This creates consumer demand for products and services to be available on a world-wide basis, and therefore for access to foodstuffs, products, brands and services sourced from overseas • Societal values in developed nations increasingly embrace the need to support developing-country producers and communities through international trade, influencing consumer behaviour and public policy agendas in support of responsible global sourcing.

Technology factors	• Improvements in transport technology (eg intermodal transport, containerisation, refrigeration and packaging for transport) 'shrink' distance for global logistics, acting as an enabler for global sourcing
	• Developments in ICT support and enable:
	   — 'Virtual organisation': sourcing expertise and collaboration regardless of location (eg off-shored administrative centres)
	   — Global supply (eg through access to international supply market information, improved supplier management and monitoring, and enabling developing-country suppliers to be competitive)
	   — Global logistics (eg computerised transport planning and delivery tracking)
	   — General improvements in business communication (eg through email)
	• The global development agenda prioritises technology transfer: the process whereby more developed nations share technological capability with less developed economies. This may be achieved as trading partners support their subsidiaries, suppliers or joint venture partners with technology consultancy or training; access to design patents; investment funding for new technology or R & D; or finished technology products, such as computers and equipment. However, international agencies and national governments also support technology transfer, creating enabling conditions for sourcing and production.

Environment factors	• Some resources and commodities may only be available from certain geographic regions (eg mineral, oil and gas deposits), or from different geographic regions at different seasons (eg agricultural produce) • Resources and commodities may be available more cheaply from certain geographic regions, because of their relative abundance of supply • Global sourcing can contribute to environmental management standards, where developed-country buyers invest in supplier management and development to comply with higher international standards. • The need for resource-efficiency and waste reduction (to support profitability) and environmental commitments (eg emissions targets) can best be met through strategic, co-ordinated supply chain planning and collaboration.

Continued . . .

FACTOR	EXAMPLES
Economic factors	• Increasing competition places pressure on firms to achieve or maintain cost leadership through efficient low-cost sourcing. • Macro-economic pressures (including global financial crisis, recession, credit 'crunch' and sovereign debt crises) places pressure on firms to reduce sourcing and production costs to protect profit margin • Global sourcing offers significant cost efficiencies, as firms are able to select the lowest-cost supplier of goods and services from anywhere in the world • Significant differentials in labour costs, particularly for labour intensive operations such as agricultural and craft production, create a cost advantage in sourcing from low-cost countries • Additional cost advantages may be secured by lower operating costs (passed on to the buyer, or exploited through offshoring) • Country-specific costs (such as labour costs, tax regimes, exchange rates and compliance costs) encourage strategic global sourcing, as companies seek to match the economic advantages available to local competitors
Political factors	• International trade organisations (including the World Trade Organization) and policies have tended to support increasingly free international markets (reducing protectionist barriers to trade, such as customs procedures, tariffs and quotas) • Trading blocs and agreements, such as ASEAN (The Association of Southeast Asian Nations), EFTA (The European Free Trade Agreement) and NAFTA (the North American Free Trade Agreement) facilitate direct investment and the movement of goods and labour • Host government policies may be aimed at encouraging global operators to base themselves in their countries (eg via tax incentives) in order to stimulate local economic activity and improve infrastructure and living standards. (In recent years, however, this has been countered by political activism against globalisation and the influence of the World Trade Organization on domestic economies.)
Legal factors	• Some organisations may seek to reap cost advantages from less stringent legislative and regulatory regimes eg in regard to quality, health and safety, human and labour rights, intellectual property protection (design rights, patents and copyright) and so on. • The gradual international harmonisation of technical standards has (to an extent) enabled the globalised sourcing of standardised components, compatible systems and so on.
Ethical factors	• International trade is promoted by the United Nations and World Trade Organization as a means of raising living standards, promoting technology transfer, and supporting international harmony and conflict resolution. • Sourcing from developing countries can contribute to standards of living, human and labour rights through: — The stimulation of economic activity, employment and entrepreneurship — The injection of sales revenue, wages and grants into communities — Corporate investment in infrastructure (eg transport networks, telecommunications, worker housing, education and skills development or technology transfer) to support capability development and supply security — Corporate investment in supplier development and support (eg development loans, managerial secondments, worker training) — The raising of labour conditions, standards and wages (where buyers promote and enforce CSR policies and standards through the supply chain)

Competitive advantage through global sourcing

1.11 The main business case argument for global sourcing arises from the potential for competitive advantage through factors such as the following.

- Cost efficiencies and supply flexibility, as firms are able to select the lowest-cost supplier of goods and services from anywhere in the world
- The ability to differentiate the corporate brand (eg by having a global presence, offering access to products from valued countries-of-origin, cost leadership, or promotion of sustainable procurement and fair trade practices)
- The ability to attain cost leadership in a market, by taking advantage of lower country-specific costs (eg skilled labour costs, taxation regimes, exchange rates and trade tariffs) and favourable factors such as tax breaks
- Support for supply chain agility and 'local' supply presence in global markets
- The need to keep pace with competitors who are pursuing competitive advantage through these means

1.12 The general arguments for and against global sourcing strategies, from the point of view of the buying organisation, are summarised in Table 2.2.

Table 2.2 *Arguments for and against global and local sourcing*

BENEFITS OF GLOBAL SOURCING	DRAWBACKS OF GLOBAL SOURCING
Availability of required materials and/or skills: increased supply capacity and competitiveness	Exchange rate risk and currency management issues etc
Competitive price and cost savings (scale economies, low labour and production costs)	Sourcing and transaction costs (risk management, insurances, tariffs, transport)
Less onerous constraints and costs re environmental and labour compliance	Cost savings and lower standards may create sustainability, compliance and reputational risk
Leverages technology (eg for virtual organisation, e-sourcing)	Different legal frameworks, time zones, standards, language and culture
International trade (arguably) promotes development, prosperity, international relations etc	Additional risks: political, transport (lead times, risk exposure), payment, supplier standards monitoring and so on
The opportunity to develop expertise, contacts and supply networks in countries identified as potential markets	Environmental impacts of transport and haulage (especially by air freight)

1.13 Global sourcing will have to be carefully implemented and managed to ensure that the drawbacks and risks – for both buyer and supply chain – are minimised. An organisation sourcing globally will have to pay attention to sustainability issues such as: fair pricing; the monitoring of suppliers' labour and environmental standards; quality management (to protect consumers); and transport planning (to minimise carbon footprint).

1.14 The Responsible Purchasing Initiative report *Win/Win: Achieving Sustainable Procurement with the Developing World* argues that: 'Responsible purchasing from developing countries is increasingly an economic and reputational imperative. Purchasers working in conjunction with their suppliers can start to improve labour conditions for workers in their supply chain and limit any harmful environmental impacts, resulting in business benefits for both purchasers and suppliers. Due to cheaper labour costs, sourcing from developing countries is increasingly popular, and *can* be a win-win solution.'

Globalisation and low cost country sourcing

1.15 Although global sourcing is not limited to low-cost countries, it is often identified with low cost country sourcing: that is, a procurement strategy in which buyers from high-cost countries (such as the UK, US, Western Europe, Canada and Australia) source from countries where country- or region-specific factors enable low costs of production and supply (such as China, Vietnam, India, Indonesia, and some countries in South America and Eastern Europe).

1.16 The key principle of low cost country sourcing is thus to obtain sourcing efficiencies by identifying and exploiting cost differentials between countries or geographical regions. In addition, brands can produce larger quantities for the same overall cost, allowing the generation of additional revenue and profits.

1.17 Low cost countries may be competitive for any of the following reasons.

- Cheap skilled labour costs, due to low market rates for labour, wage regulation, low or non-existent minimum wage provisions and lack of worker representation (eg trade unions for collective bargaining on terms and conditions). This may create a significant cost differential in labour-intensive operations such as agricultural, craft production and services.
- Abundance of raw materials and resources (minerals, oil, agricultural land, fish stocks and so on) for supply and production

- Low production costs, eg due to low regulatory and compliance burdens (such as worker compensation, 'polluter pays' taxes and emissions penalties) or low energy and resource costs
- Currency value and exchange rates, making production 'appear' low-cost in the importer or outsourcer's currency terms
- Favourable taxation regimes, designed to attract direct foreign investment
- Lack of bargaining power in the market and supply relationships, allowing buyers to apply price leverage.

1.18 It should be obvious that some of these factors pose sustainability issues and risks, with the potential for exploitation of vulnerable suppliers and workers: we will highlight these issues in the next section of this chapter.

1.19 The British Standards Institution *(Sustainable Procurement Guide)* sums up the purchaser's dilemma as follows. 'In a global, price-sensitive market there is a strong incentive to source commodities from low-labour-cost economies, which may be based on exploitative labour practices. Here the buyer is faced with a moral dilemma: (i) to restrict procurement to developed economies with strict labour and child laws (but ignoring the consequential effects on the economies of developing countries); (ii) to adopt a fair-trade policy which has the potential to drive up prices, but at the same time righting some fundamental wrongs and considerably reducing an organisation's exposure to reputational damage; or (iii) just to buy at the lowest price.'

1.20 It is also important to note that some low-cost developing countries pose significant business, supply and sustainability risks to buying organisations, and may *not* be an appropriate target for low cost country sourcing.

- They may lack political or economic stability, modern technological and logistics infrastructure which are considered essential for security of supply (and personnel).
- They may lack compatible legal regimes, for the effective handling of contract management and contractual disputes.
- They may lack adequate quality, labour, human rights and environmental management standards: exposing the buying organisation to compliance and reputational risk, and offering little infrastructure to support CSR policies.
- Where they are geographically remote, there may be difficulties and costs of monitoring supply chain standards (particularly if there is also a lack of ICT and transport infrastructure).
- They may suffer endemic corruption at all levels of government and business, raising cost, ethical and compliance issues of bribes, diversion of funds and so on.
- The buying organisation may lack expertise and awareness in identifying and assessing the risks, cultural differences and barriers and so on.

2 Overview of sustainability issues

Sustainability issues in globalisation

2.1 A number of sustainability-based arguments have been put forward *in favour* of globalisation.

- International trade stimulates local economic activity in developing nations. This leads to improved productivity and output, and helps to create employment, leading to greater prosperity, educational development and other standard-of-living benefits (particularly if foreign investors also operate community and infrastructure development policies).
- Smaller developing nations particularly benefit from the wider scope of markets for their products, since their domestic economy may have represented too small a market to allow development and resulting economies of scale.
- The siting of operations in developing countries may bring investment in technology, infrastructure, education and skill development which the host country could not afford on its own.

- There may be improvements in human rights, labour conditions and environmental management in developing economies, where foreign investors and buyers operate ethical and CSR policies, monitoring and enforcement (even if this is primarily done to protect their own reputations…).
- Global consumers benefit from more product and service choice and competitive pricing (where the cost advantages of low-cost country sourcing are passed on by firms).
- It has been argued that international trade is a primary mechanism for positive international relations and a deterrent to conflict.

2.2 However, it should be obvious from TV footage of violent protests outside World Trade Organization meetings that there is a contrary viewpoint! Those opposed to globalisation argue that:

- It encourages the exploitation of labour in developing nations (eg poor wages, poor conditions, child and forced labour) for lower-cost production. This is partly supported by more relaxed employment protection and health and safety laws.
- It 'exports' the developed world's problems of over-consumption, pollution, deforestation, urbanisation and carbon emissions to developing nations.
- It encourages unsustainable environmental practices (eg mono-culture premium crops for export, leaving little agricultural land – or poor soil quality – for the production of staple foods for the domestic population)
- It undermines governments in the management of their own domestic economies, particularly through the influence of the World Bank (loan conditions and so on) and the power of global corporations (whose turnover exceeds the GNP of some nations…)
- It encourages the exploitation of developing-country markets, through globalised marketing: using them as dumping grounds for poor-quality, obsolete and excess goods, and leading to increased foreign debt.
- It encourages the homogenisation, commoditisation and erosion of cultures, through globalised consumption, media and the anglicising of language.
- It exacerbates unemployment in developed nations, where justified expectations of pay and conditions make labour 'uncompetitive' with low-cost-labour competitors.
- It disadvantages small and local suppliers in domestic supply markets, who may not be able to compete on price with cheap foreign imports (particularly if also disadvantaged by exchange rates).

2.3 The fair trade advocacy organisation Traidcraft argues that: 'International trade has the potential to alleviate poverty when each link in the supply chain benefits appropriately. However, the last few years have seen a fundamental shift in who gains from international trade. In the current trend of globalisation, companies pursue flexibility, lowest raw material prices and cheap labour. Increasingly, benefits to companies at the top of global supply chains are reaped at the expense of those at the bottom.'

2.4 We will discuss the implications of these sustainability issues further. However, it should be noted that for critics, globalisation is a social justice issue: businesses committed to global sourcing, production and marketing must increasingly be prepared to justify the sustainability of their policies and practices. Meanwhile, as we will see in Chapter 3, the role of organisations such as the United Nations and International Labour Organization is to seek ways of ensuring that the benefits of globalisation reach more people – and that globalisation does not exploit the poorest and most vulnerable in society.

Sustainability issues in supply chains

2.5 In the following sections of this chapter we will explore the sustainability issues highlighted by the syllabus, in relation to global supply chains. To give you a broader overview, however, Table 2.3 provides a summary of economic, social and environmental issues in supply chains, identified by the British Standards Institution *(BIP 2203 Sustainable Procurement Guide)*.

Table 2.3 *Overview of some supply chain sustainability issues*

ECONOMIC ISSUES	SOCIAL ISSUES	ENVIRONMENTAL ISSUES
Job creation (eg creating markets for recycled products and green technology)	Creating a diverse base of competitive suppliers (eg minority-owned suppliers)	Emissions to air (eg green-house gases and pollutants)
Achieving value for money (utilising whole life costing and value definition)	Fair employment practices (eg fair wages, avoiding child and bonded labour, workforce equality and diversity)	Releases to water (eg chemical effluent) and land (eg chemical fertilisers)
Supporting SMEs (eg facilitating access to contracts, paying on time)	Promoting workforce welfare (eg health and safety, freedom to join or form a union)	Sustainable use of resources (eg sustainable forestry, protection of biodiversity)
Reducing barriers to entry (facilitating fair and open competition)	Supporting skilling and development (eg apprenticeships)	Energy (support for renewables) and water conservation and management
Ensuring business viability to provide stable employment	Community benefits (eg investment, volunteering, sponsorship)	Minimisation of waste and by-products (eg recyclng and waste or landfill prevention)
Ensuring supplier agreements are competitive and fair, to promote business viability	Fair trade and ethical sourcing practices (eg fair pricing policies)	Minimisation of impacts (eg noise, vibration, dust, traffic congestion, land degradation)

2.6 We will now go on to assess the main cultural and social sustainability issues, highlighted by the syllabus, that may arise for organisations with global supply chains, or developed-country buyers sourcing from developing-country suppliers.

3 Cultural and social issues

Language and cultural barriers

3.1 Culture is the shared ways of behaving and understanding that are distinctive to a particular group of people. An influential writer on culture, Geert Hofstede, defines it as 'the collective programming of the mind which distinguishes the members of one category of people from another'.

3.2 Different nations and regions may have significantly different norms, values and assumptions, which influence how they do business and manage people. A range of cultural barriers may hamper attempts to develop and enforce sustainability standards in cross-cultural supply chains.

- Cultural or religious norms around gender roles, or ethnic or religious superiority or hostility (often based on historic conflicts), may militate against supplier or workforce diversity and equal opportunity policies.
- Cultural norms differ in regard to the propriety of personal gifts and hospitality. In some cultures, these are essential for courtesy and relationship development – while in most Western law and ethical frameworks, they are considered corrupt and unethical (as potentially being, or being seen to be, an inducement to influence business decisions). Bribery and corruption diverts funds from productive supply chain activities – and from the paying of adequate living wages to workers.
- Respect for status and seniority, and the importance of 'face' (maintaining dignity and respect in public), may create a barrier to giving or receiving honest feedback; the raising of problems and difficulties; the ability of suppliers to say 'no' to buyers when it is in their interests to do so; or the ability of suppliers to indicate that they do not understand something.
- Improvement of labour conditions often depends on freedom of association and representation for workers, and the consultation and involvement of workers. This may not be the norm in authoritarian or paternalistic cultures.
- Individualistic cultures may generally present more of a barrier to sustainability than collectivist

cultures, in which the focus is more naturally on the collective interest and the welfare of future generations.

- Different communication, relationship and learning styles (eg preferences for rote-learning and rules vs preference for participative, active learning) may impede training and management efforts.
- Language differences may impede the communication and management of sustainability standards and policies. This includes not just the obvious issue of foreign languages, but the level of education of target audiences, their understanding of technical jargon and terminology, different use of symbols and measures (eg miles or kilometres, pounds or dollars) and so on. Inconsiderate communications by buyers may undermine respect and trust, which are the foundations for collaborative supply chain relationships.

3.3 Sensitivity to cross-cultural and language issues is obviously important in developing relationships of trust, and managing the process of gaining supply chain 'buy-in' to sustainability policies and standards. However, respect for cultural and linguistic difference may also be seen as an ethical and sustainability issue in itself.

- Assumptions of cultural superiority reflect a potential power imbalance or 'asymmetry' in negotiation and buyer-supplier relationships, which may weaken the less powerful party's ability to be heard, and protect its interests (an ethical issue). It may also cause resentment and resistance, and weaken the potential to seek genuine win-win solutions (a sustainability issue for organisations seeking collaborative and committed supply chains).
- In addition to creating risks of communication failure, insensitive use of the buyer's language (without adequate translation or interpretation for the supplier's language and cultural context) may exacerbate power imbalance in buyer-supplier dealings: making it difficult for the most vulnerable voices to be genuinely heard.

Labour standards and forced working

3.4 According to Blackburn *(The Sustainability Handbook):*

- Over 12 million people work as slaves or in some form of forced or compulsory labour: women and girls make up more than half of those subject to economic exploitation. Workers may be forced to pay 'deposits' or may have salary, benefits, property or documents withheld by employers, in order to force them to continue work. There may be enforced overtime working.
- An estimated 250 million children aged 5–14 work in the developing world, many in agricultural harvesting and garment 'sweatshops'.

3.5 Working conditions may be poor (compared with international standards) in terms of health and safety; the hygiene and amenities of the working environment; hours of work and entitlement to rest breaks; rights of representation (eg by trade unions or employee associations) for the purposes of collective bargaining, consultation and dispute resolution; employment security (permanent employment contracts, guaranteed work, dismissal and redundancy protection and so on), and adequate pay and benefits (including provision for sickness, worker compensation and other welfare issues).

3.6 Suppliers in developing countries may have little or no knowledge of labour laws and standards, and implementation may be weak or absent. The Responsible Purchasing Initiative *(Win/win: Achieving Sustainable Procurement with the Developing World)* suggests that this may be due to factors such as the following.

- Lack of sufficient national budget to promote or enforce labour laws, as governments lack the capacity to monitor company practice
- Lack of government prioritisation of labour issues, particularly since poor producers have little power or resources for lobbying to influence the policies that affect them
- Owners, managers and workers not being aware of their own laws
- Workers not being covered by employment laws, if they are informally or casually employed (eg

small holders, home workers, temporary and contract workers). This is increasingly the case, where suppliers are only given short-term contracts by purchasing organisations, to facilitate opportunistic buying and flexibility.

- Developing countries deliberately 'turning a blind eye' to violations of standards, or reducing protection for workers, in order to attract foreign business and maintain international competitiveness
- 'Employers selecting vulnerable workers, desperate for an income, because they are less likely to join trade unions, which would help them resist poor working conditions' (Traidcraft: *Are international supply chains increasing poverty?*)

Wages and social security payments

3.7 In the poorest economies, small owners, producers and suppliers may struggle to earn, or pay, a basic living wage. By definition, purchasing organisations seek to maximise the profit potential of sourcing from low-cost countries, and may use price leverage and competitive sourcing to squeeze producers' profit margins – potentially resulting in poverty wages for factory workers, and prices below the cost of production for farmers.

3.8 In addition, the infrequent updating of minimum wage laws, in adverse economic conditions (or in the attempt to remain competitive), may leave the most vulnerable workers potentially exposed by rising costs of living.

3.9 In many developing countries, large numbers of workers lack social security coverage or provision. The Responsible Purchasing Initiative estimates that 'For as many as half of the world's workforce, there is no unemployment or incapacity benefit, old age pension or social housing. In general, medical care is not free and provision of free education varies across countries. Where government provision is lacking, it falls to individuals to cover these costs for their families out of their earnings, in addition to the usual outgoings on accommodation, food, transport, clothing etc. Therefore, benefits such as day care, free transport or medical check-ups are key parts of an overall employment package. The more a supplier provides, the more it demonstrates commitment to its workforce and should be evaluated positively and rewarded by a buyer.'

Inequalities of workers

3.10 The distribution of wealth and opportunity is a global sustainability issue. Overall, the gap between rich and poor is widening, in terms of gross domestic product (GDP) per capita, incomes and private consumption. The British Standards Institution (*Sustainable Procurement Guide*) states that the poorest 40% of the world's population accounts for just 5% of global income, while the richest 20% accounts for three-quarters of world income. The wealthiest 20% account for almost 80% of total private consumption, and the poorest 20%, just 1.5%.

3.11 Many people lack access to educational opportunities, basic skills (including literacy and numeracy) and technological infrastructure and tools (such as telephone, internet or even electricity) that would enable them to aspire to economic participation on more equitable terms.

3.12 Access to economic benefits and workforce participation (or 'equal opportunity') varies widely worldwide. A high proportion of vulnerable temporary and part-time workers (who may not be covered by employment laws) are women. The participation of women and ethnic minorities in some areas of economic activity, and particularly at supervisory and managerial levels, is still an issue, even in developed nations. Increasing representation in supervisory and managerial roles is not just a matter of equity: it also lessens the risk of exploitation, especially at work sites where a high proportion of the workforce is of a different sex, ethnicity or class to management.

3.13 The Responsible Purchasing Initiative *(Win-Win)* notes that equality and diversity issues are not just about pay and conditions, and may be more acute in developing countries for various reasons. 'For example, in worksites with a high proportion of women workers, purchasers need to be alert to circumstances that could have a disproportionate impact on women, such as late product changes causing forced overtime at short notice (putting women at risk when returning home late at night), or all-male supervisors (enabling sexual exploitation at work in return for ordinary work considerations eg request for shift or job role changes).' Women are arguably more vulnerable to intimidation and sexual exploitation, in conditions where there is little employment security and women workers are desperate to keep their jobs.

3.14 The British Standards Institution argues that: 'Tackling such inequalities at all levels is central to creating a fairer world. Long-term growth is dependent on a thriving global community and environment. This means we have to reconsider the relationship between ethical and economic goals, which are too often perceived as opposing choices.'

3.15 It is worth bearing in mind that this is not just an issue in global supply chains, but also in the buying organisation's own employment practices. In the UK, the Equality Act 2010 has introduced a raft of new and clarified measures, including: introducing a new public sector duty to consider reducing socio-economic inequalities; using public procurement to improve equality; introducing gender pay and equality reporting; banning discrimination within and outside the workplace; extending the scope to use positive action to benefit disadvantaged groups; and extending measures to protect disabled people from discrimination.

Health and safety standards

3.16 Many workers, especially in low-cost countries (and vulnerable industries such as construction and extraction) continue to labour in unsafe working conditions. This may be due to:

- Poor knowledge and implementation of health and safety standards
- Lack of national arrangements for employer liability insurance, worker compensation and enforcement of health and safety standards
- Lack of priority for worker health and safety (and related processes such as risk assessment and work consultation, education and training), with corners being cut to reduce costs and save time – especially when responding to low-value orders placed with short lead times
- Lack of adequate budget to attend adequately to health and safety (eg the adequate maintenance of machinery and work environments; the provision of safety equipment and protective clothing; or the sourcing of high-quality inputs)
- A high proportion of workers subject to particular health and safety risk, including pregnant workers (eg in countries with no pregnancy or maternity benefits), young-age workers, night-shift or long-shift workers, and part-time and casual workers (who may lack adequate health and safety briefing, training and awareness).
- Undeveloped work sites, with insufficient fire exits, overcrowding or unsafe and poorly maintained buildings
- Low quality and consumer safety standards (eg in regard to permissible materials).

What can responsible purchasers do?

3.17 We will be exploring sustainable responses to these kinds of issues throughout this Course Book. However, for a brief overview, we summarise some responsible purchasing actions in Table 2.4.

Table 2.4 *Responses to social and cultural issues of sourcing from developing countries*

Language barriers	• Be sensitive to language issues and use translation and interpretation where appropriate • Seek feedback and check understanding: be sensitive to verbal and non-verbal indicators of uncertainty • Check that buyer and supplier share a clear understanding of objectives and terms, to avoid contract failure and disputes
Cultural differences	• Learn about cross-cultural issues in dealings with specific supplier countries, and cultivate behavioural flexibility • Invest time up-front in getting to know suppliers and establishing rapport and trust • Be prepared to promote and enforce minimum ethical and sustainability standards, regardless of cultural norms • Use understanding, sensitivity and support when communicating, implementing and enforcing standards, expectations and requirements • Require buyers and suppliers to subscribe to a Code of Ethics, to reduce bribery and corruption
Labour standards	• Assess whether minimum (national or international) labour standards are in place • Work with suppliers and worker organisations to realise better workplace conditions • Consider using a Code of Conduct (eg in relation to forced and child labour) for suppliers
Wages and social security	• Pay fair prices which enable suppliers to offer adequate wages to their workers • Develop an understanding of social security provision in supplier countries, and consider this when analysing supplier prices or comparing prices across countries
Equality	• Investigate and encourage equal opportunities for women and minorities, where they are under-represented in supervisory and managerial roles • Consider potential risk and exploitation issues for vulnerable groups • Consider positive action at a community level (eg investing in community projects; offering work experience, training and apprenticeships; and so on)
Health and safety	• Become knowledgeable about the risks of relevant environments and production processes • Encourage and support suppliers in making effective health and safety commitments and ongoing risk assessments

4　Environmental issues

4.1　The syllabus does not explicitly give place to environmental issues, in the way that it does to social issues. However, it does address environmental sustainability standards and management systems (covered in Chapter 3), and it will be helpful to have an awareness of the kinds of environmental issues that will be addressed by such measures.

4.2　The British Standards Institution *(Sustainable Procurement Guide)* identifies three main environmental issues arising from industrial development.

- Resource depletion and the increasing stress on environmental systems – water, land and air – from the way we produce, consume and waste resources
- Biodiversity loss across ecosystems from rainforests to fish stocks
- Climate change and its consequences

Resource consumption

4.3　Population growth and economic development together create accelerating resource consumption: increasing numbers of people consuming at increasing rates. Insofar as that consumption is of non-renewable resources, or outpaces resource renewal – there is a major sustainability problem.

- For *non-renewable resources* (such as fossil fuels and minerals), the focus is on developing adequate supplies of alternatives (eg biomass fuels, and nuclear, wind, solar, hydro and geo-thermal energy) – before the current resources are so depleted as to cause economic or social disruption.
- For *renewable resources* (such as wood, grain, cotton, fish and other biomass), the focus is on: (a) harvesting at a sustainable rate, not exceeding the rate of replenishment; and (b) consuming at a sustainable rate, not exceeding the combined rate of harvest, re-use and recycling of the resource.

4.4 Resource depletion can be delayed by reducing the consumption rate. This may involve measures such as challenging requirements; supporting recycling and re-use; and increased resource efficiency (supported by technology). Businesses can also provide incentives and support to accelerate the research and development of substitutes – and procurement functions have a key role in securing their adoption (initially, perhaps, at higher cost), to stimulate demand for innovation.

Waste management

4.5 The UK's *Environmental Protection Act 1990* defines waste as any substance which constitutes a scrap material, an effluent or other unwanted surplus arising from the application of any process; any substance or article which requires to be disposed of which has been broken, worn out, contaminated or otherwise spoiled; and anything which is discarded or 'otherwise dealt with as if it were waste'.

4.6 Each year in the UK, households, commerce and industry together generate about 100 million tonnes of waste, most of which currently ends up in landfill. Even biodegradable waste (previously regarded as desirable) generates methane, a powerful greenhouse gas and potential contributor to climate change.

4.7 It is recognised by the EU and member governments that the management of waste is a crucial element of environmental sustainability, and there is tight regulation on the management, movement and disposal of waste, particularly in areas of significant health, safety and environmental risk: hazardous waste, dangerous goods, waste electronic and electrical goods and so on. Ongoing targets have also been set for waste and landfill reduction, and the take-up of re-use and recycling programmes.

4.8 This drives a sustainable procurement focus on issues such as: reduction of waste materials sent to landfill (due to limitations in landfill capacity); increase in the biodegradability of product and packaging materials used; reduction in the amount of packaging specification for purchases; reduction in packaging designed for products; design for disassembly, re-use and recycling; reverse logistics capability for take-back and disposal; and compliance with relevant waste management regulations.

Water management

4.9 Water is becoming increasingly scarce on a global scale. Drought, salination (increasing salt concentration), contamination, population growth and increasing consumer, agricultural and industrial water consumption are all contributing factors. A recent report by the International Water Management Institute (IWMI) suggests that one third of the world population faces some form of water scarcity, whether physical (when resources cannot meet demand) or economic (poor infrastructure and unequal distribution, due to lack of investment).

4.10 Blackburn (*The Sustainability Handbook*) notes that more and more companies are beginning to see water supply and management as an area of important business risk and opportunity. This is certainly true for some large industrial users of water, such as those in beverages and bottling, textiles and apparel, biotechnology, electronics, and agricultural and food processing. In addition, there are pressures on high-risk water polluting industries such as mining, agriculture and manufacturing, to control run-offs, leakage, liquid spills, wastewater discharge and so on.

EXAMPLE: COCA COLA ENTERPRISES

The Coca Cola Company is often cited as a case study for risk management and sustainability planning in the area of water management. Both Blackburn and Senge (*The Necessary Revolution*) focus on the long journey to put water sustainability at the centre of the beverage business.

'In the past, the emphasis has been on operational performance: efficiency, wastewater treatment, managing water within the plant. Traditionally, little attention was paid to where or how plants got water for their bottling operations, or overall conditions of water availability for the larger community. It took a real wake-up call before we started to think beyond the four walls and pay attention to the larger system.' (Senge)

Features of Coca Cola's sustainability approach included:

- Partnership with WWF. 'The expertise, stature and combined public and commercial influence of the two sectors working together may be crucial to fundamental sustainability challenges like water.'
- A comprehensive inventory and risks assessment to determine security of supply (including water sources and uses, and potential future government restrictions on water).
- An action plan for: water risk surveys and mitigation; water treatment, recycling and reclaim; water saving initiatives (eg using alternative 'rinsing' methods); and efficient waste water treatment.

Other issues in Coca Cola's CSR and sustainability policies include: reducing beverage calories in schools; calculating and reducing carbon footprint; expanding a hybrid (green energy) truck fleet; and internal and external recycling programmes.

Climate change and 'carbon footprint' reduction

4.11   Climate change is perhaps the 'hottest' topic in environmental politics, raising the profile of the issue for governments and pressure groups worldwide. The science of climate change is still under debate, but there is fairly widespread political consensus on the prevailing theory that excess levels of greenhouse gases (GHGs) in the atmosphere, including carbon dioxide (CO_2), may cause global warming and changes to global climate patterns, resulting in a range of severe environmental, social and economic consequences.

4.12   In order to mitigate the effect of human-caused global warming, communities and corporations are urged to reduce greenhouse gas emissions, and to reduce their 'carbon footprint': that is, the total impact of their activities on the amount of carbon dioxide in the atmosphere, measured in tonnes of CO_2. Many nations, including the UK, ratified the Kyoto Protocol, committing to binding targets to reduce GHG emissions. In the UK, the Climate Change Act 2008 created a legally binding long-term framework to cut carbon emissions.

4.13   Procurement-led measures to reduce emissions might include: minimising the use of fossil-fuel energy in all activities, and sourcing or generating 'green' energy; reducing the air freight of goods; planning road haulage to minimise fuel use and emissions; carbon offsetting; developing products with a lower carbon impact; sourcing inputs with low carbon impact (and carbon labelled); and mobilising and supporting key suppliers and logistics providers in reducing their carbon emissions.

Pollution

4.14   Pollution is the contamination of air, water, soil or food stocks by harmful substances. The use of cars and trucks, increased chemical wastes, nuclear wastes, and accumulation of rubbish in landfills have all been the subject of legislation specifically aimed at decreasing pollution. Traditional air pollution (including auto emissions, smog, dust and smoke) have largely been stabilised by national and international regulations, but remain a problem in rapidly developing economies such as China and India.

4.15   Companies need to determine if they or their supply chains generate or emit hazardous chemicals or emissions from their operations, and if so, properly handle, control and ultimately dispose of them in ways that will not harm people or the environment.

5 Stakeholder conflicts and trade-offs

5.1 It should be clear from our discussion so far that there is a potential conflict between the needs of stakeholders in supply chains.

- The pressures on buying organisations to minimise costs, in order to generate profits and create shareholder value (traditionally the primary objective of business) or value for money (a primary objective of public sector procurement)
- The need for suppliers to charge prices that will enable them to generate adequate revenues to pay their workers a living wage and benefits, and to invest resources in improved working conditions, additional employment and capacity and capability development

5.2 CIPS (*Buying Matters*) argues that two of the key objectives of current purchasing practice – in response to internal and external pressures on buyers – can work against product quality, suppliers' incomes and good labour practices.

- The continual search for improved profitability, through lower prices and better deals – conflicting with suppliers' need to price adequately to sustain quality, conditions and livelihoods
- The need to produce quickly (eg just in time supply) and the need for flexibility to respond to customer or business demand, including peak seasonal orders – conflicting with suppliers' need to plan ahead, in order to maintain labour contracts and investments

5.3 We will now look at these two areas of conflict in more detail.

The profit motive

5.4 In the private sector, the primary objective of business is to generate (if not necessarily to maximise) profits. Both buyers and suppliers seek to make a profit.

- Profit means that the business has covered its costs and is not 'bleeding' money in losses. This is important for the business to survive in the long term.
- Profit belongs to the owners or shareholders of the business, as a return on their investment: a share of profits is paid to them in the form of a 'dividend'. Strong and consistent profits are important to maintain the share capital of the company.
- Profits which are not paid to shareholders ('retained profits') are available for reinvestment in the development of the business, enabling it to acquire assets, meet long-term borrowings, update plant and equipment, and build up reserves for future contingencies – without the cost and risk of borrowing funds.

5.5 The profit motive in buying organisations may militate against the interests of suppliers and other stakeholders in various basic ways. Procurement staff may be under pressure to continually reduce sourcing costs – by measures such as:

- Sourcing from low labour cost countries (where by definition, workers are poorly paid)
- Sourcing from high-productivity, low-cost suppliers. In manufacturing, this may be enabled by 'sweatshop' labour conditions, forced or child labour, forced overtime and so on. In agriculture, it may be supported by intensive techniques which degrade environments and create poor conditions for livestock
- Sourcing from suppliers whose low prices are enabled by cost-saving short-cuts in quality, safety or environmental standards, which may create downstream risks for customers or workers
- Opportunistic supplier switching (creating income insecurity)
- Price leverage over less powerful suppliers (squeezing prices and wages back up the supply chain)
- Sourcing cheaper products or materials with poor environmental performance.

5.6 In addition:

- Sustainable procurement policies and fair trade pricing may be (or may be perceived to be) more expensive, and thus counter to short-term profitability.
- If an organisation is not securely profitable, financial survival will be the overriding objective, and 'discretionary' social and environmental sustainability concerns may be seen as an unaffordable luxury in the short term.
- The *maximisation* of profit is essentially a 'win-lose' or 'zero-sum' game for the supply chain: the interests of the buyer (forcing supplier prices down to minimise costs) directly conflict with the interests of suppliers (by narrowing or eliminating their profit margins).

5.7 Two main sustainability arguments can be made to counter these effects. Firstly, the buying organisation, with the support of its shareholders, can choose not to *maximise* profits, but to earn *adequate* profits while promoting equity, fair trade and the sustainability of its supply chain. And secondly, a business case for sustainability may be made on the basis of long-term added value and profitability.

5.8 We will examine how the conflicting priorities of sustainability and cost reduction can be managed in Chapter 4.

Demand management and supply flexibility

5.9 Supply chain speed, flexibility and 'agility' are increasingly sought after in order to minimise wastes and inventory costs for the buying organisation. You should be familiar from your CIPS studies with the concept of just in time (JIT) supply, whereby inventory is 'pulled' through the system in response to (rather than in anticipation of) demand: eliminating the use of buffer stocks. An article in *The Guardian* (15/5/03) sums up the concept in practice as follows. 'Every time you buy a product in a supermarket, the scanner and computerised till records your purchase. This enables the supermarket to send their supplier last-minute and very precise orders: for example, they will send an e-mail to Kenya at midday with the order for exactly what produce they need on that evening's flight to be on the shelves the next day. This reduces waste and increases profits for the company. But because orders can go up and down dramatically this means that sometimes suppliers have to meet large orders at very short notice.'

5.10 In addition to deliberate short-lead time purchasing, urgent and last-minute orders may arise from buying inefficiencies such as the following.

- Poor demand forecasting: underestimating demand or failing to anticipate peaks in demand (resulting in urgent orders), or overestimation of demand (resulting in orders being cancelled or reduced, or returned on 'sale or return' terms)
- Poor critical path management. Slippages in project schedules may result in orders being placed late – and because the final delivery date can rarely be moved, this simply squeezes suppliers' lead times.
- Inefficient decision-making eg lengthy procedures to get sign-offs for contracts; failure to understand the nature of supplier lead times
- Poor communication between buyers and suppliers on demand forecasts, lead times, clarification of requirements, project plans and critical paths, and so on.

5.11 Whatever the cause, the requirements of buyers for speed and flexibility of supply make it difficult for suppliers to estimate and plan adequately to meet demand. This can be a problem in any supply chain, but is particularly acute where a power imbalance exists between the buyer and supplier.

- Order volumes may be increased or decreased, or orders cancelled (owing to unforeseen fluctuations in demand), or delivery schedules altered and lead times shortened (owing to urgent orders) – often at short notice.
- Buyers may keep their options open for opportunistic buying by using last-minute, short-term or no-obligation call-off contracting with suppliers – rather than establishing long-term, stable, guaranteed-volume contracts for recurring supply.

- Many developing-country suppliers, particularly small agricultural producers, have no written contract with the purchaser, and have to rely on verbal agreements, which are vulnerable to change or cancellation with no remedies for the supplier.
- Payment terms often provide no protection for suppliers. Suppliers may lack power to insist on any form of deposit at the time of ordering, or stage payments to reflect their investment if an order is reduced or cancelled. Purchases may be made on a 'sale or return' basis, with little incentive for buyers to estimate demand accurately, and no certainty of revenue for the supplier.

5.12 Lack of long-term stable supply contracts, low-value short-lead-time orders and/or lack of sharing of accurate demand forecast information are unsustainable in various ways.

- They pass the risk and cost of demand fluctuations back up the supply chain – with an ultimate impact on the most vulnerable members (such as developing-country producers and women, migrant or temporary workers).
- They impose unnecessary production costs on suppliers to meet urgent orders (eg overtime or extra shifts, and urgent supply orders at premium prices) or wasted costs of cancelled, reduced or returned orders.
- They may force suppliers to keep stocks of work in progress, in order to meet just in time or urgent orders: forcing them to bear related costs and risks (capital tied up in stock, storage and insurance costs, risk of deterioration and obsolescence and so on).
- They create a disincentive for suppliers to engage workers under permanent employment contracts, because they have no long-term contracts to supply. Flexible contracts, temporary contracts and casual working perpetuate income insecurity, worker vulnerability and poor enforcement of labour standards. They may also create quality risks because of the use of unskilled, untrained labour.
- They put suppliers under pressure to produce more quickly and at lower cost, exacerbating the risk that corners will be cut on quality, working conditions and health and safety. Suppliers may have to hire in short-term labour, enforce excessive overtime hours, or outsource or subcontract work. All these practices can reduce ethical and quality standards.

Short-term commercial gains versus long-term security of supply

5.13 There may well be a conflict (and resulting trade-off) among the internal stakeholders of a buying organisation between:

- The pressure to make short-term commercial gains (for example, through price leverage of suppliers; opportunistic buying and just in time supply; or exploitation of available resources) and
- The need to support the long-term availability of supplies (for example, through support for supply chain viability; long-term, stable and mutually beneficial supply chain relationships; fair trade; supplier development; minimisation of negative economic, social and environmental impacts on supply chains and host communities; and managed consumption of non-renewable resources).

5.14 There may be pressure for short-term commercial gains from shareholders and investors, to provide a short payback horizon on their investments, and to strengthen corporate results and market confidence (impacting on the availability of share and loan finance). Senior management and procurement professionals may also be under pressure to deliver such gains, because of the way value is defined, and performance measured, in the organisation.

5.15 There may be a perceived conflict of payback horizons: investment in the short term, to protect long-term supply. Sustainable procurement can, as we have seen, incur up-front costs and investment. Many procurement functions – and organisations generally, under recessionary and/or cashflow pressures – look for short-term return on investment, or short payback periods. However, the returns on investment from sustainable procurement are often long-term in nature, accruing through whole life cost savings, improved security of supply and mitigation of supply risks. These returns represent long payback periods – and may, like reputational benefits, be difficult to quantify.

5.16 The longer-term perspective is essentially the original argument for sustainability. It is against the organisation's long-term interests to undermine the future security, quality and cost of supply, by increasing the risk of supplier failure; restricting supplier capacity and capability development; exacerbating quality and productivity problems in the supply chain; fostering negative and uncooperative supply chain relationships; accelerating resource depletion (and resulting rising costs); or arousing the resistance of stakeholders in host communities and countries.

5.17 The Responsible Purchasing Initiative *(Taking the Lead)* argues as follows.

- The implementation of sustainable and responsible sourcing practices requires concerted and consistent action over a long period.
- With only short-term targets and decision-making horizons, buyers may focus on immediate deliverables (cost, inventory, speed of response) at the expense of more strategic objectives such as reputation leadership and innovation, which support the organisation's longer-term goals.
- Longer perspectives and targets allow the input and involvement of suppliers and other stakeholders: allowing them to shape events and co-ordinate their own actions in support of them. This can enable better and more lasting results, less waste, support for innovation, and better performance from a more committed and efficient supply chain.
- Short-term decision-making creates supply, sustainability and reputational risk, because suppliers are not able to anticipate or plan for their impacts (as we saw in our discussion of demand management).
- Without a longer-term strategic context and rationale, short-term tactical actions can damage trust and confidence in the supply chain.

5.18 Here are some measures to support managers and procurement professionals in developing long-term, sustainable sourcing strategies and targets.

- Developing long-term sustainable sourcing strategies for key expenditure areas, and ensuring that all supply market, supplier relationship and supply chain management policies are aligned with these strategies.
- Gaining independent scrutiny and endorsement of sourcing strategies, and periodic independent reviews of sourcing strategy effectiveness, to help build trust and confidence
- Incorporating sustainability in definitions of success and performance measures (such as 'Triple Bottom Line' accounting or a 'balanced scorecard' approach). This will need to be championed by senior management, and embedded in mission and values statements and HR management systems.
- Two-way feedback and communication of supply chain performance against desired social, labour and environmental standards and identified risk or problem issues, to facilitate collaborative problem solving
- Encouraging the use of whole life costing for sourcing decisions
- Developing strong cross-functional collaboration on procurement projects, to provide balancing perspectives.

5.19 The downside risk of this trade-off must also be minimised, however, by ensuring that:

- A sound business case can be made for investing in sustainable supply, on the basis of whole life costs and risk management
- Investment is focused on strategic, high-risk items, suppliers and sustainability issues (rather than a generalised 'save the whales' orientation)
- Momentum and stakeholder confidence are gained by ensuring some 'quick wins': measures with low cost implications and quick payback periods.

Supplier resistance to buyer-driven sustainability initiatives

5.20 So far, we have broadly assumed that conflicts of interests involve the possible downside to buyers of sustainability measures in favour of the supplier. However, it is very important to note that suppliers may themselves resist buyer-driven attempts to improve sustainability standards in the supply chain. Resistance from supplier stakeholders may arise from the perception of:

- Externally imposed pressure to change, in areas which may or may not be culturally relevant or commercially viable in the supplier's operating context – and may or may not be adequately supported by co-investment, supplier development or gain and risk sharing by customers
- The costs of developing sustainable products and services, processes, improvements in terms and conditions for workers, and sustainability management systems – which, again, may not be adequately or reliably offset by sales revenue, or gain-sharing by customers
- The costs and risk of buyer-specific innovations and adaptations, where required as part of sustainability standards, which may not be transferable to other customers, and may lock suppliers in to unprofitable customer relationships.

5.21 The task of overcoming stakeholder barriers to responsible procurement is therefore not *just* presenting a robust business case to internal stakeholders – but also influencing (and collaborating with) suppliers to implement and enforce sustainability standards through the supply chain, for mutual benefit and value gains.

Chapter summary

- In recent decades there has been a trend towards increasing globalisation of economic activity. This includes globalisation of markets, supply, production, and finance. As far as procurement is concerned, the main driver is the search for competitive advantage.
- The trend towards globalisation has not always been welcomed. Critics suggest that it may lead to undesirable practices such as exploitation of local workers.
- Responsible purchasers adopt a proactive stance to improvement of labour standards and health and safety standards throughout the supply chain.
- Key environmental issues of concern to procurement specialists include resource consumption, waste management, water management, climate change, and pollution.
- Procurement professionals must deal with trade-offs between sustainability and other objectives. For example, long-term security of supply may conflict with short-term commercial gains.

Self-test questions

Numbers in brackets refer to the paragraphs where you can check your answers.

1. What is meant by (a) globalisation of markets and (b) globalisation of supply? (1.2, 1.3)

2. What aspects of global sourcing may help to achieve competitive advantage? (1.11)

3. In what ways can globalisation arguably contribute to sustainability? (2.1)

4. List criticisms that have been made in relation to globalisation. (2.2)

5. List possible cultural barriers that may impede sustainability in cross-cultural supply chains. (3.2)

6. List possible reasons why workers in low-cost countries may have to endure unsafe working conditions. (3.16)

7. What measures can be taken to address excess consumption of (a) non-renewable resources and (b) renewable resources? (4.3)

8. What measures can procurement professionals take to minimise climate change and reduce carbon footprint? (4.13)

9. List possible adverse consequences of seeking to lower sourcing costs by the use of low-cost country suppliers. (5.5)

10. Explain the potential conflict between short-term commercial gains and long-term security of supply. (5.13)

CHAPTER 3

Sustainability Initiatives and Standards

Assessment criteria and indicative content

2.1 Analyse how the major labour codes can help to achieve improved sustainability in supply chains

- Standards set by the United Nations (UN) and the International Labour Organization (ILO)
- The role of the UN and ILO in pursuing improved sustainability
- Labour codes of conduct such as the Ethical Trading Initiative (ETI) and the Agricultural Ethical Trading Initiative (AETI)
- Social Accountability International (SAI) and the standard SA 8000

2.2 Analyse how the leading standards on environmental purchasing can help to achieve sustainability in supply chains

- The role of the International Organisation for Standardisation (ISO) and the environmental standard ISO 14001
- The European Union's Eco-Management and Audit Scheme (EMAS)
- Other standards for environmental purchasing produced by standards organisations
- Industry standards and standards set by organisations

2.3 Analyse how leading standards can achieve improved fair trade

- The World Fair Trade Organisation (WFTO) and its principles and charter of fair trade
- Fair trade Labelling Organisations International (FLO) and global fair trade organisations
- Fair trade standards that affect the workplace and producers

Section headings

1. The role of codes and standards
2. Labour codes
3. Fair trade standards
4. Environmental management standards
5. General sustainability and sustainable procurement
6. The UK sustainable procurement agenda

Introduction

The syllabus focuses on the use of standards, codes of conduct and collaborative initiatives, as a way of promoting systematic attention to sustainability issues – and consistent minimum standards of sustainability performance.

In this chapter we will review the major codes and standards highlighted by the syllabus, in the areas of labour and employment, fair trade and environmental management. We will also summarise the British Standard (BSI 8903) dealing specifically with sustainable procurement. Finally, we will look at the UK's sustainable procurement agenda, as an example of the embedding of sustainability leadership in public procurement policy.

In later chapters of this Course Book, we will look in more detail at how sustainability standards can be implemented in practice (through the sourcing cycle and supply chain management) and how compliance with standards can be monitored and managed.

1 The role of codes and standards

1.1 According to the Responsible Purchasing Initiative (*Buying Matters)* the first step for purchasing organisations wishing to have a fair and positive impact on their supply chains (especially overseas) is to ensure that their sourcing is in line with **national laws** and **international agreements** (such as the fundamental International Labour Organization conventions and international environmental protocols).

1.2 As a minimum, organisations would be expected to comply with – and to purchase from suppliers who comply with – relevant legislation in their own country of operation. A wide range of statutes and regulations exists in areas such as human rights law (covering issues such as freedom from servitude and discrimination, freedom of association and so on); corporate law (including corporate governance and accountability); employment law (including equal opportunity and diversity, health and safety, employment rights, employee relations and minimum wages); and environmental protection law (covering issues such as pollution, wastes, climate change mitigation and liability for environmental damage).

Codes and standards

1.3 In addition to legislation and regulation, however, various international and governmental agencies, NGOs, commercial organisations and multi-stakeholder associations have developed a range of voluntary codes of practice and benchmark standards: voluntary initiatives established to support sustainable supply chain management, emphasising progress towards better conditions rather than superficial compliance.

- **Codes of conduct** (and/or Codes of Ethics) specify expected or acceptable ways of behaving.
- **Standards** specify desired levels of attainment in a particular area of conduct or management (such as sustainable procurement, ethical employment or trading, or environmental management). Attainment of the requirements of a given standard often entitles the organisation to include reference to that attainment on products or corporate communications (eg in the form of a standards mark or logo).
- **Inspection regimes** (audits) are designed to provide assurance that business practices in supply chains are in line with the stated CSR intentions of organisations, and with the requirements of the standards to which they subscribe.

1.4 The CIPS Knowledge Works document *Standards in Procurement* defines a 'standard' as: 'an agreed and repeatable way of doing something. A standard is a collective work that is created by bringing together the expertise and experience of all interested parties, such as manufacturers, sellers, buyers, users and regulators of a particular material, product, process or service. Standards are designed for voluntary use and do not generally impose any regulation, but some laws and regulations may refer to standards and even make compliance with them compulsory. There are many different types of standards, ranging from British Standards to labelling standards such as the Fairtrade trade mark, the Forest Stewardship Council Standards mark and the European Flower mark.'

1.5 Codes and standards vary in a number of ways.

- Some codes and standards are mandatory (such as the UK Competition Commission's Grocery Supply Code of Practice), while some are open to voluntary participation (such as Social Accountability 8000).
- Some are independently verified (such as Fair Trade and the Environmental Management Audit Scheme), for the purposes of certification, while others are used primarily as benchmarking, self-assessment and self-development tools for internal use.
- Some are based on minimum internationally-agreed standards (such as the ILO's core conventions), while others seek to develop above-minimum good or best practice on particular issues. (Examples include industry codes such as the UK Considerate Construction Code, or the Global Good Agricultural

Practices standard; environmental standards, such as ISO 14001 and EMAS; and 'consumer-facing' standards such as Fairtrade or Rainforest Alliance certification.)

How codes and standards help improve supply chain sustainability

1.6 The British Standards Institution *(Sustainable Procurement Guide)* notes that: 'Organisations are coming under ever greater scrutiny by various stakeholder groups (including NGOs, investment analysts, consumers, employees and competitors) who are increasingly **evaluating their commitment** to ensuring a fair and equitable working environment, environmental responsibility and transparent business practices. This climate means that organisations will be called upon more and more to demonstrate their social and environmental responsibility. **Assurance** is likely to become more important.'

1.7 Many organisations deal with sustainability-related risks in global supply chains by requiring suppliers to commit to codes of business conduct and environmental management systems, reflecting their own CSR policy commitments. Code or standard compliance would typically form part of supplier pre-qualification and tender evaluation criteria, and be embedded in supply contracts. However, this only provides assurance from direct or first-tier suppliers – and sustainability (and related reputational) risks may well occur at lower tiers of increasingly long and complex supply chains.

1.8 CIPS argues that: 'Standards and standards-related information provide frameworks and best practice solutions that help to manage business critical decisions and relationships... Standards can be a powerful tool for many organisations... providing a framework for sustainable growth and profitability through streamlining business efficiency.'

1.9 In general terms, the use of formal codes of conduct and standards allows purchasing organisations to identify and manage sustainability-related risks, especially in developing- and low-cost-country sourcing, by:

- Taking advantage of the local knowledge, expertise and perspectives of multiple stakeholders involved in standards development
- Raising awareness of social and environmental issues and expectations among purchasers, managers, suppliers and other key stakeholder groups
- Securing greater visibility of the business practices and environmental performance of suppliers at all levels of the supply chain
- Selecting the standards that they desire their suppliers to achieve and maintain, in the context of agreed minimum and good practice standards – and in line with their own organisational CSR commitments and policies
- Receiving assurance that minimum legal and ethical labour standards are being met, in countries where relevant internally agreed standards (based on ILO conventions) are not effectively enforced. Most governments have ratified the conventions, but there may be little funding or political appetite for monitoring and enforcement, and sanctions for non-compliance may be weak.
- Receiving assurance that suppliers' management of ethical and responsibility issues is systematic and robust (as measured against management systems standards)
- Communicating assurance to customers and consumers, regulatory bodies, investment analysts, NGOs and other key stakeholders, in order to enhance and protect corporate brand and reputation
- Gaining a sustainable source of competitive advantage, as buyers use compliance to choose between comparable suppliers
- Lightening the regulatory burdens on the supply chain, as standards offer 'a more flexible and business-orientated approach which helps to maintain market relevance' (CIPS Knowledge Works)
- Opening global markets for small producers, as standardisation promotes 'inter-operability' (compatibility of standards and processes) along the supply chain
- Improving business processes, which in turn can lead to increased efficiency and sustainable profitability

- Facilitating supplier and supply chain development with the assistance of guidance documents, common standards, improvement benchmarks, audit checklists, independent inspection and verification regimes, and other resources available around agreed standard frameworks
- Using codes and standards as a tool to encourage and facilitate two-way communication in the supply chain around sustainability risks, concerns and aspirations (including communication on relevant issues with workers, communities and other stakeholders).

Issues in the use of supply chain standards

1.10 There are a number of potential issues in the use of standards in supply chains.

- The implementation of supply chain codes is likely to be ineffective without a range of enabling or support activities undertaken by purchasing.
- There may be equity, sustainability and implementation issues in 'imposing' or 'enforcing' codes in ways that fail to take the needs, perspectives and constraints of suppliers (and other stakeholders) into account.
- Standards-related development activities and audits impose costs, which may have a disproportionate impact on the most vulnerable suppliers, if not supported by the purchasing organisation.
- There may be a pre-occupation with auditing and compliance – at the expense of helping suppliers to improve their social and environmental performance. (Many organisations are now moving to what is called a 'beyond auditing' orientation, for this reason.)
- The proliferation and duplication of codes (and related audits) by different purchasers may divert supply chains' attention and resources away from development. Multiple codes and audits can cause audit fatigue; supplier confusion; high costs; inefficiency; and focus on compliance at the expense of improvement.

1.11 An article in *Supply Management* ('Purer Source', Emma Clarke, 4 January 2007) highlighted research from the Institute of Development Studies, commissioned by the Ethical Trading Initiative to assess the impact and effectiveness of its Base Code (discussed in the next section). The findings revealed that:

- While child labour, health and safety failures and working hours had fallen as a result of implementation of labour codes, in other areas it had made little or no impact. Union membership showed no sign of increase in the sites visited; women were still denied equal access to employment and training; and there was little progress in ensuring that workers received a living wage.
- Observed reductions in the level of child labour appeared to be due to enforcement of the law, rather than the implementation of labour codes.
- In some cases, the use of codes may even have worsened conditions in supply chains. (For example, the US Fair Labour Association's code of conduct stipulates that employees shall not be required to work more than 48 hours per week and 12 hours' overtime, except in extraordinary business circumstances. This sends the message that a 60-hour week is broadly acceptable – whereas the ILO convention clearly states that working weeks should only exceed 48 hours in exceptional business circumstances.)

Applying codes and standards effectively

1.12 We will be discussing how standards can be embedded in the supply chain throughout the rest of this Course Book. However, essential 'complementary enabling activities' for supply chain code implementation (Responsible Purchasing Initiative: *Win/Win*) include:

- Public and senior management commitment to labour standards, reinforced by the benchmarking of responsible procurement programmes against best practice
- Facilitating the building of workers' and suppliers' capacity to improve: eg providing good practice guidance and worker training
- Working with local organisations to raise awareness of labour standards, and collaborating with

organisations experienced in bringing about workplace improvements in the particular country or culture

- Involving suppliers' management and workers in the adoption of codes and the planning and implementation of improvements, since 'ultimately, the sustainability of code implementation rests with workers and suppliers'
- Sharing good practice within the supply chain, industry and multi-stakeholder organisations. 'Supplier *development* can help improve the practices of specific suppliers, and supplier *co-ordination* can help share good practices and initiatives between groups of suppliers to bring about improvements.'
- Effective auditing: for example, using unannounced audits and worker interviews to get at the truth of labour practices; and disclosing audit results (as Apple has recently done, for example, to make transparent its efforts to address labour issues at the Chinese plants of its original equipment manufacturer, Foxconn).
- Being willing to address purchasing practices which limit the improvement of working conditions (such as price leverage, urgent orders and last minute changes – discussed in Chapter 2)
- Recognising and rewarding good performance and improvement (eg supplier awards or 'preferred supplier status' to recognise improvement, progress or standards attainment), recognising that 'in some contexts, the owners or managers of suppliers are under peer pressure not to improve conditions'.

1.13 The British Standards Institution notes, however, that: 'When using standards, the most important issue for buyers is to ensure: (a) that you know what the standard requires, (b) that this is communicated properly to your suppliers and (c) that they clearly understand the requirements.'

1.14 We will now outline some of the main relevant standards for supply chain sustainability.

2 Labour codes

2.1 Codes for minimum acceptable standards in the employment and management of labour are usually based on the 'conventions' or treaties developed by the International Labour Organization (ILO). It is increasingly common to include Supplier Codes of Conduct based on ILO minimum standards in supply contracts.

The International Labour Organization (ILO)

2.2 The ILO is the UN's specialised agency promoting human, civil and labour rights. It develops consensus documents (Conventions), and less formal codes of conduct, resolutions and declarations (Recommendations). Here are some examples.

- The *Declaration on Fundamental Principles and Rights at Work* (1998). This sets out eight core ILO Conventions, the principles of which are binding on all ILO member states (which includes most member states of the UN). The Conventions cover four core principles: elimination of child labour; abolition of forced labour; equality (freedom from discrimination); and freedom of association (worker representation and collective bargaining). We will identify specific provisions under these principles in the context of the SA 8000 standard, a bit further on.
- The *Declaration of Principles Concerning Multinational Enterprises and Social Policy* ('The MNE Declaration'), on the contribution of multinational enterprises to economic and social progress, and how to minimise and resolve problems arising from their actions. The MNE declaration makes recommendations for: general sustainable development and compliance policies; employment (increasing employment opportunities and standards, building links with local supply chains, and promoting equal opportunity, employment security and fair treatment); training (encouraging skill development); work/life conditions (providing equitable and competitive remuneration, benefits and conditions, recognising the need for work/life balance, respecting minimum employment ages, and maintaining high standards of health and safety); and industrial relations (respecting freedom of association, collective bargaining and representation, and allowing for consultation and fair grievance and dispute procedures).

2.3 The general aims and objectives of the ILO illustrate their sustainability concerns: Table 3.1.

Table 3.1 *Objectives of the ILO*

OBJECTIVE	COMMENT
Decent work for all	Decent work considers the aspirations of people in their working lives, such as their aspirations for opportunity and income; rights, voice and recognition; family stability and personal development; and fairness and gender equality
Employment creation	The ILO identifies policies that help create and maintain decent work and income. These policies are formulated in a comprehensive Global Employment Agenda
Fair globalisation	The ILO seeks ways of ensuring that the benefits of globalisation reach more people.
Rights at work	The ILO identifies four fundamental principles relating to workers' rights: freedom of association and collective bargaining; elimination of forced labour; elimination of discrimination; and elimination of child labour
Social dialogue	The ILO defines social dialogue to include all types of negotiation, consultation and exchange of information between, or among, representatives of governments, employers and workers on issues of common interest
Social protection	Access to an adequate level of social protection in the form of medical cover, social security payments etc, is recognised by international labour standards and the UN as a basic right of all individuals. It is also widely considered to be instrumental in promoting human welfare and social consensus on a broad scale, and to be conducive to and indispensable for social peace and thus improved economic growth and performance.
Working out of poverty	People should have the ability to improve their situation not only in terms of income but also in terms of respect, dignity and communication. Improvements in these areas will lead to economic, social and political empowerment.

The Ethical Trading Initiative

2.4 The concept of **ethical trade** focuses on the meeting of minimum labour and human rights, as set out by the ILO labour standards. The Ethical Trading Initiative is a multi-stakeholder association of companies, NGOs and trade union organisations committed to working together to identify and promote internationally agreed principles of ethical trade and employment, and to monitor and independently verify the observance of ethics code provisions.

2.5 The ETI publishes a code of labour practice (the **Base Code**) giving guidance on fundamental principles of ethical trading practices, based on international labour standards (including the ILO's core conventions). The principles covered by the Base Code are as follows.

1 Employment is freely chosen (ie freedom from forced labour).
2 Freedom of association and the right to collective bargaining are respected.
3 Working conditions are safe and hygienic.
4 Child labour shall not be used (exploited).
5 Living wages are paid.
6 Working hours are not excessive.
7 No discrimination is practised.
8 Regular employment is provided.
9 No harsh or inhumane treatment is allowed.

2.6 The ETI also asks member organisations to follow certain **Principles of Implementation**, which complement the base code. These ensure that ETI standards are communicated, implemented and enforced fairly in the supply chain, and that costs and risks are not borne disproportionately by suppliers.

2.7 This is not an approach based on certification or product labeling (like FairTrade): ETI members work together to identify and share good practice. Subscribers to the ETI Base Code include Marks & Spencer, Tesco and GAP.

The Agricultural Ethical Trading Initiative (AETI)

2.8 The AETI, created in 2002, is an example of a multi-stakeholder initiative in a specific area of trade. It represents a collaboration between UK purchasing organisations, NGOs, agricultural producers, the South African Department for Labour and union members of the ETI to address the specific issues of racial discrimination and sexual harassment in agricultural production (vineyards and farms) in South Africa.

- Member producers undertake to meet certain minimum requirements and workplace standards.
- The association organises monitoring, inspections and training and awareness courses to support improvements.
- International buyers support the initiative by only purchasing from member producers.

The Social Accountability (SA) 8000: 2001 standard

2.9 SA 8000 (developed and administered by Social Accountability International) was one of the world's first auditable social certification standards, and is now the most widely recognised global standard for managing human rights in the workplace. It is both:

- A management system standard for addressing workplace conditions and independently verifying factory compliance (based on ISO standards) and
- A code of conduct for workplace conditions and labour rights (based on the conventions of the ILO, UN and national laws).

2.10 It addresses management and reporting requirements on nine key 'elements', as shown in Table 3.2.

Table 3.2 *Elements of SA 8000*

Child labour	• No use or support of child labour • Policies and procedures for remediation where children are found working • Adequate financial and other support to enable children to attend school • Conditional employment of young workers
Forced and compulsory labour	• No use or support of forced or compulsory labour or human trafficking • No requirements for worker 'deposits' (financial or otherwise): no withholding of salary, benefits, property or documents to force personnel to continue work • Rights for personnel to leave premises after the working day • Rights for personnel to terminate their employment
Health and safety	• Provision of a safe and healthy workplace and prevention of occupational accidents • Appointment of a senior manager for occupational health and safety (OHS) • Instruction on OHS for all personnel • Systems to detect, avoid and respond to workplace hazards • Recording of all accidents • Providing protection equipment and medical attention for work-related injury • Hygiene (toilets, drinkable water, sanitary food storage) • Worker rights to remove from imminent danger
Freedom of association and the right to collective bargaining	• Respect for the right of all personnel to form and join trade unions and bargain collectively with their employer • Not interfering in workers' organisations or collective bargaining • Informing personnel of these rights and freedom from retaliation • Allowing workers to elect representatives (where the law restricts rights) • Ensuring no discrimination against personnel engaged in worker organisations • Ensuring representatives have access to workers in the workplace
Discrimination	• No discrimination based on race, national or social origin, caste, birth, religion, disability, gender, sexual orientation, union membership, political opinion or age • No discrimination in hiring, remuneration, access to training, promotion, termination or retirement • Prohibition of threatening, abusive, exploitative, coercive behaviour at workplace or company facilities.

Continued . . .

Disciplinary practices	• Treating all personnel with dignity and respect • Zero tolerance of corporal punishment, or mental or physical abuse • No harsh or inhumane treatment
Working hours	• Compliance with laws and industry standards • Normal work week (not including overtime) not to exceed 48 hours • One day off after every six consecutive working days (with some exceptions) • Overtime to be voluntary, not regular and no more than 12 hours per week
Remuneration	• Respecting the right of personnel to a living wage • All workers paid at least the legal minimum wage • Wages sufficient to meet basic needs and provide discretionary income • Deductions not made for disciplinary purposes (with some exceptions) • Wages and benefits clearly communicated to workers • Payments made in a convenient manner (eg cash or cheque) • Overtime paid at premium rate • No use of short-term contracts or false apprenticeships to avoid legal obligations
Management systems	• Facilities seeking to gain and maintain certification must go beyond simple compliance to integrate the standard into their management systems and practices

2.11   Companies endorsing the standard, and/or seeking certification under it, must select suppliers and contractors based on their ability to meet the SA 8000 standards, and require by contract that they do so. Hundreds of facilities have been certified under the scheme so far, mainly in the clothing, textile and chemical industries in China, India, Brazil and Vietnam (Blackburn, *The Sustainability Handbook).*

'Jo-In'

2.12   The Joint Initiative on Corporate Accountability and Workers' Rights is an example of a multi-stakeholder initiative to: (a) develop best practice standards and (b) harmonise various codes used by purchasers, in order to reduce confusion and unnecessary audits arising from duplication.

2.13   'Codes of conduct have been an important part of efforts to improve labour standards in global supply chains. Over the last ten years these codes and systems for their implementation have proliferated. Brands and retailers are faced with multiple industry standards and suppliers are confused by the numerous codes and initiatives. Local organisations are frustrated by the many initiatives making demands on their time. Better co-ordination and co-operation is essential to address this confusion. It is also important to develop a shared understanding of the ways in which voluntary codes of conduct contribute to better working conditions' (www.jo-in.org)

2.14   Jo-In is a multi-stakeholder collaboration between the Ethical Trading Initiative, Social Accountability International, the Clean Clothes Campaign and Fair Wear Foundation (representing the garment industry), the Fair Labour Association and Workers' Rights Consortium. It also encourages broad stakeholder involvement in the implementation of codes of conduct, including governments, trade unions and employer associations.

2.15   Its own Draft Code of Labour Practice includes minimum provisions in regard to: child labour, non-discrimination, freedom of association and collective bargaining, forced labour (linked to the ILO fundamental conventions), and health and safety, wages, hours of work, harassment and abuse, and the employment relationship (building on ETI and SA 8000).

3   Fair Trade standards

What is 'fair trade'?

3.1   'Unfair' trading arises when large buyers exert their bargaining power to force down the prices of small suppliers, to levels that bring economic hardship to producers, exacerbating poor wages and working conditions for their workers, and bringing no economic benefit to their communities. Fair trade issues arise most acutely in developing economies, where workers and small producers are particularly vulnerable. The media has recently highlighted the plight of banana, coffee and tea growers, and textile and garment trade workers.

3.2   Traidcraft defines **ethical trade** as 'the main approach used by companies that are serious about improving the social conditions up to minimum international norms in their supply chains'. It defines **fair trade** as a more proactive and participative approach: 'an approach to bringing about positive social impact in the supply chain... which requires standards of behaviour from buyers, not only of suppliers. Fair Trade recognises that all parties have to be involved in reducing poverty through trade – local communities, workers, homeworkers, smallholders, suppliers, buyers and consumers'. (Traidcraft, *Corporate Social Responsibility: Does it Make any Difference?*)

3.3   The goals of Fair Trade (as expressed by Traidcraft, *Fair Trade in the Wider World),* are as follows.

- To improve the livelihoods and wellbeing of producers by improving market access, strengthening producer organisations, paying a better price and providing continuity in the trading relationship
- To promote development opportunities for disadvantaged producers, especially women and indigenous people, and to protect children from exploitation in the production process
- To raise awareness among consumers of the negative effects on producers of international trade, so that they can exercise their purchasing power positively
- To set an example of partnership in trade through dialogue, transparency and respect
- To campaign for changes in the rules and practice of conventional international trade

3.4   Traidcraft also argues that, while the same principles underpin both CSR and Fair Trade, there are some fundamental differences between them.

- CSR seeks to render trading activities benign – while Fair Trade advocates change in the international trading system to bring about greater structural equity.
- CSR relies mainly on buyer power in the supply chain to enforce compliance with unilaterally developed standards – while Fair Trade seeks to consult and involve supply chain partners and local communities in developing standards and monitoring impacts.
- CSR involves voluntary compliance with agreed minimum standards – while Fair Trade seeks proactively to have a positive developmental impact.
- CSR can be counter-productive when it involves unreasonable demands and/or the elimination of vulnerable suppliers from the supply chain. ('If a company adopts CSR approaches only as a means of limiting the risk to its brand and applies these in a generalised top-down manner, this is likely to result in culturally insensitive actions that will backfire on the claimed social objectives'.) Meanwhile, Fair Trade aims explicitly to improve the livelihoods of small producers and their families, through developing standards in consultation with them to address their priorities.

3.5   Started over 60 years ago, Fair Trade has developed into a worldwide concept, seeking to ensure decent living and working conditions for small-scale and economically disadvantaged producers and workers in developing countries. It involves an alliance of producers and importers, retailers, labelling and certifying organisations – and, of course, consumers willing to pursue ethical consumption by support for certified Fair Trade products. Products sold by Fair Trade organisations now include food, household products, soft furnishings and clothing.

3.6 Meanwhile, the comparatively new discipline of 'fair trade marketing' involves 'the development, promotion and selling of fair trade brands and the positioning of organisations on the basis of a fair trade ethos' (Jobber, 2007). Recent years have seen a significant increase in both awareness and sales of Fair Trade goods, with sales showing annual growth rates of 20% to 30% – and this is likely to provide a strong influence on sustainable procurement policies.

3.7 Fair Trade is one of the clearest examples of buying organisations forgoing commercial and negotiating leverage and opportunism, in order to support supply relationships based on sustainability, fairness and justice.

3.8 Traidcraft *(Corporate Social Responsibility: Does it Make any Difference?)* describes the general Fair Trade requirements for suppliers and buyers: Table 3.3.

Table 3.3 *Fair Trade responsibilities of suppliers and buyers*

RESPONSIBILITIES OF SUPPLIERS (PRODUCERS IN DEVELOPING COUNTRIES)	RESPONSIBILITIES OF BUYERS (IMPORTERS IN DEVELOPED COUNTRIES)
Marginalised, but organised and able to export	Pay a Fair Trade price (covering costs of sustainable production and living) and a premium to invest in development
Democratic and transparent management	Buy from disadvantaged producers (including registered producers where Fair Trade labelling applies)
Decent working conditions and a fair wage	Provide business and financial support (including advance payment where necessary)
Workers have freedom of association	Long-term co-operative and transparent trading relationships
Equal opportunities for all, particularly the most disadvantaged	
Long-term co-operative relationships	
Commitment to invest in the development of their organisation and the welfare of producers and workers, product quality and environmental stability	

3.9 Fair Trade products are marketed in two different ways.

- The traditional or integrated route is where goods are produced, imported and/or distributed by dedicated Fair Trade organisations, under standards developed by the World Fair Trade Organisation (WFTO).
- The other route to market is through Fair Trade labelling and certification, whereby goods sourced from producers in developing countries are certified by an independent third party verification body, to guarantee that their production chains respect the International Fair Trade standards developed by FLO (Fair Trade Labelling Organisations) International.

3.10 Standards developed by the fair trade movement primarily aim to improve the situation of small producers, farmers and workers at the 'bottom' of global supply chains in areas such as agriculture, arts and crafts. There are two main recognised standards.

- The World Fair Trade Organisation (WFTO)'s principles and charter of fair trade
- Fairtrade Labelling Organisations (FLO) International's labelling scheme

The World Fair Trade Organisation (WFTO)

3.11 The WFTO has developed a charter of fair trade, consisting of 10 key principles that fair trade organisations must follow in their day-to-day operations, which are monitored: Table 3.4.

Table 3.4 *WFTO Standards*

STANDARD	COMMENT
Creating opportunities for economically disadvantaged producers	Fair Trade is seen as a strategy for poverty alleviation and sustainable development. Its purpose is to create opportunities for producers who have been economically disadvantaged or marginalised by the conventional trading system
Integrity	Transparency and accountability in dealings with trading partners
Capacity building	To develop producers' independence by providing continuity, during which producers and their marketing organisations can improve their skills and access new markets
Promotion	Promoting Fair Trade using honest adverting and marketing techniques
Fair payment	Pay a fair price which not only covers the cost of production but enables production that is just and sound and takes into account the principle of equal pay for equal work by men and women
Gender equity	Women are appropriately paid for their labour and are empowered in their organisations
Working conditions	Provision of a safe and healthy working environment for producers
Children's rights	Fair Trade Organisations respect the UN Convention on the Rights of the Child as well as local laws and social norms
The environment	Fair Trade actively encourages better environmental practices and the application of responsible methods of production
Trade relations	Trading with concern for ongoing social, economic and environmental wellbeing.

Fairtrade Labelling Organisations International (FLO)

3.12 FLO International has developed standards mainly covering agricultural products. There are two basic standards.

- The 'hired labour standard', to be implemented in formal **workplaces**
- A standard to be implemented where small-scale **producers** are organised in co-operatives
- Standards are independently certified, and products originating from certified sites may carry the Fairtrade mark on their packaging.

3.13 The FLO standard is the only standard which guarantees suppliers a minimum price, so that suppliers know in advance that any costs incurred to reach standard will be recovered by sales of the product.

3.14 The requirement under the standard for fair trade production sites is that:

- Workers are paid a fair wage
- A 'premium fund' is developed to benefit workers and the community. Expenditures from the fund are decided by workers or members of the co-operative, and may be used to address gaps in social security provision.

3.15 In addition, the standard places obligations on purchasers to ensure that:

- Trading terms are based on written contracts
- Contracts specify mutually agreed price and payment conditions (including pre-payment where requested by producers)
- Contracts specify delivery schedules allowing 'sufficient lead time for production without excessive working hours' and recognising 'seasonal factors affecting the producer'.

4 Environmental management standards

4.1 The CIPS Practice Guide on CSR highlights the fact that 'the law is a floor': it represents minimum acceptable standards – not good practice. 'There are in most cases few or no globally accepted norms on environmental behaviour, and so suppliers, often at several tiers' remove, may be operating perfectly legally – but with environmental impacts that would be unacceptable if our representative organisations or companies were creating them.'

4.2 The syllabus focuses on voluntary standards – *not* (as in the case of law and regulation) addressing particular environmental 'content' issues (such as waste, pollution, GHG emissions, land use or end-of-life disposal), but addressing the 'process' issues for organisations in managing their environmental impacts and responsibilities – regardless of context, industry or sector.

4.3 An **environmental management system (EMS)** is a structured and documented system which manages an organisation's environmental performance. An EMS can be seen essentially as a tool of risk management.

4.4 There are a number of recognised standards in relation to environmental management, all drawing on a similar framework. The main ones, highlighted by the syllabus, are the International Organisation for Standardisation's ISO 14001: 2004 and the European Union's Eco-Management and Audit Scheme (EMAS).

ISO 14001: The Environmental Management System Standard

4.5 The International Organisation for Standardisation (ISO) is the world's largest developer and publisher of International Standards. It is a non-governmental organisation (NGO) made up of a network of the national standards institutes of over 150 countries worldwide. Its role is to develop international standards which:

- Make the development, manufacturing and supply of products and services more efficient, safer and cleaner
- Facilitate trade between countries and make it fairer
- Provide governments with a technical base for health, safety and environmental legislation and conformity assessment
- Share technology advances and good management practice
- Disseminate innovation
- Make life simpler by providing solutions to common problems
- Safeguard users of products and services.

4.6 Launched in 1996, **ISO 14000** is a series of international standards on the design, implementation and control of environmental management systems (EMS). An EMS gives an organisation a systematic approach for assessing and managing its impact on the environment: that is, the environmental consequences (and risk exposure) of its operations. The standard is designed to provide a framework for developing such a system, as well as a supporting audit and review programme.

4.7 **ISO 14001** specifies the practical requirements for an environmental management system, focusing on environmental aspects that the organisation can control, and over which it can be expected to have influence. It enables companies to identify elements of their business that impact on the environment and produce objectives for improvement supported by regular review for continual improvement. As a detailed specification, it is also the standard against which an organisation can be audited (by an independent third party) and certified.

4.8   Other standards in the ISO 14000 series are guidelines.

- ISO 14004 provides guidance on the development and implementation of environmental management systems.
- ISO 14011 provides guidance on the audit of an environmental management system (now superseded by ISO 19011).
- ISO 14020+ provides guidance on eco-labelling (discussed further below).
- ISO 14040 provides guidance on lifecycle issues.

4.9   The major requirements for an EMS under ISO 14001 include the following.

- An environmental policy statement which includes commitments to: prevention of pollution; continual improvement of the EMS leading to improvements in overall environmental performance; and compliance with all relevant legal and regulatory requirements
- Identification of all aspects of the organisation's activities, products and services that could have a significant impact on the environment (whether or not regulated): focusing on environmental aspects that are within the organisation's control or ability to influence
- Establishing performance objectives and targets for the EMS, taking into account legal requirements and organisational policy commitments and information about significant environmental protection issues
- Implementing an EMS to meet these objectives and targets, including: training of employees, establishing work instructions and practices, establishing performance metrics and so on
- Establishing a programme for periodic auditing and review of environmental performance against the environmental policy and legal and regulatory framework
- Taking corrective and preventive actions when deviations from the EMS are identified
- Undertaking periodic reviews of the EMS by top management to ensure its continuing performance and adequacy in the face of changing environmental information.

4.10   An organisation can make a self-assessment and self-declaration, or be audited and certified by a third party, if desired, to demonstrate compliance to customers, clients and regulatory bodies. Benefits claimed for an EMS based on ISO 14001 by various Environmental Protection Agencies include the following.

- Improvements in compliance and reduced costs of non-compliance; improvements in overall environmental performance
- Enhanced predictability and consistency in managing environmental obligations
- Increased efficiency and potential cost savings when managing environmental obligations
- Enhanced reputation and relationship with internal and external stakeholders

ISO 14020+: Eco-labelling Standards

4.11   The ISO 14020+ standard provides principles and protocols for third-party audit and labelling based on environmental criteria. Different categories of eco-labels are required to meet different criteria.

- Type 1 eco-labels ('seal of approval': ISO 14024) must have third party certification on multiple award criteria (based on the product's impacts throughout its lifecycle), and is only awarded to the best environmental performers. As an example, the European Union 'Flower' mark is a label awarded only to products which are kindest to the environment: this voluntary program helps public and private consumers identify officially approved green products, across a wide range of products and services.
- Type 2 eco-labels (ISO 14021) are self-declared by suppliers (eg 'made of x% recycled material'). The standard provides guidance on the terminology, symbols, testing and verification methodologies.
- Type 3 eco-labels (ISO 14025) embody environmental claims giving quantified product information based on a full lifecycle analysis. The standard requires third party certification, quantitative

information and multiple attributes with lifecycle consideration. Car companies such as BMW and Volvo are currently leading the way in this area.

The Eco-Management and Audit Scheme (EMAS)

4.12 The European Eco-Management and Audit Scheme (EMAS) is a voluntary EMS certification process, created under European Community regulations. The aim of EMAS is to recognise and reward organisations which go beyond minimum compliance and continuously improve their environmental performance.

4.13 Registration under EMAS can be obtained by an organisation or site by a full audit programme – or by 'upgrading' from ISO 14001, where the audit concentrates on the fulfilment of *additional* EMAS requirements. EMAS registration includes all requirements of ISO 14001 *plus* requirements for an organisation to:

- Issue a public, externally verified report on its environmental performance
- Have a verified environmental audit programme, conducting periodic audits to assess environmental performance
- Have no apparent failures of regulatory compliance, with legal compliance status periodically reported to the regulator.

4.14 The features of EMAS which add value to ISO 14001 are said to be as follows.

- A stricter and more systematic framework for measuring, evaluating and improving environmental performance. A comprehensive initial environmental review is required (unlike ISO 14001, in which it is only 'recommended'). 'Environmental core indicators' in key areas enable the documentation and benchmarking of performance, year on year or against other organisations. Internal environmental audits evaluate the EMS, environmental performance and compliance (where ISO 14001 merely audits the EMS requirements of the standard).
- Enhanced legal security, with the requirement for proof of full legal compliance. This is more stringent than ISO 14001 which merely requires identification of legislation relevant to the organisation and a commitment to assess the level of compliance. As a result of the regulatory compliance assurance, EMAS registered organisations may benefit from fewer environmental inspections, easier permit applications (and lower related costs), and enhanced access to public contracts within the EU.
- Requirement for active involvement of employees and their representatives (not required in ISO 14001, although both standards include employee training). EMAS also requires the organisation to demonstrate influence over suppliers and contractors, in order to support standards enforcement (where ISO 14001 requires relevant procedures to be 'communicated' to suppliers).
- Transparent external communication, with requirements for open dialogue with external stakeholders, and external reporting (neither of which are requirements of ISO 14001). Public information on environmental performance, validated by an independent and accredited or licensed environmental verifier, is released via a periodic environmental statement.
- Reliability. Registration is formally made by a public authority, after verification by an independent, accredited or licensed environmental verifier. Data from the environmental statements is verified, and periodic inspections check for improvement of environmental performance.
- EMAS registration confers the right to use the EMAS 'Performance, Credibility, Transparency' logo, and also leads to ISO 14001 certification.

PAS 2050: 2011

4.15 As an example of other environmental purchasing standards produced by standards organisations, Publicly Available Specification (PAS) 2050 was launched in 2008 by the British Standards Institution (BSI). It builds on existing methods established through ISO 14040/14044, by specifying requirements for the assessment of greenhouse gas (GHG) emissions arising from products across their lifecycle, from initial sourcing of raw materials through manufacture, transport, use and ultimately recycling or waste.

4.16 The standard is designed to help organisations and consumers to understand the 'carbon footprint' of goods and services, and may also be used for a variety of processes for analysing, improving, comparing and communicating the emissions carbon footprint performance of products and services. For organisations, PAS 2050:

- Supports internal assessment of the lifecycle GHG emissions of their goods and services
- Facilitates the evaluation of alternative product designs, sourcing and manufacturing methods, raw material choices and supplier selection, on the basis of GHG emissions
- Provides a benchmark for programmes aimed at reducing GHG emissions
- Allows for comparison of goods or services on the basis of GHG emissions
- Supports reporting (and promotion) on corporate social and environmental responsibility.

Corporate and industry standards

4.17 Corporate standards, codes of practice and supplier audit and monitoring systems may be developed by large purchasing organisations, as an expression of their own environmental concerns and commitments. In the private sector, we have already highlighted examples such as Marks & Spencer's Plan A CSR framework, Coca Cola's water management standard, and the Virgin Group's sustainable tourism policy. Almost any corporate website will nowadays include corporate social responsibility or environment pages, including policy statements; a charter or principles; and the key standards expected of suppliers.

4.18 You should browse some corporate websites in areas of your own interest, and develop a portfolio of 'mini-case studies', in the form of corporate sustainability policies and supply chain standards.

4.19 Codes of practice and standards are also produced by industry associations, particularly for industries which are vulnerable to environmental risks in their supply chains. Examples include the following.

- **Global GAP (Good Agricultural Practice)** is a private sector body which sets voluntary standards for the certification of production processes of agricultural and aquacultural products. The standards 'are primarily designed to reassure consumers about how food is produced, by minimising detrimental environmental impacts of farming operations, reducing the use of chemical inputs and ensuring a responsible approach to worker health and safety as well as animal welfare.'
- Standards include: the Integrated Farm Assurance standard (IFA); the Compound Feed Manufacturer standard (CFM); the Animal Transport standard (AT); the Plant propagation material standard (PPM); the risk assessment on social practice (GRASP: an add-on to the IFA standard, with an assessment of basic worker welfare criteria); and the Chain of Custody standard (CoC).
- The **4C Association** is a platform for stakeholders in the coffee sector to address sustainability issues in a 'pre-competitive' manner. Almost 200 organisations (including coffee farmers, traders, roasters, retailers and civil society organisations) work together to improve the economic, social and environmental conditions of 'those who make their living from coffee'.

  The Common Code for the Coffee Community (4C Code of Conduct) is a baseline standard for sustainability in the coffee sector. It includes 28 social, environmental and economic principles for the sustainable production, processing and trading of coffee. For each principle, criteria are categorised according to sustainability as 'green' (desirable), 'yellow' (practice should be improved) or 'red' (practice must be discontinued). A producing group will only be certified to sell 4C Compliant Coffee if its practices meet a minimum average of 'yellow', as confirmed by independent verification.
- The **Forest Stewardship Council** is a non-governmental, multi-stakeholder organisation dedicated to the economically, socially and environmentally responsible management of forests. It facilitates the development of standards, ensures independent monitoring of certified operations, and protects the FSC trademark in order to provide consumers with assurance that forestry products originate from well managed and sustainable forests.
- The **Global e-Sustainability Initiative (GeSI)** and the **Electronic Industry Citizenship Coalition (EICC)** have conducted extensive research into the key challenges surrounding the supply of metals, the

ability to trace and track sources of metal used in electronic products and the industry's ability to influence conditions in supply chains. More generally, GeSI's role is to identify areas where the ICT sector can make the biggest contribution to sustainability, ensuring that member companies are focusing on leverage issues. It published a major report in May 2008 identifying 10 key sustainability issues for the ICT sector: climate change; waste and materials use; equality of access to ICT; freedom of expression; privacy and security; employee relationships; customer relationships; supply chain issues (including poor labour and environmental standards); product use issues (including health, safety and wellbeing); and economic development.

Based on these findings, GeSI has developed a number of tools, including: a 'materiality matrix', plotting the significance of sustainability criteria for companies and their stakeholders; supplier assessments (E-TASC: Electronics – Tools for Accountable Supply Chains); and a validated GeSI/EICC audit programme.

The effectiveness of environmental standards in achieving sustainability

4.20   Research findings from across the EU suggest that implementation of an EMS typically leads to:

- Significant environmental performance improvement, and a reduction in environmental impacts and risk events
- Enhanced competitive performance, if the EMS is fully integrated throughout an organisation
- Financial benefits, including reductions in energy use and more efficient resource use. Some EMAS registered organisations in the manufacturing sector, for example, have reported that annual energy savings alone exceed the annual costs of maintaining the scheme.

4.21   However, ISO 14001 in particular has been criticised for the fact it does not consistently guarantee full compliance with environmental regulations: it only provides a framework for organisations to set their own objectives, in the absence of mandatory reporting requirements.

5   General sustainability and sustainable procurement

5.1   Crossing syllabus boundaries, we will briefly outline some of the major standards which span social and environmental sustainability considerations.

The UN Global Compact

5.2   The Global Compact was launched in 2000, setting out ten principles for business, derived from the Universal Declaration of Human Rights, the International Labour Organization (ILO) Declaration on Fundamental Principles and Rights to Work; and the Rio Declaration on Environment and Development.

5.3   The ten principles include: support for human rights (freedom of association and collective bargaining, and elimination of forced and child labour); labour rights (elimination of labour discrimination); environmental responsibility (embracing a precautionary approach, and developing and sharing environmentally friendly technologies); and anti-corruption measures (working against bribery and extortion).

5.4   This is said to be the largest and most prestigious of all global sustainability codes: adopted by thousands of corporations and dozens of international NGOs and labour federations. However, criticisms focus on the lack of a system for transparent assessment and reporting on what endorsing companies have actually done to implement the principles.

ISO 26000: 2010 Guidance for Social Responsibility

5.5   ISO 26000:2010 is designed to provide: 'harmonised, globally relevant guidance for private and public sector organisations of all types based on international consensus among expert representatives of the main stakeholder groups, and so encourage the implementation of best practice in social responsibility worldwide.'

5.6 The Standard provides voluntary guidelines: it is not a management system standard, and is not intended to be used for certification purposes (like ISO 90001 or 14001) or for regulatory or contractual use. Guidance is given on:

- Concepts, terms and definitions related to social responsibility
- Principles and practices relating to social responsibility
- Core subjects and issues of social responsibility
- How to integrate, implement and promote socially responsible behaviour throughout the organisation and supply chain
- How to identify and engage with stakeholders
- How to communicate commitments, performance and other information related to social responsibility.

5.7 The core subjects and issues identified by the standard are shown in Table 3.5.

Table 3.5 *ISO 26000 core subjects*

CORE SUBJECT	ISSUES
Organisational governance	
Human rights	Due diligence; human rights risk situations; avoidance of complicity; grievance mechanisms; discrimination and vulnerable groups; civil and political rights; economic, social and cultural rights; and fundamental principles and rights at work
Labour practices	Employment and employment relationships; conditions of work and social protection; social dialogue; health and safety at work; and human development and training in the workplace
The environment	Prevention of pollution; sustainable resource use; climate change mitigation and adaptation; and protection of the environment, biodiversity and restoration of natural habitats
Fair operating practices	Anti-corruption; responsible political involvement; fair competition; promoting social responsibility in the value chain; and respect for property rights
Consumer issues	Fair marketing, factual and unbiased information and fair contractual practices; protecting consumers' health and safety; sustainable consumption; consumer service, support and complaint and dispute resolution; data protection and privacy; access to essential services; and education and awareness
Community involvement and development	Community involvement; education and culture; employment creation and skills development; technology development and access; wealth and income creation; health and social investment

BS 8903: 2010 Sustainable Procurement

5.8 In 2006 the British Standards Institution launched the BS 8900 Guidelines, designed to help organisations to develop an approach to sustainable development, and to connect existing technical, social and environmental standards.

5.9 BS 8903: 2010 is the world's first standard specifically addressing sustainable procurement. As a guidance standard, it does not 'specify' the steps to sustainable procurement, but provides information and recommendations – recognising that procurement processes and practices vary so widely across organisations and sectors that a more prescriptive approach would be impractical.

5.10 The standard defines sustainable procurement; presents the business case for sustainable procurement; and gives recommendations on 'how to do sustainable procurement' and embed sustainable procurement principles and practices across an organisation and its supply network. The fundamentals (principles) and enablers (supporting factors) are closely aligned to the core themes of the Flexible Framework: the benchmarking and development framework developed by the UK Government's Sustainable Procurement Taskforce.

5.11 The general thrust of the 'how to' sections of the standard is shown in Table 3.6.

Table 3.6 *BS 8903: 2010*

Fundamentals *Organisational and procurement policies and strategies that should be in place to provide context and priorities for sustainable procurement decision-making*	**Organisational policy and strategy**. The first step is to establish what sustainability means for your organisation and what the key priorities are. Procurement objectives must be aligned with corporate sustainability policy and strategy.
	Procurement policy and strategy: clearly written statement(s) outlining key sustainability intentions and priorities for procurement: aligned with organisational drivers; informed by sustainable procurement risk and opportunity assessment; and capturing economic, social and environmental objectives, targets and KPIs.
	Risk. Understanding of sustainability risks and opportunities in the supply chain is key to identifying objectives, priorities and KPIs.
Procurement process	**BS 8903** follows a generic procurement process and identifies the sustainability considerations that should be addressed at various points across this process. (This will be explored in Chapter 4.)
Enablers *Ways of working, competencies, practices and techniques that should be in place (and utilised by managers or buyers) on an ongoing or periodic basis, to support the sustainable procurement process*	**Leadership and governance**. Sustainable procurement requires (a) senior management support and endorsement and (b) systems, structures and controls in place to ensure consideration, resourcing and accountability.
	People. Relevant staff and stakeholders need to develop competence (eg whole life costing) and awareness (of values and goals). This may be developed through training, networking, knowledge-sharing and work experience, both internal and through the supply chain.
	Risk and opportunity assessment. Once sustainability risks and opportunities have been identified, they should be prioritised using a combination of: spend; scope to make a difference; and influence over the market to effect change. Risk management should be applied over the life of the contract: not as a 'one-off' exercise.
	Engagement. Sustainable procurement depends on building relationships, aligning thinking and communicating in a timely and effective way, to secure 'buy-in' (especially among participant stakeholders).
	Measurement. Performance measures should include: • Practice measures (management performance indicators) providing information on the organisation's capability and efforts in managing sustainability (eg percentage of staff trained in sustainable procurement, or number of contracts with sustainability criteria included) • Operational indicators providing information on the outcomes of sustainability initiatives (eg reduction in waste sent to landfill, eco-efficiency savings, or reduction in supply chain overtime hours)

5.12 The standard also highlights a set of fundamental values for sustainable procurement.

- A **sound** approach: based on fairness, openness and transparency, non-discrimination and competition
- An **ethical** approach: ensuring integrity, encouraging diversity, avoiding corruption and ensuring activities comply with ILO standards for pay and working conditions across the supply chain
- A **holistic approach**: considering the effects of procurement decisions on quality of life, the environment and society
- A **risk/opportunity-based approach**: using risk and opportunity assessment to identify and prioritise issues at all stages of the product lifecycle, in an ongoing process of continual improvement
- A **leadership approach**: requiring buyers to adopt leadership qualities to help build capacity and competence within supply chains and the marketplace
- A **value-adding approach**: delivering against a wide range of organisational objectives, beyond financial and efficiency savings, from CO2 emissions savings to innovation strategies.

6 The UK sustainable procurement agenda

The Sustainable Procurement Action Plan

6.1 Government has a crucial role in furthering sustainable development through its own large-scale procurement of goods, services, labour, property and other resources.

6.2 In the UK, the Sustainable Procurement Task Force (under Sir Neville Simms) was established in 2005, charged with drawing up an action plan to bring about a step-change in public procurement.

6.3 The task force drew on a range of governmental and non-governmental organisations to analyse the key barriers to sustainable procurement and presented a National Action Plan for overcoming them. The report *Procuring the Future* delivered its findings and recommendations in June 2006.

- *Lead by example*. Many public sector procurers lack clear direction from the top of their organisation on the priority to be given to delivering sustainable development objectives. To address this, a clear commitment from government should be cascaded down through both government targets and performance management systems that are independently monitored.
- *Too much guidance*. Procurers complained of guidance and information presented in an incoherent manner – a 'one size fits all' approach. Policies should be rationalised into a single integrated framework which meets the needs of procurement.
- *Raise the bar*. The existing minimum standards for central government should be properly enforced and extended to the rest of the public sector.
- *Build capacity*. The public sector must develop its capabilities to deliver sustainable procurement, including areas such as whole life costing.
- *Remove barriers to sustainable procurement* – whether actual or perceived. All public organisations were called upon to examine their budgeting arrangements to make sure they encourage and support sustainable procurement.
- *Innovation*. The public sector must capture opportunities for innovation and social benefits and must manage risk better through smarter market engagement.

6.4 The National Action Plan put forward three building blocks for moving the sustainable procurement agenda forward.

- *Prioritisation of spend*. Ten priority areas were identified for action nationally.
- The *flexible framework* guides public sector leaders in actions to make sustainable procurement happen, and to benchmark sustainable procurement development and maturity.
- *Toolkits* providing expert advice and support to public sector procurers, including 'Quick Win' minimum sustainable specifications in key spend categories with potential to make an immediate impact.

The European Integrated Product Policy (IPP)

6.5 In 2003 the European Commission published the Integrated Product Policy (IPP) outlining its strategy for reducing the environmental impact caused by products throughout their lifecycle. The IPP is based on five key principles.

- **Lifecycle thinking**: aims to reduce a product's environmental impact from the cradle to the grave. In doing so it also aims to prevent individual parts of the lifecycle from being addressed in a way that results in the environmental burden being shifted to another part.
- **Working with the market**: establishing incentives in order that the market moves in a more sustainable direction and rewarding companies that are innovative, forward-thinking and committed to sustainable development
- **Stakeholder involvement**: aims to encourage all those who come into contact with the product

(industry, consumers and the government) to act across their sphere of influence and encourage the purchase of more environmentally aware products and how they can better use and dispose of them

- **Continuous improvement**: the IPP seeks to encourage improvements that can be made to decrease a product's environmental impacts across its lifecycle.
- **Policy instruments**: the IPP approach requires a number of different initiatives and regulations to be enacted. The initial emphasis will be placed on voluntary initiatives although mandatory measures may be required.

Chapter summary

- The increasing trend towards sustainability is supported by legislation, codes of conduct, published standards, and inspection regimes.
- Various codes have been published to promote minimum standards in labour conditions. These include the ILO Declarations, the Ethical Trading Initiative, the Agricultural Ethical Trading Initiative, and the SA 8000 standard.
- Fair trading standards have been published by such organisations as Traidcraft, the WFTO and FLO International.
- Environmental management standards include ISO 14001, ISO 14020+, the European EMAS scheme, and PAS 2050.
- Social and environmental sustainability is supported by the UN Global Compact, ISO 26000 and BS 8903.
- In Europe, sustainable procurement is supported by the UK Sustainable Procurement Action Plan and the European Integrated Product Policy.

Self-test questions

Numbers in brackets refer to the paragraphs where you can check your answers.

1   Explain some of the general ways in which codes and standards differ among themselves. (1.5)

2   List some of the 'enabling activities' that are needed to facilitate implementation of supply chain codes and standards. (1.12)

3   Describe two of the declarations issued by the ILO. (2.2)

4   List the principles outlined in the ETI Base Code. (2.5)

5   List the goals of fair trade organisations. (3.3)

6   List the ten key principles of fair trade laid down by the WFTO. (Table 3.4)

7   What is an environmental management system? (4.3)

8   What features of EMAS are said to add value to ISO 14001? (4.14)

9   What are the ten principles of the UN Global Compact? (5.3)

10   What are the fundamental values for sustainable procurement outlined by BS 8903? (5.12)

11   What were the key recommendations of the report *Procuring the Future*? (6.3)

12   What are the five key principles underlying the European Integrated Product Policy? (6.5)

CHAPTER 4

Developing Responsible Procurement

Assessment criteria and indicative content

 2.4 Critically assess the main principles that will help achieve responsible procurement to help promote sustainability

- The implications of responsible procurement
- The responsible use of power in supply chains
- Managing conflicting priorities
- Reducing operational, financial and reputational risks

Section headings

1. Principles of responsible procurement
2. Implications of responsible procurement
3. Power in supply chains
4. Managing conflicting priorities
5. Sustainability risk management
6. Sustainability through the procurement cycle

Introduction

In this chapter we look at some of the main principles of responsible procurement, and their implications for supply chains and supply chain management. We start by exploring some general principles and models of responsible procurement.

We then look in overview at some of the implications of responsible procurement for the organisation and the procurement function. We consider the relationship between responsible procurement and organisational objectives, and the importance of strategic alignment and stakeholder buy-in. We also acknowledge a range of different sustainability issues and priorities faced in different economic sectors and industries. Sustainability standards and policies are not 'one size fits all' – and you need to develop the ability to contextualise your thinking (especially when dealing with exam case studies...).

Next, we focus on the three sustainability principles highlighted by the syllabus: the responsible use of power in supply chains; the management of conflicting priorities; and the management of risk.

Finally, we set the scene for the following chapters (and the next section of the syllabus), by giving an overview of the procurement cycle, and identifying the main sustainability implications of each stage. This will be followed up in detail in Chapters 5–7.

1 Principles of responsible procurement

1.1 We have already discussed what might be called the 'principles' of responsible procurement, in exploring sustainable procurement issues and standards. Different policy and standards frameworks articulate the core principles of sustainable procurement in different ways. We will outline a representative sample here.

1.2 The Responsible Purchasing Initiative report *Taking the Lead* sets out ten **responsible procurement principles**: see Table 4.1.

Table 4.1 *Responsible procurement principles*

PRINCIPLES FOR SENIOR MANAGEMENT	
1 Embed responsible procurement in job descriptions, competency frameworks and performance reviews	Responsible procurement practices flow from the top down: commitment needs to be unambiguous.
	Responsible procurement should not be compromised by the delivery of other work objectives.
2 Adopt a 'balanced scorecard' approach to objectives and rewards	Require buyers to deliver across a range of objectives: not just cost. Measure and review progress. Adopt a similar process with external suppliers.
PRINCIPLES FOR BUYERS AND BUYING ORGANISATIONS	
3 Make buyers accountable for delivering sustainable standards	Accountability supports effective implementation. Buyers are responsible for reconciling responsibility with other sourcing priorities, and for working with suppliers to achieve agreed standards using agreed approaches.
4 Build robust sourcing strategy for key categories with complex and/or high risk supply chains	Sourcing strategy is an opportunity for cross-functional and stakeholder input. It brings focus to key priorities, and avoids short-term tactical decision-making which can have negative consequences in the supply chain.
5 Subject sourcing strategies to independent review	Independent challenge and endorsement provide a stronger mandate for change, and improve the organisation's accountability for procurement actions.
6 Give suppliers a 'voice'	As key stakeholders, suppliers can provide important input to stratgic thinking, implementation and governance.
PRINCIPLES FOR SUPPLY CHAINS	
7 Insist on the use of supply and employment contracts, and include sustainability standards	Contracts protect and promote the interests of individuals and organisations by creating an agreed basis for dealings.
8 Identify vulnerabilities in the supply chain: apply measures to monitor and manage them	Vulnerability assessment can be used to look at the potential impact the organisation and its supply chain has on the external world. Make this a formal process and subject it to independent scrutiny.
9 Manage relationships professionally	Segment relationships and focus resources on the more complex ones. Relationship management is a key part of implementing change. Good practice should be cascaded to suppliers, for their own supplier dealings.
10 Encourage collective worker representation	Encourage worker representation to protect individuals from exploitation and provide a forum for problematic practices to be addressed. (If necessary, take steps to support 'whistle blowers' in exposing breaches.)

1.3 The report also identifies six 'key success factors' for an organisation to manage responsible purchasing effectively.

- **Leadership and accountability:** securing executive sponsorship and visible commitment; ensuring that skilled employees lead the agenda; embedding sustainability into procurement 'business as usual' (not managing it as a separate activity); and making procurement accountable for delivering improvements

- **Knowledge of the consequence of buying actions:** developing market and supply chain knowledge; requiring procurement professionals to think about the impacts of their decisions and to work jointly with suppliers to overcome problems; being alert to supply chain vulnerabilities
- **Managing conflicting priorities:** acknowledging the potential for other functions to resist responsible purchasing; giving purchasers the ability to prioritise (in line with overall responsibility objectives); and aligning policies, measurement and rewards cross-functionally to eliminate conflicting behaviours.
- **Thinking and acting beyond short-term horizons:** setting long-term targets reflecting organisational values; and developing sourcing strategies for key expenditure areas, as a framework for decision-making.
- **Managing relationships in the supply chain:** building secure, trust-based, relationships with suppliers; segmenting relationships to prioritise management; insisting on good practice in relationships between other parties in the supply chain; and aligning sourcing strategies, supplier relationship management and supplier development towards delivering long-term sustainability objectives.
- **Responsible use of power in supply chains:** understanding how power and influence are being used; using power positively to improve supply chain standards; and making sure that power is exercised responsibly at vulnerable points of the supply chain.

Basic steps in establishing responsible purchasing

1.4 The *Buying Matters* consultation document takes a more process-oriented approach to core principles, by setting out 'six steps to more responsible sourcing': Table 4.2.

Table 4.2 *Six steps to more responsible sourcing*

1 Understand existing legislation	Ensure that sourcing is in line with national laws and internatinoal agreements (eg ILO Conventions and environmental protocols such as the Kyoto Protocol).
2 Establish a senior management champion	The champion's role is to review procurement practices; develop a robust business case for sustainable procurement; and drive internal stakeholder 'buy-in'.
3 Develop company policies	Develop clear and agreed policies, including commitments (a) to promotion of human rights in the supply chain; and (b) on key aspects of the treatment of suppliers.
4 Train buyers	Train buyers to understand the impact of purchasing decisions, including how they might be supporting or undermining better conditions at the sites of production.
5 Collect data and set benchmarks	Indicators of desired behaviours can encourage steady improvement. Supplier feedback on the impact of purchasing practices also provides useful input.
6 Assess and reward buyers' and suppliers' performance on responsible purchasing	Measure and manage buyer and supplier performance. Recognise and reward improvements to reinforce positive practices and learning.

1.5 It also helpfully summarises the 'components' of responsible purchasing: Table 4.3.

Table 4.3 *Components and indicators of responsible purchasing*

Good relationships with suppliers	*Aim*: Buyers aim for long-term, stable, trusting, risk-sharing relationships. *Business case*: Stable, mutually beneficial supplier relationships support product delivery, continuous improvemnet, efficiency and innovation. Frequent supplier turnover costs time and money. *Social concerns addressed*: Supplier uncertainty, leading to temporary employment and lack of investment. *Suggested indicators*: Transparent criteria for supplier selection; firsti-tier supplier locations known; products bought in a fixed-term or ongoing relationship (rather than spot purchase); stable or growing value purchased per supplier year on year; low turnover ('churn') of first-tier suppliers
Clear, timely communication	*Aim*: Suppliers know the terms of trade which govern the relationship, receive clear communications about the buyer's expectations and are able to feed back on their own needs in a two-way relationship *Business case*: Poor communication jeopardises delivery and quality. Well-informed suppliers feel valued and invest in improvement. *Social concerns addressed*: Suppliers are unable to plan ahead, without feedback on products or demand forecasts. *Suggested indicators*: Terms of trade explaining policies on ordering, poor quality etc; suppliers are aware of complaints mechanisms; regular two-way exchange of information on products and sustainability issues.
Sustainable prices and pricing	*Aim*: Prices allow both supplier and buyer to benefit, and enable those further along the chain to adequately cover living and production costs. *Business case*: Cost pressures may lead to corner-cutting on OHS and exploitative management practices: posing quality and reputational risk. *Social concerns addressed*: Adequate profit margins are vital to ensure that workers have a living wage. Higher margins enable social improvements. *Suggested indicators*: Mechanisms for negotiated price adjustment; use of relevant pricing models (eg national minimum price or fair trade); suppliers have collective bargaining agreements in place (re worker wages).
Clear lead times and payments	*Aim*: Suppliers have consistent and transparent payment terms and an order timetable, identifying specification and delivery dates (lead times) *Business case*: Short lead times pose quality risks. Late payments pose risks to supplier viability and security of supply. *Social concerns addressed*: Fluctuating or urgent orders drive insecure employment and overtime. Long payment terms affect supplier liquidity. *Suggested indicators*: Time of payment is set in contract; prompt or early payment made; late, frequent and large changes in volume or price avoided.
Respect for human rights in the supply chain	*Aim*: Buyers and suppliers work towards minimum standards. Buyers give preference to suppliers demonstrating improving conditions. Buyers manage their own practices to support supply chain standards. *Business case*: Improving social practices are often reflected in productivity, quality and reduced reputational risk. *Social concerns addressed*: Where standards are not met, working with suppliers to improve conditions is more effective than ending relationships. *Suggested indicators*: Suppliers aware of minimum standards; systems in place to support compliance; buyers understand the impact of practices; improvement included in buyer job descriptions, reviews, rewards etc.

2 Implications of responsible procurement

2.1 This syllabus caption invites us to consider the impacts of implementing a responsible procurement strategy – on the organisation, procurement and other functions.

2.2 We will confine ourselves to a fairly broad overview of some key issues. The impacts will depend to a large extent on the content of the strategy (what measures it advocates, and whether these 'fit' existing structures, resources and capabilities) and the process by which it is developed and implemented (including stakeholder and change management issues). You will need to consider the specific details of an exam case study organisation, or an organisation of interest to you which you might use as an example in the exam.

The impact of responsible procurement on the organisation

2.3 A robust approach to sustainable procurement will have several implications for organisation structure, both as a whole and within the procurement function – depending on the specific approach adopted.

2.4 Processes may need to be aligned or re-aligned, creating a more 'horizontal' process flow in the interests of sustainability. CSR and sustainability explicitly cut across 'vertical' barriers and the separation of functional specialisms (often called 'silos' in a vertical or compartmentalised structure), emphasising the flow of sustainable value through the value chain.

2.5 Mechanisms may need to be developed or adjusted to facilitate:

- The allocation of clear responsibilities and accountabilities for sustainability within the procurement function
- The integration of sustainability responsibilities, objectives and targets within the current work of the procurement function where possible
- Liaison, cross-functional teamworking, consultancy or other forms of partnership between procurement and other functions on sustainability issues (or to integrate sustainable procurement perspectives into projects)
- The championship of sustainable procurement by representatives of the procurement function: that is, a change agency role.

2.6 The organisation may decide to centralise responsibility for sustainability, CSR or global citizenship, under a dedicated director or manager. This would create a visible presence, a 'hub' for sustainability information, a point of co-ordination and oversight for initiatives and so on. There may be a matrix-style support staff who work with or within the company's functional departments and business units (eg in a 'business partner', consultancy or centre-led action network model – similar to the ways in which procurement is commonly organised).

Skills and resources for sustainable procurement

2.7 The deployment of sustainable procurement policy may require new knowledge, awareness and skills. Education may have to be provided on sustainability issues and policy frameworks. Awareness training may be required to change attitudes to sustainability issues (and particularly, say, their priority in relation to former priorities which may have focused on cost). Skills training may be required to utilise new systems, tools of analysis (eg lifecycle analysis or whole life costing), negotiating techniques and so on.

2.8 Knowledge, awareness, skills and principles will have to be supported with adequate resources: authority to carry out allocated responsibilities; information (eg on corporate social responsibility targets and performance feedback); budget allocation (to cover short-term investment in sustainability); and so on.

Implications for procurement processes and tasks

2.9 We have already highlighted the need for procurement professionals to examine and change practices (such as flexibility, price leverage and opportunistic spot purchasing) which act as barriers to the improvement of social and labour conditions in supply chains. Chapters 5–7 specifically address the implications of responsible procurement for core processes and tasks – and we will give an overview of the responsible procurement cycle in Section 6 of this chapter.

Implications for other functions

2.10 The implementation of responsible procurement will have operational impacts on other functions in the organisation.

- Sustainability will become a key decision-factor in the requisitioning, specification and selection of the inputs to their activities and processes. The business need for requisitioned purchases and unsustainable specifications may legitimately be challenged by procurement and/or sustainability specialists.

- Sustainability principles may impact on their processes, procedures and practices: eg to reduce the carbon footprint of transport operations and office working, or to re-engineer production operations, in order to minimise waste.
- There may be new operational requirements: eg for reverse logistics, disassembly or recycling.
- New materials, technologies and systems may need to be developed and/or incorporated in operations – and new skills learned to manage and utilise them.
- There may be new risks (eg in innovation or transparency to stakeholders).
- There may be a need for increased cross-functional collaboration, consultation and information, in order to align sustainability decisions and activities.

Sectoral differences and issues

2.11 It is worth noting, for the purposes of exam case studies, that the implications of responsible purchasing may be somewhat different in the private, public and third sectors of the economy.

2.12 **Private sector** organisations vary enormously in activity and size, and the challenges of responsible procuremet will be different for a major multinational organisation than for a small or medium enterprise (SME). Private sector corporations, particularly large transnational corporations, are perceived to be major contributors to environmental exploitation and damage, over-consumption, social inequity and social costs. Now that society demands transparency and accountability for such impacts, and has become more vigilant (owing to increasing global information and activism), sustainability is no longer 'optional' in the private sector.

2.13 Competition and the profit motive are very strong drivers for private sector business. Responsible purchasing may be supported by competitive pressures for sustainability or constrained by competitive pressures for cost leadership in a market. As we have already discussed, there is a vital need for responsible purchasing to be justified by a robust business case, often based on risk and opportunity management, whole-life value and sustainable supply.

2.14 **Public sector** organisations are owned by the government on behalf of the State, which represents the public. This means that their primary mission, purpose and strategic driver should be the wellbeing and best interests of the public, both for present and future generations: by definition, 'sustainability'.

2.15 Public sector activity is financed by the state, mainly via taxation – as well as any revenue the organisation's activities may generate. This means that core drivers for sustainability will be the need for transparency and accountability in the use of public funds; and the potential for sustainability efficiencies and cost-savings.

2.16 However, the massive buying power of the UK public sector is envisaged as a key driver of sustainable development in all sectors: 'setting an example both to business and consumers in the UK and to other countries', as well as 'making rapid progress toward its own goals on sustainable development' (National Action Plan).

2.17 The key drivers for responsible procurement in the **third sector** (including charities, co-operatives, clubs and associations, trade unions, professional bodies and pressure and advocacy groups) include the following.

- The values of stakeholders (eg volunteers, donors, supporters and members), which are often directly related to the mission and purpose of the organisation
- The management of reputational risk, which is significant because of dependence on volunteer labour, political support and discretionary funding

- The need for transparency, accountability and stewardship in the management of funds, since third-sector funding often comes from persons or organisations not themselves benefiting from the services provided
- The need for economic sustainability. Cost disciplines are important, because of the scarcity of funds; pressure to devote as much as possible of their income to beneficiaries; or expenditure limits set by funding authorities or trustees.

EXAMPLE: OXFAM GB

The following is an excerpt from Oxfam's published sustainability policy.

'An accepted definition of sustainable development is "achieving economic growth, environmental protection and social progress at the same time". Much of Oxfam GB's programme work seeks to achieve sustainable development for people living in poverty. But Oxfam also needs to be aware of the impact of all its activities on the environment and on communities...

'Oxfam's activities impact on the environment and communities through its:

- **supply chain's employment conditions,**
- **direct and indirect use of non-renewable carbon fuels in its buildings and for passenger and freight transport via road and air,**
- **use of scarce/non-renewable raw materials in the supply chains of the items it purchases,**
- **use of harmful materials or high energy consuming processes in the production of the items it purchases,**
- **disposal of waste products,**
- **relationships with local communities where activities take place,**
- **welfare of staff, visitors, volunteers, neighbours and other stakeholders.**

'Oxfam will follow the principles of Reduce, Re-use, Repair, Recycle in managing its environmental impact. Using the 4Rs will not only minimise environmental impacts, it also makes sound economic sense.'

Industry differences and issues

2.18 Clearly, the organisational characteristics, operational priorities and sustainability issues of an oil drilling company are likely to be very different from those of an airline, management consultancy, hospital or food retailer – and these differences are likely to be apparent at least to some extent in their approaches to responsible procurement. We can only make some general comments here: start collecting and analysing your own examples – and pay close attention to the context and characteristics of case study organisations in the exam.

2.19 In an **extractive** industry, there will invariably be environmental sustainability concerns around issues such as: the over-extraction and consumption of non-renewable resources; environmental damage and degradation as a result of extraction activity (eg open cast mining); wastes, emissions and pollution (eg oil spills, dust and noise pollution, toxic waste disposal, slag); carbon emissions and other impacts of transport to and from remote locations; and ongoing environmental impacts from refining and use (eg burning of fossil fuels). There may also be social impacts on local communities, caused by the use of fly-in-fly-out workers, for example, and social sustainability and ethical issues arising from dangerous and difficult conditions for workers.

2.20 **Agriculture** has a distinct set of sustainability priorities: changing methods to protect and replenish natural resources such as water, soil and seed quality; maintaining or increasing productivity to feed growing populations (posing dilemmas around genetic modification, the use of pesticides and deforestation, say); growing consumer demand for organic and non-genetically modified produce; maintaining viability in the face of changing or difficult weather conditions; the impact of supermarket price leverage on farmers and small producers; and so on. Many of the social issues of purchasing from developing-country suppliers are highlighted by global agricultural and food supply chains.

2.21 In **manufacturing** industries, processes may be particularly prone to unnecessarily high resource and energy consumption, waste products, pollution and emissions – as well as industrial accidents and the handling and storage of hazardous substances. Each of these areas will be high priority for sustainability measures, with potential for 'quick wins' and measurable economic benefits. As we have seen, offshored or globalised production (with outsourced, licensed or owned-and-managed facilities in overseas countries) may also be prone to quality, health and safety, labour, human rights and environmental problems, especially in low-cost countries with less onerous regulatory regimes.

2.22 In the **retail** sector, the main focus of procurement is on selecting products that will appeal to consumers. Increasingly, this will include Fair Trade brands and products differentiated and branded on the basis of sustainability features. Additional responsible procurement issues may include the following.

- Reducing waste sent to landfill (including plastic bags and packaging materials)
- Reducing transport impacts of distribution
- Ethical supply chain relationships (where retailers have significant buying power), prompt payment and fair trade (eg not exploiting sale or return terms)
- Issues relevant to particular retail specialisms: the take-back of end-of-life electrical and electronic products, for example, or the potential for large supermarket chains to support or exploit small producers.

3 Power in supply chains

3.1 Power is an aspect of any relationship – not just obvious ones such as leader-subordinate or buyer-supplier. It also applies to inter-organisational relationships, as well as interpersonal ones. Power is essentially exercised in supply chains to appropriate or claim a larger share of the value or value gains created by the process.

3.2 From your studies for other modules, you should be aware of French & Raven's classification of the sources of power, and it is worth considering how those ideas might apply to supply chain relationships.

- **Legitimate power** may be exercised by an organisation, for example, by virtue of formal delegated authority: eg the role of an agent or lead logistics provider. Power is also legitimised by law, contract terms and agreed standards, and any of these might be appealed to in order to reinforce an organisation's interests.
- **Expert power** may be exercised by an organisation which is acknowledged as having knowledge or skills that are highly valued within the supply chain: for example, specialist service providers, owners of patents on processes or parts, a buying organisation willing to offer business consultancy to less experienced suppliers, or a developed-country organisation able to support technology transfer to developing markets.
- **Reward or resource power** is exercised by organisations recognised as having control over resources that are scarce and/or valued by the supply chain. In the broadest sense, this may be the power of a buyer to offer or withhold valued business; or the power of a supplier to control access to strategic or critical supplies.
- **Referent power** may be exercised by an organisation which has a strong brand or reputation, or is a recognised leader in the industry: other organisations will seek to emulate it, or be associated with it.
- **Coercive power** may be exercised through the aggressive use of competitive leverage by a dominant buyer or supplier (especially in a monopoly position).

3.3 The term 'structural power' (Cox) is often used to describe power that is built into a situation, context or relationship. Supply chains can be seen as having 'structural properties of power', as there are inherent balances and imbalances of power between buyers and suppliers of different sizes, in the criticality and substitutability of different materials, in the degree of 'lock in' created by relationship-specific investment and so on.

3.4 Traidcraft *(Are International Supply Chains Increasing Poverty?)* argues that 'the last few years have seen a fundamental shift in who gains from international trade. Increasingly benefits to companies at the top of global supply chains are reaped at the expense of those at the bottom. This shift has been possible due to the weakening position of workers and small producers at the bottom of the chain, in relation to increasingly powerful companies at the top.'

- As a result of trade liberalisation and political lobbying, the rights of multinational companies have increased, while protection for workers and small producers has reduced (in order for developing countries to attract foreign investment).
- Mergers and acquisitions increasingly consolidate market power in the hands of a few large global companies. (For example, 75% of all food bought in the UK is sold through four companies: Tesco, ASDA, Sainsbury and Morrison.)
- A few large brands control access to consumers, creating oligopoly markets, in which suppliers are forced to trade with a small number of powerful buyers.
- The power of retailers enables them to use a number of techniques to pass the risks and costs of doing business down the supply chain: for example, price squeezing, delaying payment, shortening lead times, changing requirements at short notice and so on.

3.5 The Responsible Purchasing Initiative makes it a key principle of responsible purchasing that: 'Good procurement professionals are aware of the power they exercise and use it responsibly to avoid abuses in the supply chain.'

Irresponsible use of power in supply chains

3.6 Resource power and coercive power are clearly open to abuse in power-imbalanced or structurally 'asymmetric' supply chain relationships: that is, relationships which are essentially *unequal* in terms of power, influence, 'voice', scale, or dominance of a market or sector (eg in terms of percentage of turnover, or control of access to the market). As part of the sustainability risk management process, buyers should seek to identify areas of the supply chain, and sustainability issues, which are vulnerable to the abuse – or unhelpful use – of power.

3.7 The use and leverage of power is a widely used technique, underpinning many buying strategies. The buying power of large global purchasers gives them the ability to bargain hard with suppliers – and in the case of small, less powerful suppliers, to dictate and enforce prices and terms of trade to suit their own interests. This may, as we have seen, have adverse effects.

- Disempowering suppliers, especially at lower levels of the supply chain, creating vulnerability and the risk of exploitation (which in turn can have social, economic and environmental consequences)
- Squeezing suppliers' profit margins so that they are unable to pay living wages or invest in improved labour conditions, quality and business development
- Forcing suppliers to pursue unsustainable practices (such as enforced overtime, forced working and corner-cutting on health and safety and quality)
- Passing 'top-down' pressures down the supply chain, creating knock-on effects of poverty and disempowerment to progressively more vulnerable suppliers, producers and workers
- Robbing the buying organisation of the potential benefits of supply chain input (for decision making and innovation), feedback (for learning) and commitment
- Stimulating scrutiny from regulatory bodies, media and pressure groups, owing to the recognised unfairness and unsustainability of such relationships.

3.8 Coercive, arbitrary, unfair or abusive exercise of power in supply chains may be seen as a source of sustainability risk, on several grounds.

- It may be **unlawful or unethical.** Key examples include: abuse of a monopoly or dominant market position under competition or 'anti-trust' laws; unfair treatment of suppliers in a public sector tender situation, under EU public procurement directives; or abuse of a position of influence for personal gain, under relevant codes of professional ethics (such as that of CIPS).

- It is generally **counter-productive**: aversive forms and use of power may secure short-term compliance, but they generally cause resentment, resistance (from corner-cutting to active sabotage), and loss of potential value arising from long-term, stable relationships, trust, commitment, continuous improvement and synergy. This is why adversarial relationships, based on overt competitive leverage, are not considered suitable for all supply situations! They are rarely likely to achieve long-term best value for money, or potential for mutually satisfying partnerships.
- It presents a **source of sustainability risk.** The irresponsible use of power, and its manifestations and consequences elsewhere in the supply chain, may not be visible, predictable or controllable by buyers. The risks may not be mitigated by standard methods of protection such as contracts and requirements to comply with standards, law and regulation.

Responsible use of power in supply chains

3.9 Even in relatively dominant relationships with suppliers and contractors, power may be exercised constructively through less coercive and damaging influencing strategies.

- Mutual obligations, expressed through negotiated supply contracts and service level agreements
- The offer of approved or preferred supplier status or public acknowledgement for performance and/or improvement
- Fair competitive pressures to meet price and non-price criteria (eg through fair and transparent competitive tendering)
- The potential for ongoing, stable, mutually beneficial business relationship, as an incentive for compliance and continuous improvement

3.10 Here are some measures that may be taken to improve the responsible use of power by buyers.

- Training buyers to be aware of the power they exercise; how power and influence are used; and their potential sustainability impacts on supply chains
- Developing an understanding of the end-to-end supply chain, and points of vulnerability (eg through supply chain mapping, discussed in Chapter 8) – as part of an emphasis on robust risk management
- Establishing effective oversight and governance of sourcing strategies and supply chains: eg through independent review of sourcing strategies, accountability structures and sustainability reporting mechanisms
- Effective mechanisms for supply chain control, audit and feedback gathering, so that the impact of buying decisions and practices can be assessed
- Capture and dissemination of learning from critical incidents and supplier feedback, in order to solve problems and initiate changes in purchasing practice

3.11 It should also be noted that power can be *intentionally used to positive effect* in supply chains and supplier relationships.

- Expert power may be used to develop and empower suppliers and supply chains, eg through technology transfer and support for business development.
- Referent power may be used to share and benchmark best practice standards, and to secure supply chain emulation of the buyer's sustainability standards, through sustainability leadership and role modelling.
- Reward power may be used to exercise responsible influence over the supply chain, to secure compliance with desired sustainability standards: eg through the use of sustainability criteria for access to contracts, supplier awards, and financial incentives for the achievement of improvement targets.
- Reward power may be used to develop required capabilities and sustainability standards in the supply chain, through investment in supplier training and development.
- Reward power may be exercised responsibly by the buying organisation through fair and sustainable pricing, rather than price leverage.

Power and dependency

3.12   *Cox et al* depicted the key issues of power and dependency in supply chains in a simple matrix: Figure 4.1.

Figure 4.1 *The power/dependency matrix*

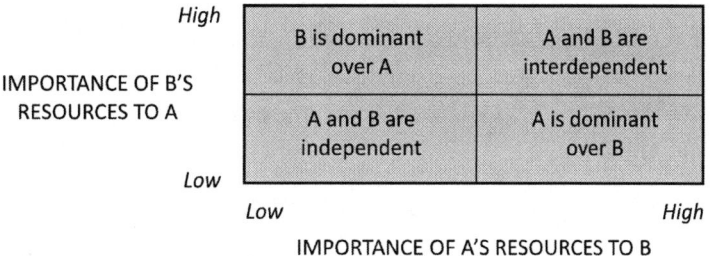

3.13   Where B is important to A, but A is not important to B, there is an asymmetrical relationship, in which B is the dominant partner in the relationship. This is inevitably the situation for most small developing-country farmers and producers in relation to large global buyers.

3.14   For buyers, the dangers of over-dependency on suppliers are obvious enough (what happens if our strategic supplier seeks more lucrative business elsewhere?) However, responsible purchasing emphasises that there are also dangers in an over-dominant position.

3.15   Responsible buyers may be reluctant to take too much of a supplier's turnover, or to insist on relationship-specific adaptations – even though the supplier might be keen to get more business. This is a responsibility and sustainability issue: protecting the supplier from risk, if the buyer, for whatever reason, terminates the relationship. Buyers may also benefit from suppliers having a good range of customers: being more attuned to the market, and supported by multiple customer resources for supplier development. This is an issue that should form part of regular communication between buyer and seller.

4   Managing conflicting priorities

4.1   In Chapter 2 we discussed a range of potential conflicts arising between the needs of stakeholders in supply chains. The Responsible Purchasing Initiative highlights the fact that responsible purchasing values and priorities may come under particular pressure from *internal stakeholders:* that is, from the priorities and expectations of purchasing's internal customers and collaborators in senior management and in other functions of the organisation.

4.2   Managers at all levels may be resistant to responsible procurement, if:

- It is perceived as being irrelevant to – or, worse, incompatible with – the critical success factors for which they are responsible and accountable
- It is perceived as being 'soft' or subjective, without a sound business case to justify effort and investment
- It is perceived as a public relations exercise: something to which 'lip service' can usefully be paid without the need for meaningful action.
- It is perceived as the preserve of the procurement function, without significant implications for other functions – or as an attempt by the procurement function to bolster its influence and status through additional policy and red tape
- It threatens the *status quo*, established norms and procedures, and established competencies and relationships: in other words, if it involves disruptive change.

4.3   There may also be specific divergences or conflicts of priority between responsible procurement and the objectives of other functions or departments in the organisation.

- The preference of design and engineering functions for highly-specified materials and components, or favoured suppliers, may be challenged on sustainability grounds.
- The objective of operations functions to achieve flexible, just in time production may be challenged by responsible purchasers seeking to guarantee suppliers adequate lead times and fewer changes to orders. Operations may resist trade-offs on specification criteria to support sustainable sourcing – or the need to adjust processes and practices for sustainability.
- The priority of the finance function for cost management and profitability may conflict with that of responsible procurement for longer-term, values-based performance measures (eg lifecycle costing and the balanced scorecard); and fair trade pricing and sustainability investment, at the short-term expense of cost minimisation.

4.4 There are a number of related issues in regard to conflicting priorities.

- Short-term operational requirements (eg for last-minute and urgent orders) will often prevail over strategic sourcing principles. This problem is particularly acute where procurement is carried out by part-time buyers situated in user departments, embedded in their culture and priorities, and reporting primarily to operational managers.
- With procurement resources typically thinly spread in an organisation, there may be a lack of capacity to drive and implement change at the departmental level – however good the intentions at an executive level.
- The accepted business case for sourcing strategies, and procurement performance measures, are often based on securing short-term cost reductions (eg through price leverage).
- Conflicting priorities can result in incongruent, disjointed and inconsistent actions and communications from different points of contact with the supply chain – causing confusion, inefficiency and risk. 'Mixed messages', apparent 'changes of mind' and demands for conflicting deliverables (low price, better sustainability) may heighten supplier uncertainty, particularly in low-cost countries where there are already language and cross-cultural barriers to understanding. And uncertainty, as we have seen, tends to put vulnerable producers and workers at greater risk.

4.5 One of the main challenges of responsible procurement is therefore to ensure that:

- Progress in implementing more sustainable sourcing practices is not compromised or jeopardised by competing expectations, pressures and priorities
- The actions and communications of all units and functions of the organisation are broadly congruent and consistent, in terms of the values they reflect, the standards they expect in the supply chain, and the impact they aspire to have on the supply chain

4.6 Here are some key mechanisms for managing conflicting priorities within the organisation.

- Communicating, promoting and reinforcing sustainability values and policies in such a way as to secure cross-functional stakeholder 'buy-in'
- Emphasising the benefits of sustainability and risks of non-sustainability for each stakeholder group – and ensuring that benefits can actually be demonstrated
- Incorporating sustainability goals, value and aspirations in corporate mission, value and policy statements, to ensure value and strategy alignment
- Co-opting senior management champions for cross-functional leadership
- Clear, cross-functional communication of (a) the social, labour and environmental standards expected in the supply chain and (b) methods of working with suppliers to achieve these standards (as agreed with suppliers)
- Aligning performance measurement and reward systems cross-functionally, in order to reinforce congruent and consistent action (such as adherence to the agreed critical path on projects)
- Risk and vulnerability impact assessments, to mitigate the negative consequences on supply chains of priority conflicts in the buying organisation
- Capture and dissemination of learning from critical incidents, and attempting to identify and resolve root causes (eg through cross-functional responsibility 'circles' and task force groups)

- Maintaining consistency in sustainability efforts, so that they become 'business as usual' – and give time for benefits to accrue

Value and strategy alignment

4.7 Organisations generally measure the relevance and value of any activity by whether it will 'fit' (and ideally further) its overall purpose, goals and strategic plans. An organisation's mission (definition of purpose) and vision (strategic intent or desired future state) typically 'cascade' down to goals and objectives (targets or aims which the organisation will pursue in order to fulfil its mission and vision), and strategic, tactical and operational plans to achieve them.

4.8 One of the key points arising from this 'hierarchy of objectives' is that, in order to secure widespread acceptance and support, responsible procurement will have to be embedded in the guiding **value system** of the organisation, from the top down. Consider the following high-level statement of strategic intent from The Body Shop, for example: 'Tirelessly work to narrow the gap between principle and practice whilst making fun, passion and care part of our daily lives.'

4.9 If an organisation is to achieve its corporate objectives, the plans set for each unit and function – while specific to their own roles – must be co-ordinated with each other so that they contribute towards overall objectives. This integration or **alignment** needs to happen in two directions.

- *Vertical alignment* is about ensuring that the goal of every activity contributes towards the overall objectives of the business. So, for example, sustainable procurement plans should support corporate sustainability and CSR policies.
- *Horizontal alignment* is about ensuring that the plans of every unit in an organisation are co-ordinated with those of other units, so that they work effectively together – and present a consistent, coherent face to the world (and especially to the supply chain). Sustainable procurement policies and principles should be communicated and embedded cross-functionally.

Cost barriers to responsible procurement

4.10 One of the biggest challenges faced by sustainable procurement is the perception that it is a more expensive option, and that sustainability fundamentally conflicts with procurement's core aims of cost management and value for money.

4.11 Sustainable procurement may well be more expensive, for a variety of reasons.

- It may involve the purchase of products and services which are innovative or new to the market, and therefore command a price premium.
- It may prevent organisations from buying opportunistically to secure the best available price (eg with longer-term, more stable contracts with suppliers) or from pursuing price-maximising strategies (eg because of concerns about fair trading, supplier viability, or exploitation of low-cost labour) or from selecting lowest-cost suppliers (eg to support diverse, small or local suppliers).
- It may involve more labour and management intensive processes (such as supplier monitoring, verification of sustainability standards, disassembly and sorting for recycling).
- It may require the development of new processes and capabilities: for example, reverse logistics, recycling and re-use of end-of-life or scrap materials.
- It may generally involve significant change (and change management) within the organisation and its supply chain – which also requires investment of resources.

4.12 Cost barriers may be strengthened by a number of environmental factors.

- Organisational performance may be measured by profitability (if not profit maximisation), and procurement performance may be measured by short-term cost reduction. Social and environmental benefits may be undervalued – as may longer-term cost efficiencies based on whole life costing.

- There may be lack of understanding or implementation of whole life costing, with a persistent belief that 'value' and 'efficiency' mean best price and short-term payback. (This was a finding of the *Procuring the Future* report on public sector sustainable procurement, for example.)
- Recessionary pressures may reduce consumer demand for sustainable products, services and commodities.
- The global financial crisis, credit crunch and European sovereign debt crisis have imposed severe investment constraints and budget cuts on all sectors of the economy. Sustainability is perceived as a low priority by many purchasers: a survey for *Supply Management* (27 August 2009) found that 64% of purchasers are not getting 'significant' financial benefit from sustainable procurement.

4.13 Cost barriers can be overcome in various ways.

- Where possible, sell a longer-term view of cost management to shareholders and internal stakeholders. Whole life costing, for example, can be used to demonstrate that initial investment in sustainability can reap later cost savings in running costs (eg in the case of energy-saving appliances), disposal costs (eg in the case of design for disassembly), and management (eg in the case of sustainable supply relationships based on fair and ethical trading).
- Make the business case for sustainability. Value and return on investment should be re-defined to include reputational and brand strength benefits, revenue from new market opportunities, reduced compliance costs and so on.
- Build momentum. Implement changes with relatively low-cost impacts, and/or quick payback periods: eg energy-saving light bulbs, recycled paper. Emphasise areas where outlays are actively reduced by sustainable procurement, eg reduced energy consumption and other 'eco-efficiencies'.
- Offset higher prices by seeking efficiencies elsewhere (eg lower transaction costs through long-term stable contracts).
- Access financial grants, subsidies, tax breaks and awards eg for regional development, innovation and sustainability.

4.14 It is worth noting that sustainability can help *reduce* costs throughout the supply chain, in the long term, through:

- Cheaper prices for some sustainable products (eg recycled products)
- Productivity gains (from health and safety, workforce stability and morale)
- Waste reduction and resource efficiency
- A reduced burden of regulation and compliance (eg from voluntary measures).
- Improved supplier relations, resulting in collaborative efficiencies and improvements
- Reduced supply risk and failure costs
- Whole life cost efficiencies: taking into account factors such as quality, durability, low maintenance and usage costs and recycling potential
- Reduced costs of capital, by increasing appeal to lenders and investors (particularly those focused on ethical and sustainable investments)
- Reduced costs of compliance, liability and contract disputes.

5 Sustainability risk management

Risk and vulnerability

5.1 **Risk** is defined by CIPS as 'the probability of an unwanted outcome happening'. Probability is the measure of the *likelihood* that a given event or result *might* occur. The International Standard on risk management (ISO 31000: 2009) defines risk simply as: 'the effect of uncertainty on objectives'. This highlights the fact that risk *can* be positive (in the form of 'upside risk' or opportunity) as well as negative.

5.2 Risk is effectively unavoidable. Negative risk can never be eliminated from business, but it can be identified and mitigated: either by reducing the *likelihood* of a risk event's occurring (eg by placing preventive controls in place) or by reducing the *impact* of its occurrence (eg by having insurance and contingency plans in place). This is the basic aim of risk management: reducing residual (remaining) risk to an acceptable level.

5.3 The term **vulnerability** is used to describe factors that make an organisation more prone to risk, or points at which it is more prone to risk, in terms of either the probability of the risk event occurring, or the impact of its occurrence. For example, complex supply chains and lack of visibility of lower-tier labour practices might be identified as a vulnerability to the risk of worker exploitation and reputational damage. Excessively lean supply chains may create a vulnerability to supplier insecurity or failure.

5.4 Since resources for risk monitoring, control and mitigation are typically limited, the concept of vulnerability is important in supporting the *prioritisation* of risks. It enables managers to focus on areas in which the organisation is most exposed to risk.

5.5 The management of supply chain vulnerability and risk has come to the fore in business thinking over recent years. Factors such as supply base rationalisation, supply partnerships and the development of lean and agile supply chains have increased the dependency of buying organisations on their supply networks – and disruption or variability of supply can have severe consequences for supply chains.

Risk management and sustainability

5.6 Throughout this Course Book so far, we have touched on the fact that risk and opportunity management are at the heart of responsible procurement.

- Sustainability-related operational, financial and reputational risks are key drivers for responsible procurement, and key components of the business case for investment in sustainability.
- Risk, vulnerability and opportunity assessment offers a sound and systematic approach to:
  — Raising the visibility of the end-to-end supply chain and points of vulnerability in relation to sustainability
  — Identifying and prioritising supply chain sustainability issues for policy-making and action: addressing key vulnerabilities, potentially high-impact risk factors, and opportunities to make significant impacts or secure 'quick win' improvements
  — Planning policies and practices to minimise or reduce sustainability risk exposure
  — Identifying and leveraging opportunities (eg sustainability-based marketing, supply chain innovation or competitive advantage).

5.7 The whole point about sustainability – as we saw in Chapter 1 – is that it addresses an identified risk to the future wellbeing of society, and, from the point of view of organisations, to the social and environmental 'eco-system' which supports their activity. Lack of sustainability poses risks to an organisation in several key areas.

- **Financial risks** impact on the organisation's ability to trade profitably. They may arise as a result of: poor corporate governance, investment or financial management (eg in regard to gearing, cashflow and liquidity); lost profits or higher costs due to poor supply chain management; higher prices due to over-consumption of scarce commodities; or financial penalties for irresponsible or illegal practices (eg 'polluter pays' taxes or damages paid to suppliers)
- **Operational risks** arise from supply chain processes, and impact primarily on production or service delivery. Such risks in the supply chain might include quality issues (eg arising from urgent orders or below-cost pricing); unmanaged health and safety hazards; and technology vulnerabilities. They also include **supply risks**: risks to the security and continuity of supply arising from supplier failure (eg as a result of unsustainable sourcing practices, excessively 'lean' supply chains or cashflow problems); supply disruption (eg as a result of industrial action, health and safety incidents or supply shortages); and the length and complexity of supply chains and logistics (pressure on lead times, transport risks).
- **Reputational risks** arise from vulnerability to the exposure of unethical, socially irresponsible or

environment-damaging activity by the organisation and/or its supply chain, potentially damaging the organisation's image, brand and credibility in its customer, investor, labour and supply markets. (We will discuss this important risk category in more detail below.)

- **Compliance and liability risk:** exposure of illegal or irresponsible activity by the organisation, incurring reputational, operational and financial penalties, including liability for workplace health and safety, and consumer or product safety problems.

5.8 Unlike traditional risk management, sustainability also explicitly recognises and seeks to manage the risks to health, safety, viability and wellbeing posed:

- By the organisation and its purchasing practices *to its supply chains*; and
- *By its supply chains* to their own natural and stakeholder environments.

5.9 The need for robust sustainability risk management practices is highlighted by a variety of factors in modern supply chains.

- The trend towards the transfer of operational management to external enterprises (eg category managers, outsource providers, lead providers, first-tier suppliers or agents) typically distances a buying organisation from the supply market and events in its own supply chain. Reduced transparency and visibility creates risk – because what cannot be seen cannot be managed.
- The trend towards globalisation has created lengthier and more complex supply chains, magnifying the risks of reduced transparency.
- The growth and consolidation of global sourcing organisations has increased their power over supply markets, and the potential for their buying practices to impact negatively on the most vulnerable members of supply chains.
- Traditional risk management techniques tend to focus on risks *to* the business organisation, and do not always adequately capture the risk the organisation *itself* poses to vulnerable social, economic and environmental resources in the supply chain.
- Increasing stakeholder and public awareness of sustainability issues (through standard-setting and reporting, activism and global information) adds an element of reputational and corporate brand risk.

Reputational risk

5.10 Charles Fombrun defines corporate reputation as: 'the overall estimation in which a company is held by its constituents. A corporate reputation represents the net affective or emotional reaction – good-bad, weak or strong – of customers, investors, employees and general public to the company's name' (*Reputation: Realising Value from the Corporate Brand*). Positive reputations take years to build – and can be damaged or destroyed in a moment...

5.11 It is increasingly recognised that reputation is an important intangible asset. A strong positive reputation can differentiate an organisation from its competitors; produce goodwill and trust in the organisation and its products (which in turn may enhance its stability and resilience in times of change and crisis); and help it to attract and retain quality staff, suppliers, investors and allies.

5.12 Conversely, a negative reputation – or reputational damage – can erode support and trust for the organisation and its products; attract hostile scrutiny from the media and pressure groups; and damage the organisation's relationships with its key stakeholders (which in turn can affect productivity, profitability, market value and so on). Some high profile examples include Wal-Mart in the US (using their size and price power to destroy small local competitors); Nike (exploitation of workers in low-cost labour countries); and Shell and BP (environmental damage from oil drilling operations). These corporations continue to enjoy market success – but have taken significant steps to strengthen and communicate their sustainability credentials, in order to 'manage the issues'.

5.13 With the rise in media, pressure group and public interest in sustainability issues, responsible purchasing has become a key dimension in the defence of corporate reputations – and the winning and preservation of credibility, consumer trust and brand strength. According to ongoing consumer attitude monitoring by research firm Populus, for example, three quarters of the UK population claims to weigh up a company's reputation before buying its products or services, and nearly three in five say they actively avoid purchasing from certain companies because of questions they have about their social, environmental or ethical track record.

EXAMPLE: NIKE

An article in *Supply Management* **(7 June 2007) reported on Nike's unveiling of an 'updated' range of CSR goals.**

'The firm, once famously criticised for poor conditions at supplier factories, says it wants to improve working conditions for the 800,000 people who manufacture its branded products. It hopes to eliminate the problem of excessive overtime by 2011. The company is also keen to increase the transparency of its supply chain operations by posting a list of the 700 factories it uses on the internet. The site will also explain the auditing tools it uses to examine its suppliers. It also intended to make its factories, shops and business travel climate neutral by 2011. [In May 2007], Nike signed a deal with a new supplier in Pakistan to make Nike footballs after problems with a different supplier last year. The contract has imposed strict guarantees on [the supplier] which is expected to meet nine workplace conditions, including making sure that employees are registered, paid hourly rates and eligible for social benefits, such as healthcare.'

In 2009, Nike was listed as one of the 'World's Most Ethical Companies' by the Ethisphere Institute.

The risk and opportunity management process

5.14 Risk management involves three key elements: risk identification, risk analysis and risk mitigation. ISO 31000 notes that: 'Organisations manage risk by identifying, understanding and trying to anticipate it. Through this process they communicate and consult with stakeholders and monitor and review the risk and the controls that are modifying the risk.'

5.15 The **risk management cycle** is an expression of the continuous process of risk monitoring and management, portrayed as a cycle: Figure 4.2.

Figure 4.2 *The risk management cycle*

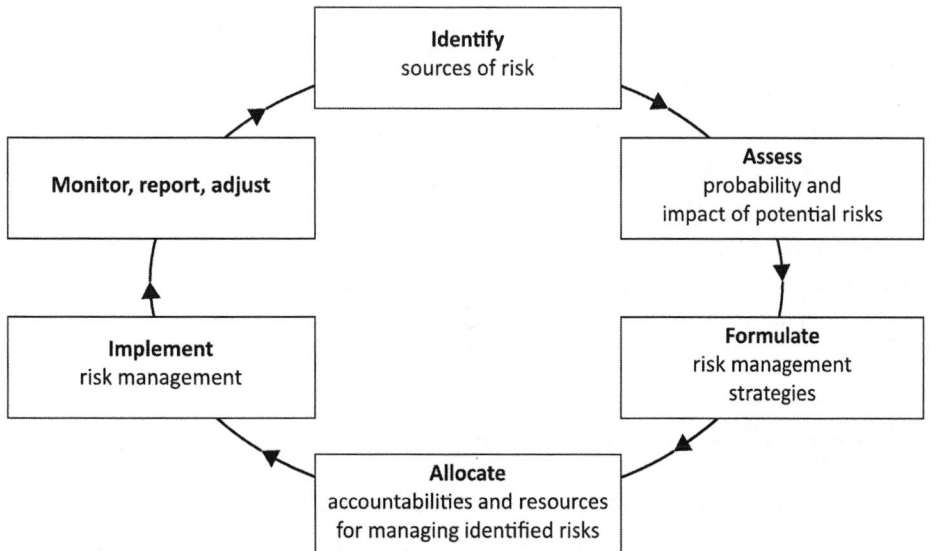

5.16 Sustainability risk management starts with developing an understanding of the organisation's sustainability objectives and how they apply to procurement. The British Standards Institution *(Sustainable Procurement Guide)* notes that sustainability objectives usually fall into two broad categories.

- Making a positive impact, based on the identification of **opportunities** to make a difference (eg reduce wastes, reduce poverty or improve labour conditions in the supply chain) and to reap related rewards
- Mitigating a risk, based on the identification of **risks and vulnerabilities**

5.17 **Risk identification** is the process of seeking to identify potential problems or areas of uncertainty: in other words, asking 'what could go wrong?' The corresponding process of **opportunity identification** seeks to identify potential areas where a positive impact can be made. Initial identification mechanisms may include any of the following.

- Monitoring of research results and reports, and risk events in benchmark organisations
- Environmental scanning (STEEPLE), supply chain mapping and supply chain appraisal (SWOT analysis)
- Critical incident investigations (investigating the causes of major or unexpected problems or successes)
- Consulting with key stakeholders (including suppliers) and industry experts, eg using brainstorming, survey questionnaires and workshops
- Periodic checks, inspections and audits of supplier premises and processes
- Conducting formal risk and opportunity assessments (for high-value projects or activities in volatile environments, and identified vulnerabilities)
- Employing third-party risk audit and risk management consultants.

5.18 **Risk and opportunity assessment** is the appraisal of the probability and significance of identified potential (negative) risk events and (positive) impacts: in other words, asking 'how likely is it and how bad/good could it be?' This is often quantified using the basic formula: *Risk = Likelihood (Probability) × Impact (Consequence)*. Quantifying risk and opportunity allows an organisation to:

- Determine how thoroughly, and how far down the supply chain, to investigate potential risks and opportunities
- Prioritise planning and resources to meet the most severe risks (or the most impactful or easily leveraged opportunities) and
- Set defined thresholds at which management action on an issue will be triggered.

We will look at tools for doing this in Chapter 8.

5.19 **Risk mitigation** is the process of lessening the adverse impact of a risk event, to a level at which the assessed residual risk is acceptable to the organisation: in other words, asking 'what can we do about it?' Risk management strategies are often classified as the Four Ts.

- **Tolerate** (or accept) the risk: if the risk is negligible, or there is no viable way to reduce the risk, no further action may, for the moment, be required, or justified. The risk may simply be acknowledged and registered – or it may be flagged for monitoring and periodic re-evaluation.
- **Transfer** (or spread) the risk: eg by taking out insurance cover, not putting all supply eggs in one basket (ie multi-sourcing) – and using contract terms to ensure that the costs of risk events and risk management will be shared with suppliers. Note that passing risk and liability down the supply chain is itself a sustainability issue: care must be taken to ensure that risks and rewards are shared equitably, and to protect vulnerable stakeholders at the bottom of the supply chain. Risk can be responsibly shared, however, by means such as clarifying liability for risks at all stages of the contract; requiring supplier insurance (eg to cover workplace accidents); and collaborating constructively with suppliers in risk identification, monitoring and management (including seeking supplier feedback on the impact of purchasing practices).
- **Terminate** (or avoid) the risk: if the risk associated with a particular project, practice or supplier is too great, and cannot be reduced, the organisation may consider ending the activity or relationship.
- **Treat** (mitigate, minimise or control) the risk: take active steps to manage the risk in such a way as to reduce or minimise its likelihood or potential impact, or both. In relation to supply risk, this may involve measures such as: risk-preventive contract development; supplier monitoring and performance management; the use of standards and codes of conduct in supplier selection; critical

incident reporting and analysis; supplier development and training programmes; and so on.

5.20 **Monitoring, reporting and review** is the process of monitoring the risk situation, and capturing learning. Risk and opportunity identification should be an ongoing process, as the supply chain risk profile may continually change, presenting new risks and opportunities – or turning slight risks into potential crises (eg if they attract media or regulatory scrutiny). A comprehensive list of identified risks should be compiled in a regularly updated **risk register**, with designated **risk owners** to monitor risk, update the register, and trigger action as required.

6 Sustainability through the procurement cycle

6.1 The British Standards Institution *Sustainable Procurement Guide* notes that deciding how and when to consider sustainability, in the procurement process, will require judgement by the buyer. 'Each procurement has different sustainability impacts, which means there will be unique opportunities to make a difference.' We will explore incorporation of sustainability into key stages of the sourcing process, as highlighted by the syllabus, in Chapters 5–7. However, it may be helpful to give an overview.

The responsible purchasing cycle

6.2 The Responsible Purchasing Initiative (*Win/Win*) suggests a responsible purchasing cycle, with specific reference to purchasing from developing countries: see Table 4.4. Stages 1 and 7 focus on the responsible purchasing programme (covering all purchases), while Stages 2–6 represent a process for each purchase.

Table 4.4 *The responsible purchasing cycle*

STAGE	CONSIDERATIONS
1 Prioritisation of categories and products within the responsible purchasing programme (discussed in Chapter 8)	• Assess sustainability risk vs importance to the organisation • Assess sustainability risk vs scope for improvement • Prioritise products and categories to focus on, to improve social and environmental impacts and mitigate risk • Identify desired relationship with suppliers in that category • Set targets for the responsible purchasing programme
2 Identification of priority issues in supply chains (discussed in Chapter 5)	• Map and understand (a) the supply chain and (b) the production processes behind the purchase • Work with internal stakeholders who requisition purchases • Draft economic, social and environmental criteria for inclusion in the contract specification
3 Supplier market engagement; development of procurement plan (discussed in Chapter 5)	• Engage suppliers to understand their perspectives and capabilities on economic, social and environmental issues • Conduct supplier market assessment re labour conditions, wages, compliance, standards and initiatives etc. • Develop a purchasing plan: approach, evaluation criteria (eg inclusion of standard or code), consultation requirements (eg multi-stakeholder approach), time-frames
4 Evaluation and shortlisting of suppliers; creation of ITT or RQF documents (discussed in Chapter 6)	• Use pre-qualification questionnaires and Invitations to tender to communicate commitment to sustainability • Shortlist suppliers, using the PQQ to assess willingness (policy), capabilities (process) and standards (performance). • Develop ITT/RFQs, clearly stating non-price criteria and weightings for selecting the winning bidder.
5 Receipt and evaluation of quotes or offers; selection of preferred supplier (discussed in Chapter 6)	• Evaluate bids on the basis of objective stated criteria • Use follow-up audits, site visits and discussions to verify • Use post-tender negotiation to discuss sustainability issues and improvement targets with preferred suppliers • Select a supplier on the basis of performance and evidence of willingness to improve.

Continued . . .

STAGE	CONSIDERATIONS
6 Creation of contract (discussed in Chapter 5) **Performance management against contract (discussed in Chapter 7)**	• Include social, ethical and environmental targets in contract • Establish key performance indicators (KPIs) for progress • Monitor supplier performance against KPIs • Manage supplier performance: agree corrective action and continuous improvement plans • Reward suppliers for sustainability attainments • Manage relationship, conflicts and grievances: in the absence of improvement, terminate responsibly
7 Update responsible purchasing programme and share and reward good practice (discussed in Chapters 9–10)	• Review the programme's implementation, effectiveness (target achievement) and supply chain impact • Identifiy and act to address root causes of poor performance and barriers to improvement • Share good practice (eg via supplier development) • Recognise and reward good performance • Update the programme and set new targets

The BSI Sustainable Procurement Guide

6.3   The *BSI Sustainable Procurement Guide* (BIP 2203) also helpfully offers an overview of the tools and skills required to support sustainable procurement (in a broader context) at each stage of a generic procurement process: Table 4.5.

Table 4.5 *Tools and skills for sustainable procurement*

STAGE	TOOLS AND SKILLS
Identify business need	• Challenge the demand: is the purchase really needed? • What are the performance requirements and desired outcomes? Establish business needs, not wants.
Define strategy	• Research the market, find out what is available and what is possible. Look for innovative solutions. • Identify sustainability impacts and opportunities. Prioritise these and focus where the most difference can be made. • Use specifications to design in sustainability wherever possible • Consider use of output based specifications to promote innovation, letting suppliers meet the need in new ways
Identify suppliers	• Ensure qualification and tender documents capture sustainability requirements • Keep the process simple and straightforward to encourage SMEs and local enterprises to take part • Advertise widely and in local media to promote supplier diversity • Communicate evaluation criteria including sustainability, so bidders understand its relative importance
Evaluate and award	• Use whole life costing techniques where relevant to evaluate bids • Evaluate and score tenders in line with published criteria which take into account sustainability • Take time to debrief unsuccessful suppliers, including sustainability performance to reinforce its importance • Negotiate for sustainability as well as cost, while suppliers are receptive • Finalise the contract, agree performance requirements: including sustainability measures and targets, incentives and penalties
Implement	• Agree review process; begin performance monitoring and ensure sustainability performance measures are clearly documented and agreed
Manage performance and relationship	• Monitor sustainability performance alongside other performance targets and agree corrective actions promptly if performance dips • Look for ways to improve sustainability performance throughout the lifecycle; pursue joint initiatives where applicable • Harness your supplier's expertise for your competitive advantage; use the supplier review process to promote understanding and dialogue, and to foster a good business relationship
Review and learn	• Take time to share learnings throughout the process. The sustainability agenda is constantly evolving; documenting good practice will enable standards to be raised and will help embed sustainablity into procurement processes and decision-making.

6.4 The guidance also provides a handy **sustainability requirement decision matrix**, suggesting particular points and methods at which different sustainability criteria can be captured and promoted for different levels of requirement: Figure 4.3.

Figure 4.3 *Sustainability requirement decision matrix*

	Pre-tender		Pre-award		Post-award	
Requirement	*Specification*	*Pre-qualification*	*Whole life cost*	*Weighted criteria*	*KPIs*	*Continuous improvement*
Recognised minimum standard (eg ETI, ILO)						
Bespoke minimum standard						
Quantifiable requirement (eg recycled content or waste recovery rate)						
Requirement can be monetised (eg energy, landfill)						
Performance requirement (eg reducing energy usage)						
Aspirational requirement (eg embedded impacts)						

Chapter summary

- There have been several attempts to establish principles of responsible procurement. This indicates the increasing importance attached to this area in modern times.
- Implementation of responsible procurement has important implications for organisational structure. In particular, there is likely to be an increased need for 'horizontal' organisation.
- Traidcraft has argued that recent years have seen a shift in power balances within supply chains, favouring multinational companies at the expense of those near the bottom of the supply chain. This creates pressure for MNCs to exercise their power responsibly.
- Implementation of responsible procurement may be resisted because it may conflict with other priorities, such as short-term profitability.
- The modern emphasis on sustainability is meant to address risks to the future wellbeing of society. However, introduction of sustainability policies can also reduce more immediate risks to an organisation (eg reputational risks).
- The BSI publishes helpful guidance on the tools and skills required to support sustainable procurement at each stage of the procurement process.

Self-test questions

Numbers in brackets refer to the paragraphs where you can check your answers.

1   List six key success factors for an organisation to manage responsible purchasing effectively. (1.3)

2   Describe the 'six steps to more responsible sourcing' identified in *Buying Matters*. (Table 4.2)

3   Explain the impact of responsible procurement on other functions in the organisation. (2.10)

4   List environmental concerns affecting (a) an extractive industry and (b) a manufacturing industry. (2.19, 2.21)

5   According to Traidcraft, there has been a shift in supply chain power in favour of large companies at the expense of smaller, overseas suppliers. Why? (3.4)

6   What are the adverse effects of irresponsible use of supply chain power? (3.7)

7   Give reasons why managers may resist a policy of responsible procurement. (4.2)

8   Describe mechanisms for managing conflicting priorities in relation to the introduction of sustainable procurement. (4.6)

9   In the context of sustainability risk management, what is meant by vulnerability? (5.3)

10   Describe risks that may arise for an organisation that fails to implement sustainable procurement. (5.7)

11   Describe stages in the risk management cycle. (Figure 4.2)

12   In the context of risk management, what is meant by the Four Ts? (5.19)

CHAPTER 5

Sustainable Specification and Contract Development

Assessment criteria and indicative content

3.1 Critically assess how sustainability can be incorporated into contract specifications

- Taking account of social, ethical, environmental and economic considerations in specifications
- International, regional and local standards for specifications
- The benefits of using standards
- Developing market knowledge

3.2 Critically assess how sustainability can be incorporated into contract terms

- Pricing and payment terms and the use of pre-payments for cashflow
- Community benefits arrangements in contracts
- Allowing for lead times and the management of capacity
- The use of fair and transparent terms that reward performance

Section headings

1 Identifying and defining requirements
2 Developing sustainable specifications
3 Developing market knowledge
4 Contract negotiation and development
5 Sustainable pricing and payment
6 Other contract terms for sustainability

Introduction

In this chapter we begin a more detailed examination of the main stages in the procurement cycle, and how sustainability can be embedded at each stage.

It is widely recognised that the best time to incorporate sustainability criteria into the sourcing process is 'at the beginning': that is, as early as possible. We therefore start with identification, definition and communication of the requirement in the form of product, service or contract specifications.

Next, we consider the processes of market engagement and market research that may be required before specifications can be finalised, in order to obtain high-quality information and stakeholder input on sustainability issues.

Contracts may be developed in draft form, following the preparation of specifications. However, contracts are basically 'agreements', and terms may need to be negotiated with suppliers: either as the primary approach to developing the contract, or as a way of refining a selected vendor's offer. We therefore start by considering briefly how sustainability considerations can be incorporated in contract negotiation. We then explore some of the main contract issues and terms relevant to sustainability, as highlighted by the syllabus.

1 Identifying and defining requirements

Early sustainability intervention

1.1 The best time to deliver sustainable sourcing is at the start of the process, when the buyer (and designer) have the greatest ability to influence sustainability. Procurement has traditionally involved fulfilling purchase requisitions and specifications drawn up by designers and users. However, there has been a trend towards early procurement involvement (in order to leverage commercial and supply market expertise) – and a sustainable procurement orientation argues that buyers need to partner with internal customers early, to achieve corporate sustainability objectives.

1.2 The BSI's *Sustainable Procurement Guide* suggests seven early points for influencing sustainability, before specifications have been agreed: Table 5.1.

Table 5.1 *Seven points of early influence on sustainability*

1 Aim to reduce consumption at the start	• Try to ensure that all purchases are really needed • Try to ensure that demand cannot be met in more sustainable ways (eg sharing, repairing or upgrading existing assets, hiring or buying, switching to re-usable products)
2 Develop understanding of business need (and sustainability impacts)	• Pre-qualification, shortlisting and contract award criteria should be drawn directly from business needs – so this is an important opportunity to reduce sustainability impacts
3 Challenge the *status quo*	• Research the market: know what is available and possible, and seek to tap into a continuous pipeline of supply innovation
4 Understand the power of your spend	• Use spending power appropriately, to influence markets, support innovation and develop sustainable solutions
5 Identify positive impacts achievable by your procurement	• What potential is there to improve labour conditions in supply chains, engage SMEs, support skilling and employment – and other socio-economic benefits?
6 Consider whole life sustainability issues	• Think beyond ownership to consider the impacts of sourcing, production, transportation, use and disposal
7 Engage the market early	• Where possible, signal sustainability requirements early (ideally, prior to formal pre-qualification or tender) • Give the market time to develop sustainable solutions

Demand or needs analysis

1.3 It is sometimes said that 'the most sustainable product that you buy is the one that you don't buy at all'. Identification and definition of requirement, as the basis for procurement strategy, is a foundational intervention point for sustainability. In order to develop appropriate procurement solutions for a given requirement, buyers need to understand the current and future needs of key stakeholders – and distinguish them from 'wants' (which may result in unnecessary consumption or over-specification). Robust definition of the business need or requirement can have a major impact on the final contract specification.

1.4 Buyers can influence the sustainability of requirement definitions in the following ways.

- Challenging customer definitions of requirement. Is there a genuine operational need for this item (or this quantity of it)? Are demand forecasting methods accurate? Could a lower specification (less resource-intensive) or generic item be used without compromising functionality or performance? What would avoid the need for this good or service?
- Challenging purchase requisitions, and seeking other ways to meet business needs: eg using substitute items in stock; outsourcing services; renting, leasing, sharing, exchange or refurbishing and repairing existing assets (instead of purchasing); or using purchased items more efficiently

- Ensuring that definitions of business need include sustainability requirements alongside performance, quality, cost and compliance requirements
- Attempting to change designer and user mindsets, to move away from prescriptive conformance specifications (which detail exactly what the required product, part or material must consist of) towards performance, output or outcome-based specifications (allowing flexibility and innovation in coming up with the best solutions to meet needs)
- Developing a knowledge bank on sustainable alternatives – or planning to access available information sources. (What internal or external expertise is available? What information is provided by suppliers, industry lead bodies, NGOs? Are eco-label or social certifications relevant to the requirement?)

1.5 The principles of the UK waste hierarchy (Reduce; Re-use; Recycle; Rethink) may offer a useful framework for discussion with internal customers: Table 5.2.

Table 5.2 *The UK waste hierarchy*

Reduce	• Ensure products are definitely needed • Ensure products are fit for purpose to avoid wasteful mistakes • Ensure products are durable and covered by a long warranty • Ensure packaging is the minimum necessary for protection • Avoid disposable products designed for single use
Re-use	• Check for redundant equipment that could be redeployed • Specify goods that are repairable and easily upgraded • Specify goods with clear and comprehensive maintenance, repair and operating instructions, supported with guaranteed stocks of parts • Give preference to suppliers that operate take-back schemes for end of life equipment and packaging
Recycle	• Specify products made from recovered or recyclable materials • Purchase products on which the materials are identified for ease of recycling • Minimise mixed-material products which are more difficult to recycle
Rethink	• Re-evaluate precedents and assumptions • Consider and evaluate options and alternatives • Consider consortium buying, if required, to gain sufficient buying power to promote sustainable performance among suppliers.

The intelligent customer

1.6 The term 'intelligent customer' is given to an internal or external customer who has strong capabilities for effective and efficient procurement. Intelligent customer qualities include: product knowledge; supply market and supplier knowledge; ability to translate internal customer requirements into specifications which enable suppliers to provide effective solutions; and procurement expertise and efficiency.

1.7 We might extend this concept to a 'sustainable customer', with strong capabilities for sustainable procurement, including: an understanding of sustainability issues; commitment to sustainability policy and targets; use of whole life product and service costing and relationship management; ability to specify clearly and flexibly for sustainability; and so on. We have argued that the procurement function must seek to be an intelligent and sustainable customer – but also to educate and support its own internal customers in being intelligent and sustainable customers.

2　Developing sustainable specifications

The role of specification

2.1　A specification can be simply defined as a statement of the requirements to be satisfied in the supply of a product or service. It translates the agreed business need into contractual requirements, describing specific requirements for the services or goods being procured.

2.2　The BSI *Sustainable Procurement Guide* argues that: 'Capturing sustainability requirements at this point is the *most effective* way of ensuring that sustainability is factored into the purchasing decision. Specifications should be used to establish minimum acceptable performance, actively excluding undesirable features and specifying in positive aspects and preferred higher-sustainability options.'

2.3　Specification is particularly important for sustainable procurement in the public sector. EU public procurement directives, for example, state that environmental and social considerations should be built into the earliest stages of the procurement process – and further opportunities to do this are limited, under competitive tendering rules, at the supplier selection and contract award stage. Design and specification thus offers the best opportunity to incorporate sustainable procurement criteria.

2.4　Incorporating sustainability into contract specifications sends a clear message that sustainability is an important element of the procurement.

2.5　An effective specification for sustainability is one that is:

- Clear and unambiguous as to what is required
- Concise (not restrictively detailed) but comprehensive (covering all points of the requirement)
- Compliant with all relevant national or international standards; health, safety and environmental laws and regulations; and the buying organisation's own sustainability policies and guidelines
- Up-to-date with current supply market sustainability developments and solutions
- Expressed in terms which can be understood by all key stakeholders
- Value-analysed, to minimise unnecessary consumption
- Integrated: incorporating sustainability principles in all elements of the specification – not just adding a separate sustainability criterion to an existing specification.

Stakeholders in specification development

2.6　In most cases, the lead role in specification development is taken by users of the product or service. After all, they may be most familiar with the requirement, and most technically 'savvy' about what is required. In less straightforward cases, however, the preparation of a specification may require cross-functional input, so that technical considerations are balanced with commercial and sustainability considerations.

2.7　Dobler and Burt (*Purchasing & Supply Management*) identify four major items that have to be brought into harmony.

- Design considerations of function
- Marketing considerations of consumer acceptance and satisfaction
- Manufacturing considerations of economical production
- Procurement considerations of markets, materials availability, supplier capability and cost

The overarching concern of sustainability could be added to this list – since each discipline's definition of sustainability, and its costs and benefits, will need to be harmonised and integrated.

2.8　Procurement professionals are in a good position to contribute the following benefits.

- *Supply market awareness:* the availability of standard and generic items (for variety reduction), the availability of suppliers with sustainability and innovation capability, the possibility of alternative suppliers and sustainable solutions, market prices and supply market risk factors (including sustainability risk factors)

- *Supplier contacts*, to discuss potential sustainable solutions in advance of specification, or to introduce pre-qualified suppliers to the design team (early supplier involvement), which may contribute to more sustainable design
- *Awareness of legal aspects* of sustainable procurement, eg the need to comply with national and international standards, and regulations on health and safety, environmental protection and (in the public sector) procurement methods
- *Purchasing disciplines*, for variety reduction, value analysis, cost reduction, whole life costing and so on

Conformance and performance specifications

2.9   As you should be aware from your earlier CIPS studies, it is common to distinguish between conformance specifications (or design specifications) and performance specifications (functional, output or outcome specifications).

- With a *conformance specification*, the buyer details the characteristics and/or content of the purchased items. This may take the form of an engineering drawing or blueprint, a chemical formula or 'recipe' of ingredients, a brand name and model number, a market grade, or a sample of the product to be duplicated. Suppliers may not know in detail, or even at all, what function the product will play in the buyer's processes. It is their task simply to conform to the description provided by the buyer.
- With a *performance specification*, the buyer aims to describe what it expects the purchased items to be able to achieve, in terms of the functions performed, the level of performance reached, or the outputs or outcomes delivered. It is then up to the supplier to furnish a product which will satisfy these requirements: the buyer specifies the 'ends', and the supplier has relative flexibility as to 'means' of achieving those ends (materials, designs and processes).

2.10   Performance or outcome-based specifications are generally regarded as being more supportive of sustainable procurement than conformance specifications.

- Conformance specifications may restrict the potential supplier base. A tight specification may be capable of fulfilment only by a small number of suppliers: in effect, the capabilities of other potential suppliers have been 'specified away'. This may particularly disadvantage SME and diverse suppliers.
- The prescriptive nature of a conformance specification may restrict innovation and the range of solutions to problems. With performance specifications, suppliers can use their full expertise, available technologies and innovative capacity to develop sustainable solutions.
- The focus on performance and functionality helps to ensure that products are not 'over-engineered' or over-specified relative to the actual requirement. At the same time, it ensures that they are 'fit for purpose' and sufficiently robust (minimising replacement and repair costs).
- The focus on performance and functionality prevents discrimination against sustainably preferable products on the grounds of non-essential design features or appearance (eg recycled content products).

2.11   It may be appropriate to use performance specifications (Lysons & Farrington: *Purchasing & Supply Management)* in the following circumstances.

- There are clear criteria for evaluating alternative solutions put forward by suppliers competing for the contract. These should be clearly communicated to potential suppliers, who may invest considerable time and resources in coming up with proposals, and will want to be assured that the selection process is fair.
- The buyer has sufficient time and expertise to assess the potential functionality and sustainability

of suppliers' proposals and competing alternatives (particularly where the technology is unfamiliar). The complexity of the evaluation process is the major disadvantage of the performance specification approach.

2.12 However, sustainability generally involves issues and risks across business processes and supply chains, so specifications will increasingly set standards or requirements for issues such as the following.

- Materials to be used in manufacture of purchased components, subassemblies or finished items: preferred sustainable materials and/or excluded unsustainable materials – or sustainability standards, attributes or functionality to be attained by materials (compliance with national or international standards, recyclability, biodegradability, renewable, sustainably managed, low-GHG emission, non-toxic)
- Processes and standards to be used in manufacture: eg ethical product testing, certified environmental management systems (eg ISO 14001), GHG emissions control (eg PAS 2050) and labour standards (eg ILO conventions)
- Sourcing and supply chain management processes: eg ethically sourced materials or products, Fair Trade certification, ethical and environmental supplier monitoring and management (to avoid risks arising from lower tiers of the supply chain) and so on
- Logistics, transport and delivery requirements: eg transport planning and fleet management for reduced fuel use and emissions; warehouse health and safety; location of distribution hubs to minimise community impacts and so on.

2.13 These issues may, alternatively, be set out in the broader definition of requirements (eg in tender documentation, requests for quotation, pre-qualification checklists and contract negotiations), to which product specifications are appended.

Preferred or desirable specifications

2.14 Ability to conform to specification is often used as a mandatory pre-qualification criterion. However, preferred or desirable specifications may be used if:

- There is uncertainty about how the supply market, or suppliers, will respond to the sustainability requirements
- There is uncertainty about whether there is a sufficient pool of potential suppliers capable of meeting the sustainability requirement
- The aim is to encourage suppliers to move towards more sustainable alternatives (eg 'preference to be given to Fair Trade certified or eco-labelled products') and to signal the importance of improvement. This may be a key component of the buyer's sustainable procurement policy: rather than excluding non-compliant suppliers (thereby excluding the potential to make a positive impact), the buyer may commit to developing supplier performance, conditional on demonstrated willingness to improve.

2.15 Where preferred or desirable specifications are used, it is important to determine in advance how suppliers which meet or exceed the desired requirement will be treated in tender evaluation, compared with those who don't.

Sustainability considerations in specification

2.16 The key considerations at the need identification and specification stage can be summarised as follows.

- **Economic considerations:** is there a genuine business need for the product or service (ie does it add value, as determined by value analysis or value engineering)? Can the need be met with less cost, resource use or variety? Can the need be met in a way that promotes greater operational efficiency? Can the need be met in a way that leverages available or emerging technology more effectively? Will the item, as specified, support or enhance customer satisfaction with the end product or service?
- **Social and ethical considerations:** does the specification unfairly exclude small or diverse suppliers?

Does the specification embody ethical and fair trade practices – and promote them in the supply chain? Does it require minimum standards for human rights, labour standards and worker health and safety (including compliance with relevant law and standards) in the supply chain? Will the item, as specified, contribute to or detract from the social responsibility of the end product or service, in terms of its production and consumption? Can the need be met in an alternative way that promotes any or all of these aims more effectively?

- **Environmental considerations:** does the specification require specific minimum standards of environmental performance in items or services specified (including compliance with relevant law and standards)? Does it promote the development of environmental management systems, capabilities and skills in the supply chain? Have the whole life impacts of the end product (eg end-of-life issues) been considered in the specification?
- Can the specification be **developed and formulated** (eg in consultation with stakeholders) in such a way as to maximise support for sustainable procurement principles and the potential for innovative solutions, which benefit society and the environment without compromising functionality and commercial objectives?

Drafting social and environmental criteria for specification

2.17 The social, environmental and economic criteria included in a specification should be shaped by the following factors.

- The sustainability objectives of the purchasing organisation (as set out in corporate CSR or sustainability policies)
- The key sustainability issues identified in the supply chain and production process (eg those posing most significant risk, or with best scope to secure improvements)
- The points of sustainability risk identified through supply chain and portfolio analysis (discussed in Chapter 8)
- The needs and priorities of supply chain stakeholders (where these are taken into account, eg as part of a Fair Trade orientation).

2.18 Here are some possible objectives for sustainable specification.

- To seek cost-effective (and where necessary, innovative) alternatives to environmentally or socially unsustainable materials, products and processes
- To minimise waste, including packaging, waste produced by the product, and waste generated by the eventual disposal of the product
- To maximise the re-use and recycling of materials
- To ensure ethical and socially responsible trading and employment practices at all tiers of the supply chain
- To maximise access to contracts for small, diverse, local suppliers
- To maximise resource and cost efficiency in sourcing, supply and production processes.

2.19 Here are some typical sustainability considerations that might be built into specifications.

- Environmental considerations such as: energy and water efficiency; use of recycled content; re-usable packaging; use of sustainable source materials (eg certified timber products, construction materials, crops); and/or eco-label equivalent performance standards
- Social considerations such as: the avoidance of substances hazardous to health in manufacture or use (eg PVC, lead paint); training requirements; fair trade certification; and/or labour requirements (eg fair working conditions, health and safety, workforce diversity and worker representation).

2.20 You should be able to identify some of the key sustainable specification criteria for different types of materials and products – and therefore priority areas for different industries and organisations.

- Vehicles: fuel efficiency
- Paper: recycled, chlorine-free, sustainable forestry management

- Office equipment: energy efficient, clean manufacturing processes, safety, end-of-life take-back, labour conditions in low-cost-country factories
- Energy: renewable
- Food and beverage: organic, fresh or seasonal, hygienic processes, minimised packaging, sustainable water management, fair trade for producers.

2.21 Note that sustainability issues may not be immediately obvious from the visible attributes of the product, or from supplier marketing messages. Paper production, for example, requires high consumption of energy, water and wood – and the use of chemicals (potential toxic pollutants). Forests may or may not be sustainably managed, to minimise deforestation, loss of topsoil and biodiversity and so on – while any paper that contains over 55% recycled content may be marketed as 'recycled'.

2.22 An example of a performance specification for sustainable paper purchase might be: 'Copier paper, 80gsm, suitable for printing on fax, laser printers and photocopiers, with a minimum 75% content of recycled post-consumer waste, Forest Stewardship Council certified as sourced from sustainably managed forests.'

The use of standards in specifications

2.23 Specifications will often refer to relevant legislation and standards, as a kind of 'short-hand' for expressing minimum acceptable process controls and performance levels. The British Standards Institution (BSI) describes a standard as 'a published specification that establishes a common language, and contains a technical specification or other precise criteria, and is designed to be used, consistently, as a rule, a guideline, or a definition'.

2.24 The buyer can simply specify that supplies be compliant with a given standard, or that the supplier's processes be accredited under a given standard scheme: for example, that all timber or timber products must be certified by the Forestry Stewardship Council (FSC), Australian Forestry Standard (AFS) or equivalent.

2.25 We have already discussed a range of international and national standards for specification, and the benefits of using standards to provide consistent terminology and assurance, in Chapter 3: review that material if you need to.

2.26 Lysons & Farrington urge purchasing staff to be aware of the major trade, national and international standards applicable to their industry and the items they buy regularly. The *advantages* of using standards are as follows.

- Clear specifications, no uncertainty or ambiguity as to requirement – and therefore less potential for error and conflict with suppliers
- Saving of the time and cost of preparing corporate specifications and related explanations and discussions
- Accurate comparison of quotations, since all potential suppliers are quoting on the same specifications
- A wider range of potential suppliers, and less reliance on (more costly) specialist suppliers, because of the general application of the standard

2.27 The main *disadvantage* of using standards, however, is that – like any generic specification – they may not accurately reflect the buyer's requirements and risk factors. They may also fail to reflect the latest technology or practices, since it takes some years for standards to be developed and updated. Full harmonisation of standards internationally has not yet been achieved, so there may be complexities in using British or European standards in Asia, for example.

2.28 It is worth noting that the use of standards in specification may itself be a sustainability issue.

- Public sector buyers are advised to exercise caution in the use of 'accreditation' brands, where these may not be established across the EU, as this would discriminate against some potential suppliers.

- Equivalent performance (eg '[eco-label] or equivalent') must be allowed for, to ensure that suppliers and products that possess the relevant requirements – but that do not have the specified accreditation – can still be considered. Some standards may set their specifications beyond a level that many mainstream suppliers are able to meet, and the cost of certification may be a deterrent for some suppliers, especially third sector and SME suppliers.
- A 'pass or fail' compliance-based approach to specified standards often fails to lead to sustainability improvements. The supplier may not understand the requirements of the standards, or the benefits which can accrue from them. An emphasis on compliance can lead to suppliers simply concealing problems – which makes them harder to address. The Responsible Procurement Initiative emphasises the importance of *progressive standards,* which allow flexibility; encourage improvements to be made; and support transparency about problems – which allow buyer and supplier to work together towards improvements.

Quick wins

2.29 'Quick wins' were established as part of the toolkit for sustainable procurement in the public sector, as part of the Sustainable Procurement National Action Plan. They are a set of published sustainable specifications for a range of commonly purchased products, such as IT equipment, white goods, paper (including tissue) and so on, in each of the priority spend areas. The products specified were chosen for their environmental and financial impact, scope for environmental improvement and 'political or example-setting function'.

2.30 'Quick wins are comprised of both a set of mandatory minimum standards at the market average level and best practice specifications. These best practice specifications are more stretching than the mandatory minimum. They are voluntary for those procurers that wish to purchase the "best in class" products in certain areas. These are likely to become the minimum over different time periods depending on the product or product group.'

EXAMPLE: QUICK WINS

The following is the basic 'Quick Wins' specification for buying furniture.

FURNITURE
Purchase of furniture produced from recycled materials and/or renewable materials. Reduces volatile organic compounds (VOC) emissions and avoids certain hazardous substances in materials production and surface treatment.

Minimum specification(s)

Timber must be purchased in accordance with UK timber procurement policy [link to policy]

Only timber and timber products originating either from independently verified legal and sustainable sources or from a licensed Forest Law Enforcement Governance and Trade (FLEGT) partner can be purchased.

NB From April 2015, only sustainably produced timber will be purchased

Best practice specification(s)

Same as the minimum specification and complies with the EU green Public Procurement comprehensive criteria [Link to criteria].

---

3 Developing market knowledge

The purpose of market research, analysis and engagement

3.1 Depending on the size, value, importance and risk of the procurement, further market research may be required before specifications can be finalised and sourcing options defined. Supply market research, analysis and/or engagement may be used for the following purposes.

- To ensure that draft specifications have accurately captured sustainability priorities, risks and opportunities in the supply market and supply chains (including those perceived and prioritised by suppliers)
- To develop an understanding of (a) the current level of sustainability capability and performance in the market or supply base (including examples of good practice which might be shared), and (b) their awareness, skills and willingness to improve sustainability performance and/or to move towards best practice
- To harness suppliers' expertise (including expertise in bringing about environmental and social improvements in a market or supply chain)
- To identify new technologies or products, innovative suppliers or advances in sustainable business practices which might be considered, as solutions to the business need
- To ascertain where there is a sufficient number of potential suppliers able to meet the buyer's sustainability standards – or whether it needs: (a) to ask and influence suppliers to progress *towards* those standards or (b) to stimulate and support innovation
- To determine how much influence the buying organisation has within the supply market and supply chains to drive sustainable procurement objectives (which will contribute to the prioritisation of sustainability issues, and to the choice of procurement strategy). You may be familiar with this concept under the name 'supplier preferencing': how the buyer is perceived by suppliers, on a matrix of attractiveness as a client, and importance of the business to the supplier
- To ascertain the level of sustainability performance that is being demanded by, and delivered to, benchmark organisations and competitors in the market. Where suppliers regularly meet sustainability requirements of other customers, or where sustainability precedents have been set in a market, this may indicate an opportunity to take a stronger position on sustainability specification.
- To promote creativity and innovation, by signaling demand for sustainability, and inviting the early input of potential suppliers to sustainability problem-solving.

Market research and analysis

3.2 Purchasing research is 'the systematic study of all relevant factors which may affect the acquisition of goods and services, for the purpose of securing current and future requirements in such a way that the competitive position of the company is enhanced' (van Weele). This may include various forms of strategic information gathering and analysis, including the following.

- Environmental audits, STEEPLE factor analysis and strengths, weaknesses, opportunities and threats (SWOT) analysis
- Vendor or supply base analysis: evaluating the sustainability performance and capability of current suppliers, and potential suppliers not currently being used. This may include capability analysis; attitude surveys; and risk and opportunity assessments. Qualitative factors, such as supplier perceptions of sustainability issues, will be as important as quantitative measures of capacity and attainment
- Supply market analysis: appraising general supply conditions and sustainability issues in the market

3.3 The Responsible Purchasing Initiative recommends supplier market assessment to evaluate:

- The livelihoods of the workers in the supply chain, whether they earn a living wage, and whether they are able to influence their terms of employment

- Existing national, sectoral or multi-stakeholder initiatives (including suppliers working with recognised NGOs or labour organisations) to improve worksites and address unsustainable practices. Where social concerns are entrenched, it may be advisable to consider a multi-stakeholder approach to the problem, to harness available local and international expertise – and appropriate resources and time may need to be built into the purchasing plan.
- The level of enforcement of, and compliance with, relevant laws and regulations
- The standards or codes of conduct currently in use.

Similar assessments may be made in relation to environmental issues and impacts (such as pollution, waste, water management, land use and environmental management).

3.4   This kind of research is conducted, on an ongoing or project basis, with the aim of providing information on the basis of which the organisation can plan to adapt to changes in the supply environment (ideally, earlier and better than its competitors) – to take advantage of new opportunities and/or to take defensive action in the light of perceived threats. It is thus potentially a key contributor to sustainability, in identifying, and shaping the organisation's response to, sustainability-related opportunities and threats.

3.5   In particular, it may shape decisions of whether or not to include a standard or code in contract specifications: reflecting available capability and willingness to pursue improvement.

3.6   In relation to a particular sourcing plan or cycle, the focus may be on vendor and market analysis. How many suppliers are there in the supply market? Where are they based? Of what type and size are they? What new products, processes and technologies are developing in the market? What sustainability-supporting capabilities are available or emerging? What are the sustainability commitments, objectives, performance, track-record and reputation of current vendors and potential suppliers in the market? What position does the buying organisation occupy in a supplier preferencing model, in relation to key suppliers?

3.7   The initial sustainability consideration will thus be: what sustainability issues will be built into the research and analysis project? Will the procurement function be looking for: financial stability and continuity of supply; supplier diversity and labour standards; environmental management systems?

3.8   The next consideration will be: what key sustainability 'issues' and trends are revealed by the analysis? What risks and opportunities arise from them? Are suppliers vulnerable to failure because of unsustainable sourcing practices by large buyers in the market? Is the buyer vulnerable to supply risk, owing to its lack of power or attractiveness in relationship to suppliers on whom it is dependent? Are resources increasingly scarce (and costly) in the supply market? Are the labour practices of lower-tier suppliers a source of reputational risk to the downstream value chain? Do new technologies offer potential for more sustainable supply?

Market engagement

3.9   'Market engagement' means entering into early dialogue with potential suppliers in relation to a given contract or requirement. This may be achieved by issuing a 'draft request' for industry or supply market comment, for example, or by committing to early supplier involvement (ESI).

3.10   The concept of **early supplier involvement (ESI)** is that organisations should involve suppliers at an early stage in the product or service development process: ideally, as early as the conceptual design stage, although this is not always practical. This contrasts with the traditional approach, whereby the supplier merely provides feedback on a completed product design specification.

3.11   The main purpose of ESI is to enable a pre-qualified supplier (with proven supply and technical abilities) to contribute technical expertise which the buying organisation may lack, by making proactive suggestions to improve product or service design, or to reduce process costs or wastes. Suppliers may provide constructive criticism of designs, and suggest alternative materials or manufacturing methods at a time when engineering changes are still possible.

3.12 In service contracting, it is common for the potential service provider to collaboratively develop and negotiate service specifications and service level agreements as part of a cross-functional team with users and purchasers.

3.13 The benefits to be gained from ESI have mainly focused on relatively short-term organisational gains via more accurate and achievable technical specifications, improved product quality and sustainability performance, reduction in development time, and reduction in development and product costs. However, there may also be some long-term benefits. ESI can, for example, be a catalyst for long-term, partnership relationships with excellent, sustainability-promoting suppliers. It can also improve the buyer's understanding about technological developments in the supply market, with potential for further exploitation.

3.14 As with most approaches, practitioners also need to be aware of potential drawbacks. The product or service may be designed around the supplier's capabilities, which (a) may be limiting, and (b) may lock the buyer into a supply relationship. This may become a problem if the supplier becomes complacent and ceases to deliver the quality, sustainability or innovation it once did – or if market developments present better alternatives. In addition, ESI may pose confidentiality and security issues (eg the risk of leakage of product plans to competitors).

Supporting sustainable innovation

3.15 One of the implications of market research and engagement in pursuit of sustainability is that, if sustainable solutions do not exist yet (or can only be supplied at unacceptably high cost or risk), the buying organisation may need to take responsibility and leadership within the market: signaling to the market what its needs are (establishing a demand for sustainable offerings), and encouraging suppliers to develop sustainable solutions.

3.16 Sustainable innovation may be defined as 'the successful exploitation of new ideas which further social, environmental or economic sustainability objectives'. A number of innovative solutions in product design, production processes and supply chain management are being demanded to meet sustainability challenges (such as resource depletion, climate change and entrenched poverty and inequality).

3.17 It is important to realise that innovation in design, procurement practices and supply markets does not necessarily involve 'brand new' ideas. Innovative supply solutions for one organisation may already be well established in another. Innovation is about the development, integration, diffusion, adoption and commercialisation of ideas – not just 'invention'.

3.18 Many best-practice procurement techniques are intended actively to stimulate innovation in the supply chain.

- Early supplier involvement and partnering
- Supplier development and best-practice sharing
- Innovation councils, or cross-functional innovation steering groups
- Forward commitment procurement (FCP): 'a commitment to purchase, at a point in the future, a product that does not yet exist commercially, against a specification that current products do not meet at a sufficient scale, to make it worthwhile for suppliers to invest in tooling up and manufacture' (Sustainable Procurement Taskforce). FCP evidences to the market that there is a need and demand for sustainable products and allows the supply chain to design them to meet the FCP specification.

3.19 Sustainable procurement can therefore support sustainable innovation in the following ways.

- Sourcing innovative products, services and processes (including new ways of thinking about procurement), as they become available and viable options
- Selecting, supporting and leveraging the capabilities of suppliers who are innovating, or have the potential to innovate, in pursuit of greater sustainability
- Supporting the buying organisation's own innovation capability, by promoting sustainable options in design, specification and sourcing.

4 Contract negotiation and development

4.1 At this stage of the procurement cycle, the sustainability criteria outlined in the contract specification need to be translated into draft contract terms and conditions, which may subsequently be finalised by negotiation with a selected supplier.

4.2 A variety of sustainability considerations will be built into contract negotiation and development, or the creation or deepening of a sourcing relationship.

4.3 For example, the sourcing process may have been leading up to a one-off purchase order; a framework agreement, call-off contract or rolling contract to fulfil requirements over a period of time; or a partnership or joint-venture agreement to pursue shared objectives and areas of interest (such as the development of 'green' brands or technologies). The **sourcing plan** (including the type and duration of the supply relationship) will depend to an extent on sustainability considerations.

- As the Kraljic procurement portfolio matrix indicates, the type of relationship sought will depend in part on supply risk. Economically sustainable supply may dictate arms' length systems contracts, for example, for routine and leverage items – and long-term relationships or partnership for bottleneck and strategic items.
- Social and environmental sustainability may best be managed in the context of more collaborative, long-term supplier relationships, because of the need for trust, continuous improvement, capability development and innovation.
- Economic and environmental sustainability may best be managed in the context of the whole life of the purchase: including issues such as whole life costs, maintenance and repair, upgrade, warranty, running costs, resource consumption and end-of-life issues such as take-back and disposal.

4.4 Another key issue may be the development of **written contracts**. Many suppliers at lower tiers of supply chains (especially in agricultural production) have no written contracts with their purchasers, and have to rely on ambiguous and changeable verbal agreements, which make it difficult to plan ahead for capacity management and labour hiring – and difficult to gain remedies for grievances. Similarly, many vulnerable workers lack formal contracts of employment which would provide them with protections. An important aspect of responsible procurement is therefore to:

- Provide suppliers with formally agreed, written contracts
- Insist on written contracts between organisations further down the supply chain
- Insist on employment contracts (whether standard, non-standard or casual) between supply chain organisations and their workers.

Contract negotiation

4.5 Negotiation may be the main approach by which a commercial agreement is arrived at in the private sector (where there is no legal requirement to use competitive tender as the primary means of supplier selection), or it may be used in support of tendering (eg to improve aspects of the preferred tender, or to ensure that all aspects of the requirement, bid and contract are understood): we will discuss post-tender negotiation in Chapter 6. Negotiation, as an approach to decision-making, stakeholder influencing and conflict resolution, will be important in:

- Securing stakeholder input and buy-in to sustainability policies
- Ensuring that stakeholders' voices and perspectives have been included in decisions which affect them
- Ensuring that contracts reflect genuine agreement between the parties, and a sharing of risk and reward that is broadly acceptable to both parties.

4.6 The choice of negotiating approach and tactics, and the ethical use of power in negotiation, is important for the following reasons.

- To support sustainability outcomes in the supply chain by using legitimate influence to drive change and improvement
- To support sustainability outcomes in the supply chain by using influence *responsibly* (eg avoiding 'hard bargaining' that would impact on the viability of producers and the livelihoods and conditions of workers)
- To maintain sustainable and sustainability-supporting supplier relationships, by *not* negotiating in an adversarial way that might damage future relationship, co-operation, trust and transparency, commitment to sustainability or resources for investment in sustainability.

Contract development

4.7 The development of contract terms will crystallise the commitments, responsibilities and rights of both parties in regard to the full range of sustainability issues; the apportionment and transfer of costs and risks; legislation and standards that will be adhered to; how performance will be monitored and measured; what commitments are made in relation to continuous improvement; how disputes will be managed; and so on.

4.8 Sustainability aspects may be built into the purchase order; standard terms and conditions of purchase; supply contracts; service level agreements; partnership agreements – and any schedules and appendices added to these documents in regard to sustainability criteria and commitments.

4.9 The BSI *Sustainable Procurement Guide* offers the following practical guidance.

- Sustainability-related requirements must be unambiguously stated and non-discriminatory.
- Buyers should generally use existing standard terms and conditions of business relating to sustainability, where these are included in the organisation's contract template. (Legal advice should be sought before deviating from standard terms.)
- Incentives and penalties should be agreed in relation to performance against sustainability and improvement targets.
- Buyers should ensure that any sustainability commitments or targets agreed in post-tender negotiation (and *not* delivered through the tender) are written into the contract – or at least captured in a supplier improvement plan or memorandum of understanding.

5   Sustainable pricing and payment

5.1 The sustainable price for a buyer to pay (purchasing price) will be as follows.

- A price which the purchaser can afford: allowing it to control its costs of production and make a profit on sale of its own goods or services
- A price which appears fair and reasonable, or represents value for money, for the total package of benefits being purchased
- A price which gives the purchaser a cost or quality advantage over its competitors, enabling it to compete more effectively in its own market
- A price which supports security and sustainability of supply, and reputational defence, by protecting the financial viability of suppliers, and ensuring that adequate resources are available in the supply chain to pay living wages, maintain adequate working conditions and invest in sustainability improvements

5.2 The sustainable price for the supplier or seller to charge (sales price) will be as follows.

- A price which 'the market will bear': that is, a price that the market or a particular buyer will be willing to pay
- A price which allows the seller to win business, in competition with other suppliers (according to how badly it needs the business, and the prices being charged by its competitors)
- A price which allows the seller at least to cover its costs, and ideally to make a healthy profit which will allow it to survive in business, pay living wages to workers, maintain adequate working conditions and invest in sustainability improvements – and to support profitability through its own supply chain.

5.3 As discussed in Chapter 2, fair pricing is a core issue of social and economic sustainability, because price leverage and minimisation strategies by powerful buyers can result in squeezed profit margins for suppliers, passed on down the supply chain – and impacting disproportionately on the supply chain's most vulnerable members, in terms of inadequate wages and working conditions (as well as enforced corner-cutting on quality and environmental protection).

Pricing arrangements

5.4 Price arrangements or agreements in contracts are basically of three types.

- **Fixed price agreements**, in which a schedule of fixed fees or payments is agreed in advance (and the supplier therefore bears all the risk of cost variances). More flexible variants, in supply markets with volatile labour or material costs, may include:
    — The use of a **contract price adjustment (CPA) clause**, stipulating that price adjustments are allowable on the basis of actual increases in material or labour costs, or appropriate indices and contract price adjustment formulae
    — The use of a **price review or re-determination clause,** stipulating that the fixed price will be opened to review and re-negotiation at the end of a specified period, in the light of cost fluctuations, supplier performance etc
    — The use of **long-term stable pricing models**, taking into account fluctuating costs of production (based on published benchmarks and indices) to establish stable pricing for a specified period (eg six months). In contexts where market prices fluctuate, this provides suppliers with consistent payments, allowing them to plan and budget ahead. Marks & Spencer has put such a model in place with its milk producers, for example.
- **Incentivised contracts** of various kinds, such as:
    — Specified bonus payments (or **incentive fees**) added to the fixed price on attainment of specified KPIs (including sustainability standards), cost savings or improvement targets
    — Formulae for sharing cost savings (eg against a negotiated **target cost**) between buyer and supplier in an agreed formula
    — Staged payments (so that the supplier only gets paid in full on completion of the project), contingency payments (eg part of the payment is linked to KPI performance) or pay-on-receipt arrangements (offering early payment for fast delivery)
    — Price penalties for performance failure.
- **Cost-plus agreements**, in which the buyer agrees to reimburse the supplier for all allowable and reasonable costs incurred in performing the contract, in addition to an agreed profit percentage. The buyer therefore bears the risk of cost variances, so most cost-type arrangements include a cost limitation clause or 'cap' on cost reimbursement. Cost-plus arrangements may be based on cost plus a fixed fee for doing the work, for example, or cost plus an incentive (higher) fee for meeting KPIs.

5.5 Fixed price agreements might be seen as fair and appropriate for procurements for which a reasonably comprehensive and accurate specification is available; fair prices can be estimated and established more or less accurately (based on more or less predictable costs); and there is relatively little risk of cost variation (or the supplier is willing and able to *bear* any risks of cost variation in order to win the contract).

5.6 Fixed price agreements are generally advantageous to the buyer, in terms of:

- Financial risk, since its total price commitment is known in advance, and the supplier bears all the risk of cost fluctuations (eg due to factors such as underestimation of costs, wage and price inflation, fluctuating commodity prices, schedule blowouts and incentive rates, exchange rate fluctuations and so on)
- Cashflow management, since the timing of payments (related to milestones or instalment deliveries) can be pre-planned
- Supplier motivation: a fixed price schedule gives the supplier a strong incentive to deliver efficiently and on time, since any cost savings (below the agreed price) are kept by the supplier – and it is also liable for any cost blowouts. In other words, the amount of the supplier's profit depends on the actual cost outcome – without a minimum or maximum profit limitation.
- Administrative simplicity and contract management costs, since the buyer will not be concerned with monitoring or auditing cost performance.

5.7 In some contexts, however, fixed price agreements may be seen as an unsustainable or inequitable passing of cost-related risk down the supply chain, impacting ultimately on its most vulnerable members. Sustainable procurement might therefore suggest the use of price review and contract price adjustment provisions within a fixed price arrangement – or the use of cost-plus arrangements.

5.8 Cost-plus arrangements are correspondingly advantageous to the supplier, since the buyer bears the risk of cost increases. There are advantages for the buyer, however, in that the final cost may be less than a fixed price contract, because the supplier does not have to quote or negotiate an inflated price in order to cover its cost-related risks. Cost-plus contracts are often used when long-term quality or sustainability values are more significant to the business need than cost minimisation.

5.9 In order to maintain the security of supply and a sustainable and equitable supply relationship, it is often seen as desirable to reduce the financial risks to both buyer (on the basis of a cost-plus agreement) and supplier (on the basis of a firm price agreement). This can be done by incorporating variations into a firm pricing arrangement, *or* by building protections for the buyer into cost-based agreements, eg by using target costing.

5.10 Incentivised contracts are suitable where it is regarded as desirable to motivate the supplier or contractor to improve performance: either as part of a long-term, continuous improvement and gain-sharing agreement (as in a supplier partnership) or where supplier performance management is critical to mitigate sustainability risks. Incentivised contracts may be used to support sustainability by:

- Applying incentives, rewards and penalties to agreed sustainability improvement targets, KPIs or standards attainment
- Ensuring that suppliers share equitably in value gains through improved performance (eg through revenue, profit or gain sharing, where suppliers are allocated an agreed percentage or flat fee bonus for cost savings or added value).

Payment terms

5.11 In UK law, under the Sale of Goods Act, any time stated for payment is not 'of the essence' (ie a vital condition of contract), unless the contract states otherwise. However, sustainable procurement recognises that extended payment terms, sale-or-return terms and (non-contracted) late payments, often have significant **cashflow** implications for vulnerable SME suppliers: potentially, threatening their liquidity to the point where they are unable to pay workers or creditors, or source supplies for continued operation.

5.12 Sustainable payment terms may therefore be based on:

- Pre-payment, payment in advance, or payment with order, in full or in the form of a deposit or 'down payment'. (The Fairtrade standard requires that: 'Trading terms are based on written contracts which specify the mutually agreed price and payment conditions, including pre-payment where requested by producers.')

- Scheduled payments, allowing suppliers to plan cashflows more dependably
- Staged pre-payments (eg on project milestones)
- Self-billing and automatic payments (on schedule, shipping or receipt, without the lead time required for supplier invoicing)
- Incentives for (or guarantees of) early or prompt payment of supplier invoices
- Buyer penalties for late payment (eg liability for interest on overdue payments, at a rate which compensates the supplier for losses directly incurred).

5.13   Such terms support sustainability in the following ways.

- Giving suppliers assurance of payment, in high-risk supply contexts (eg an unknown customer in an international market, or a known payment risk due to a history of late payment)
- Giving suppliers assurance of payment keeping pace with their own expenditures on the contract, and their commitments to workers and creditors
- Giving suppliers revenue assurance which may support their engagement of labour on permanent contracts (supporting worker protection) and investment in sustainability improvements
- Supporting the stability of supplier cashflow and liquidity
- Compensating suppliers for losses due to late payment (and creating an incentive for buyers to pay promptly)
- Acting as incentives for sustainability performance (eg if pre-payments are conditional on attainment of minimum standard or improvement)

5.14   Of course, this may be an issue of financial sustainability for the buying organisation, too. Negotiated terms should take into account the buyer's own cash flow risk, needs for short-term finance (through extended payment terms), desire for *quid pro quo* benefits (eg discounts for early payment), and assessment of supplier risks (eg the need to retain or withhold a reasonable proportion of the contract price until certain agreed performance criteria or project milestones have been met).

6   Other contract terms for sustainability

6.1   A wide range of express terms may be included in supply contracts, clearly stating the rights and expectations of both buyer and supplier in regard to price and terms of payment, delivery schedules, quality, liability for risks and costs, methods of dispute resolution and so on.

6.2   Contract terms should relate directly to the achievement of sustainability targets. As we will see in Chapter 7, for example, key performance indicators (KPIs) may be set, against which supplier progress and performance will be measured. However, we might argue that *all* contract terms potentially have an impact on sustainability – insofar as they allocate risk and reward equitably (or inequitably); impose sustainable (or unsustainable) obligations on suppliers; or offer (or fail to offer) protections and remedies for the rights of suppliers and workers in the contract relationship.

6.3   We will look at some of the main considerations in sustainability-supporting contracts, as highlighted by the syllabus.

Community benefits arrangements in contracts

6.4   The community benefits movement argues that the main purpose of economic development is to bring measurable, permanent improvements to the lives of communities hosting, or affected by, economic activity: particularly low-income, vulnerable and developing communities. Its aim is to ensure that economic development activity has flow-on benefits for host communities, in terms of the creation of employment opportunities, the improvement of working conditions, and the development of rights and amenities that improve the quality of life.

6.5 A **community benefits agreement** (CBA) is a formal contract agreed between community groups and a corporation involved in a major supply contract, project or development which might affect their interests, requiring the corporation:

- To provide specific amenities, benefits and/or mitigations to the local community (ensuring that promises made when 'pitching' a project are delivered) and/or
- To consult and negotiate with community representatives on relevant issues, including grievance mechanisms to handle any problems or complaints which may arise.

In exchange, the community groups agree to host, support, or not oppose, the project. Often, the negotiation of such an agreement requires a multi-issue, multi-stakeholder organisation, including community, environmental and labour organisations.

6.6 Similar provisions can be incorporated in standard supply contracts, where the buying organisation seeks to have a positive impact on the supplier's host community, as part of its responsible or ethical purchasing programme. Here are some typical community benefits provisions.

- Training and skilling programmes
- Local hiring and employment programmes
- Targets for the use of local, women-owned, minority-owned and SME suppliers and subcontractors
- Commitment to hiring responsible contractors (avoiding hiring contractors that have violated environmental or labour laws)
- Commitment to pay living or statutory minimum wages
- Guaranteed mitigations in excess of those required under local law (eg addressing environmental impacts)
- Commitments or targets for community investment (eg funding for community organisations and programmes; investment in infrastructure).

Allowing for lead times and capacity management

6.7 As we saw in Chapter 2, one of the key principles of current procurement practice is to seek fast and flexible 'just in time' supply, in response to changing demand patterns (eg peak seasonal orders) and unexpected peaks and troughs in customer demand. As we also noted, speed, flexibility (last minute orders or changes to orders) and poor demand forecasting and data sharing make it difficult for suppliers:

- To meet requirements and delivery schedules without cutting corners on quality, safety or working conditions (eg enforced overtime)
- To plan ahead for efficient capacity management (and related cashflow management). During peak periods, suppliers may have more production than they can handle – while during low-demand periods, they may not have enough. Such variations in the production cycle can make it difficult to maintain a stable level of working hours (resulting in non-contracted labour, enforced overtime and so on).

6.8 Contract provisions for discussion and agreement with suppliers may therefore include:

- Forward delivery dates and forecast quantities for large orders
- Guaranteed minimum order quantities where possible
- Achievable lead times between purchase order and delivery, taking into account the need to achieve desired social, labour, environmental and quality standards
- Minimum notice periods for change and/or cancellation of order (with penalties for late notice)
- Transparency and the sharing of information that might impact on purchase schedules or quantities (eg demand forecasts) and/or supplier capacity and lead times (eg supply or labour problems or competing orders).

6.9 The Fairtrade standard requires that: 'Trading terms are based on written contracts which... allow sufficient lead time for production without excessive working hours, at the same time as seasonal factors affecting the producer.'

Fair and transparent terms that reward performance

6.10 The aim of contract terms is to build sustainable supply chain relationships, incentivise performance and promote progressive sustainability improvements. Everything that we have said so far suggests that such terms should:

- Be **fair** in application: non-discriminatory and promoting fair competition; equitable in the allocation and sharing of risk and cost; and avoiding disproportionate impacts on the most vulnerable members of the supply chain
- Be **transparent**: stating rights, obligations and expectations clearly and unambiguously, in a way that can be understood (and therefore legitimately agreed to) by all parties
- **Reward performance**, by building in incentives, rewards and gain-sharing opportunities for progress, improvements and demonstration of commitment – rather than focusing on penalising non-compliance.

6.11 It may be comparatively easy to secure the **compliance** of suppliers with sustainability standards and targets, through mechanisms such as: information (widely disseminating the policy via contract managers, the corporate website or extranet, in contract terms and conditions, at supplier conferences and meetings, and so on); the use of contract incentives, penalties and sanctions; and making continued business contingent on progressive improvements or maintenance of standards.

6.12 If the buying organisation wants the added benefits of **commitment**, flexibility, innovation, proactive problem-solving, continuous improvement and co-operation – over and above what is expressly required by minimum contracted standards – they will have to make it worth the supplier's while. A range of incentives may be used.

- Contingency payments (eg part of the payment is linked to sustainability measures)
- Sustainability key performance indicators (KPIs) or improvement targets linked to recognition and rewards: extension of the contract or the promise of further business; inclusion on the approved or preferred supplier list; publicised supplier awards and endorsements; financial bonuses; and so on.
- Revenue, profit or gain sharing (eg allocating the supplier an agreed percentage or flat fee bonus for cost savings arising from reduced resource usage)
- The promise of long-term business agreements, increased business, or guaranteed or fixed order levels, allowing the planning of investments and improvements
- Opportunities for innovation: the contract gives the provider the chance to implement or devise new solutions that will develop their business and reputation
- The offer of development support (eg training or technology sharing, or financial contribution to the costs of attaining standards certification)

Statutory compliance

6.13 Buyers may also use contract terms to 'remind' suppliers of the statutory requirements imposed on them by relevant law and regulation in their country of operation (or international conventions), in order to signal the importance of compliance with minimum social, labour and environmental standards – and to clearly apportion liability for compliance-related costs or reputational risks.

6.14 In the UK, for example, it would be common for a contract to remind suppliers of the statutory requirements imposed on them by the Health and Safety at Work Act 1974; of the supplier's responsibility for compliance; and of the supplier's duty to ensure that staff working at the premises of the buyer (or the buyer's customers) comply with the health and safety requirements of those premises. A buyer may also require the supplier to indemnify it against any liability, costs, losses or expenses sustained by the buyer if the supplier fails to comply with the legislation.

6.15 Similar provisions may be used to ensure that suppliers comply with minimum wage regulations, rights to join a trade union, or other statutes that may be in place (however poorly enforced in the country of operation).

Chapter summary

- Sustainability is best addressed from the outset: when specifying requirements. Procurement professionals have an important role to play in this area.
- Incorporating sustainability into contract specifications sends a clear message that sustainability is an important element of the procurement.
- Effective market research can help to establish that sustainability objectives can be achieved by prospective suppliers.
- Contract negotiation should be shaped so as to achieve sustainability objectives. The approach to negotiation is itself a sustainability issue: the use of power in negotiations must be handled ethically.
- Buyers must agree prices that are fair for both sides. Enforcing unduly low prices is unsustainable because of the risk of supplier failure.
- Other contractual terms – eg on community benefits, or rewards for performance – can also promote sustainability.

Self-test questions

Numbers in brackets refer to the paragraphs where you can check your answers.

1   How can buyers influence the sustainability of requirement definitions? (1.4)

2   What are the Four Rs of the UK waste hierarchy? (1.5)

3   Why are performance specifications more suitable for sustainability than conformance specifications? (2.10)

4   List objectives of sustainable specification. (2.18)

5   What are the objectives of supply market research in relation to sustainability? (3.1)

6   What is meant by early supplier involvement? (3.10)

7   Why is the choice of negotiation approach important in relation to sustainability? (4.6)

8   List the factors that define a sustainable price for (a) the buyer and (b) the supplier. (5.1, 5.2)

9   Why are cost-plus pricing arrangements advantageous to a supplier? (5.8)

10 Give examples of community benefits that may be included in supply agreements. (6.6)

CHAPTER 6

Sustainable Supplier Selection

Assessment criteria and indicative content

 3.3 Evaluate how sustainability can be incorporated into supplier selection

- Checking suppliers' understanding of codes of practice and standards
- Recognition of trade unions and collective bargaining arrangements
- The use of international framework agreements
- Creating weighted evaluation criteria that take account of social, ethical and environmental issues
- Shortlisting suppliers based on objective criteria

Section headings

1 Sustainability considerations in supplier selection
2 Supplier pre-qualification
3 Supplier selection
4 Contract award
5 Supporting SME and diverse suppliers

Introduction

In this chapter we move on to supplier selection and contract award: a process which may embrace a wide range of approaches.

We will work our way through a generic supplier selection and contract award process: from pre-qualification of potential suppliers on minimum mandatory sustainability criteria; through the incorporation of weighted sustainability criteria in requests for quotation and invitations to tender; the conduct of an equitable and transparent tender process; the use of objective criteria in contract award; and the potential for post-tender negotiation to reinforce sustainability requirements.

Finally, we will summarise the issues surrounding participation of small and medium enterprises (SMEs) and diverse (minority-owned and women-owned) suppliers in competition for contracts, since this is an important area of responsible procurement in domestic, as well as global, supply chains.

1 Sustainability considerations in supplier selection

1.1 In Chapter 5 we looked at the process of specification, and some of the further information-gathering and decision-making that may be required to finalise the contract specification. Once a specification is finalised, sustainability requirements can be built through successive stages of the procurement process. As a very broad overview, this typically involves the following steps.

- Communicating the organisation's sustainability policies to suppliers
- Asking for sustainability-related capability and commitment in pre-qualification questionnaires
- Defining desired sustainability outcomes in the invitation to tender or other request documents (such as a request for quotation or request for proposal)
- Securing the agreement of the chosen vendor to achieving the specified outcomes, in the contract, purchase order or other form of agreement

1.2 The British Standards Institution *Sustainable Procurement Guide* notes that: 'Some suppliers with socially and environmentally unsustainable practices might be able to offer prices that are unrealistically low, for example, with poor labour standards. Unless robust pre-qualification, tender processes and evaluation criteria are in place to ensure good minimum standards before the supplier is taken on, the purchasing organisation will be constantly undermining its own ethical policies, exposing itself to reputational risk, and giving a signal to the market which undervalues sustainability against other issues.'

1.3 As we saw in Chapter 4, careful consideration should be given in procurement planning as to which stages of the procurement process are most appropriate for achieving the specified sustainability objectives. The approach adopted will be influenced by factors such as the following.

- The capability, maturity and number of suppliers in the market to achieve prescribed sustainability standards or improvements
- The buyer's level of influence in the market (to 'insist' on sustainability standards or improvements) – including the value and length of the proposed contract (and therefore its perceived value to the market)
- The assessed level of supply chain vulnerability to sustainability impacts, and the severity of potential impacts (and therefore the need to minimise risk)
- Any regulatory frameworks governing the procurement process (eg EU public procurement directives, which limit the use of non-price criteria)

1.4 The preferred sustainability approach and standards might, for example, be incorporated into one or more of the following elements of the supplier selection process.

- **Selective request for quotation or invitation to tender.** Where selective tender procedures are permitted or appropriate, the buyer may invite to quote or tender only those suppliers that market research has shown meet a mandatory sustainability requirement (eg use of recycled materials, or non-use of enforced and child labour).
- **Mandatory pre-qualification criteria.** A request may specify certain minimum capabilities or accreditations that respondents must have in order to pass through the screening or pre-qualification stage of an evaluation (eg having an ISO 14001-certified environmental management system or commitment to basic ILO labour conventions).
- **Specifications and statements of requirement.** As we saw in Chapter 5, prospective suppliers may be encouraged to offer items that meet or exceed published sustainability specifications and/or special conditions of contract (eg manufactured goods with an Energy Star rating above a specified threshold).
- **Qualitative requirements.** Prospective suppliers may be asked to provide information on a range of criteria, in order to allow their sustainability credentials to be evaluated, scored, rated and/or compared (eg a requirement to provide evidence of programmes in place to reduce packaging, or to describe what the supplier will do to ensure support for worker representation in its supply chain).

- **Continuous improvement commitments**. Request conditions may require the successful supplier to commit to improve sustainability over the life of the contract (eg to increase the proportion of products covered by recognised eco-labels, or the proportion of the supply chain covered by sustainability audits).
- **Contract and performance management**. Contract clauses and key performance indicators (discussed in Chapter 7) can be used to enforce and incentivise the achievement of specified levels of sustainability performance or improvement.

1.5 In general, mandatory pre-qualification requirements place more restrictions on potential suppliers, and may limit the number of bids received. This level of sustainability conformance may therefore be reserved for procurements for which:

- The organisation needs to address a high-risk sustainability impact or point of vulnerability
- Supply market research indicates that there are sufficient suppliers in the market who are willing and able to meet the requirement
- It is permissible (in the public sector) to use selective or restricted tendering procedures: generally, where there is a limited supply market able to meet criteria (eg the requirement for a particular recycling process).

1.6 Qualitative requirements can offer greater flexibility to tender evaluators. They can also be a useful means of promoting consideration of sustainability issues in the supply market, highlighting market demand for sustainability, and stimulating innovative solutions to sustainability problems.

1.7 In addition to the incorporation of sustainability criteria in supplier selection procedures, there may be a number of sustainability issues in the selection process itself.

- The process should be fair and transparent, and supportive of fair and open competition: this is generally the focus of public sector procurement rules, for example.
- In the interests of economic and social sustainability, the process should also, as far as possible, seek to engage and support small and diverse suppliers: facilitating their access to contracts; avoiding unnecessarily prescriptive or onerous requirements which might disadvantage their bids; and ensuring that buyers are aware of the business case arguments for supporting such sources of supply. (We will address these arguments in the final section of this chapter.)

1.8 Throughout these processes, it is important for procurement staff to work with internal stakeholders to co-ordinate clear, consistent communications about sustainability policies, issues and requirements. A number of staff within and beyond the procurement department may communicate with suppliers, and contradictory messages will undermine supplier trust and relationships – as well as the promotion of the sustainability message.

2 Supplier pre-qualification

2.1 'Pre-qualification' in its broadest sense is the definition and assessment of criteria for supplier 'suitability', so that only suppliers with certain minimum standards of capability, capacity, compatibility or commitment for sustainability are invited or considered for participation in a given sourcing process – potentially saving considerable time, effort and cost at the tender stage.

2.2 Pre-qualification may be carried out across a range of requirements: to prepare an approved supplier list, for example. Or it may be carried out on a procurement-specific basis, to pre-screen suppliers to receive an invitation to tender or to quote for a contract.

2.3 Pre-qualification involves two basic processes.

- The development of objective **evaluation criteria** by which potential suppliers' sustainability will be screened (and later evaluated in detail)
- The **appraisal and screening** of potential suppliers against stated sustainable procurement objectives

2.4 The starting point may be a pre-qualification questionnaire (PQQ) or request for information (RFI) including sustainability criteria – or a supplier questionnaire specifically focused on sustainability (such as that developed by Oxfam: see below). This is a key opportunity to communicate the purchasing organisation's commitment to sustainability – while also gathering required information for market analysis and supplier selection.

EXAMPLE: OXFAM GB SUPPLIER QUESTIONNAIRE

Oxfam GB's Ethical Purchasing Policy 'recognises that the globalisation of trade means that more and more of the goods and services we buy are at risk of being produced by workers in unregulated environments'. It states that Oxfam will 'strive to purchase goods and services which are produced and delivered under conditions that do not involve the abuse or exploitation of any persons and that have the least negative impact on the environment'.

'When we assess new suppliers we first ask them to complete a Supplier Questionnaire, which is risk-rated as high, medium or low ethical risk. Then depending on where production is carried out, we will also ask for an ethical audit report on the factory to be used. We make clear to suppliers that we are not looking for complete compliance with all standards at the outset; but we do expect a commitment to the standards in the code at director level, we expect continuous improvement towards the standards where necessary, and we expect risks in the supply chain to be assessed and managed.'

The Supplier Questionnaire contains four sections.

- Business details: locations, contact details, number of employees, main products and services, turnover
- Operational standards: governance and ethics; proportion of women employed; use of home-workers; quality, social and environmental policies; trade union recognition; communication of human and labour rights; wages and working hours; minimum age; health and safety; and operational and management standards achieved
- Sourcing from sub-suppliers: assessment of social and environmental risk; sourcing policy and criteria; location and type of subcontractors
- Continuous improvement: actual and planned, own and sub-supplier improvements in quality, labour, environment and health and safety

---

Pre-qualification criteria

2.5 While the specification component of tender documentation typically focuses on the specific nature of the product requirement, there is often also a **qualitative requirements** section, focusing on the experience, capacity and service levels of the prospective supplier.

2.6 In addition to assessing the sustainability of goods or services, it is important to capture information about prospective suppliers' sustainability performance, and capacity to manage the sustainability impacts of their business and supply chains. Here are some examples of qualitative requirements.

- Environmental performance (eg having an environmental management system in place to ISO 14001 standard or equivalent)
- Supply chain (eg details of measures or initiatives aimed at addressing sustainability impacts)
- Sustainability training and awareness (eg how the supplier will ensure that staff are adequately trained and made aware of associated sustainability issues)

Pre-qualification questionnaires (PQQ)

2.7 Self-administered questionnaires are an efficient way of ascertaining basic pre-qualification information. Questionnaires should be tailored to the organisation's requirements for a given procurement or category, identified sustainability issues, and identified vulnerabilities in its market or supply chain(s). At this point, however, the buyer should only be asking for the *minimum standards* required, so that a wide range of suppliers capable of meeting the requirement are able to proceed through to tender stage. It is common to ask at this stage about policies, processes and performance.

2.8 The aim of a PQQ is to gather information which will enable buyers to assess a supplier's attitude to sustainability; the standards it is currently working to; its current level of sustainability performance (eg via previously completed audit reports); and plans and commitments for future improvements.

2.9 When developing pre-qualification questionnaires, buyers should:

- Ensure that information required is proportionate to the importance, risk and complexity of the procurement, and the assessed sustainability risks (ie not placing an overly onerous information burden on suppliers for low-value, low-risk procurements – but gathering sufficiently robust information for high-value, high-risk procurements)
- Pose questions relevant to identified sustainability risks, impacts or opportunities associated with the particular procurement category.

2.10 Depending on the procurement, sustainability issues may be covered by a separate qualitative criterion with its own weighting, or incorporated within other criteria such as 'business systems and processes' or 'organisational capability.'

2.11 As with any claims made in the course of supplier selection, it is important with qualitative criteria to request information that is capable of verification by the provision of evidence, track record or references.

Appraisal and shortlisting of suppliers

2.12 At this stage of the sourcing process, the buying organisation evaluates the capability, compatibility and performance of potential (pre-qualified) suppliers in relation to specified requirements for a particular contract or procurement project, and draws up a shortlist of suppliers who will be invited to quote or tender, or to enter into contract negotiation (eg if a preferred supplier is being considered for sole supplier status or a partnership agreement).

- Weighted sustainability criteria should be included in the criteria for shortlisting suppliers.
- Where an open tender approach is used a shortlist will not be used. In such a case, tender advertisements should simply indicate clearly which social and environmental criteria will be used in evaluating tenders.

2.13 Supplier appraisal for shortlisting may be carried out by various means: pre-qualification or appraisal questionnaires completed by suppliers (although at this stage, the buyer will need to verify the truth and accuracy of information); perusal of the supplier's financial statements and reports; checking the supplier's certifications, accreditations, policy statements and so on; perusal of past audit reports; arranging to get references from customers, suppliers and relevant NGOs; and checking product samples or portfolios of work.

2.14 Once a shortlist of potential suppliers has been identified, the buyer may follow up with more labour-intensive and costly appraisal methods such as a supplier audit, site visit or capability survey for high-risk procurements or supply chains. This would involve visits to the supplier's premises by a cross-functional appraisal team (eg with experts on purchasing, quality, engineering and sustainability) which shares responsibility for the decision to approve or reject the supplier. A third-party capability or sustainability audit team may be used, for shortlisted suppliers in overseas countries where the buying organisation lacks presence or expertise.

Sustainable pre-qualification processes

2.15 The process of pre-qualification may in itself be considered a sustainable procurement issue.

- Pre-qualification criteria should be sufficiently clear and robust to allow unsuitable suppliers to rule themselves out early – saving them wasted time and cost on bid preparation.
- Prescriptive requirements may unfairly disadvantage some potential suppliers. Many small businesses,

for example, lack the resources to establish or maintain an accredited environmental or social responsibility management system. However, all suppliers can be asekd to provide information about what steps they are taking or proposing to take to improve the sustainability of their business practice and to minimise impacts appropriate to their industry.

- If suppliers are disqualified at the pre-qualification stage, it is good practice formally to notify them and provide some feedback or 'debrief' information. Making deselected suppliers aware of how their sustainability credentials fell short of requirement supports future development – and sends a clear sustainability message to the market.

3 Supplier selection

3.1 Requirements can be signalled to pre-qualified or approved suppliers in various ways, depending on the type of purchase and company policy.

3.2 The organisation may already have negotiated a framework agreement or standing contract with a supplier, to meet a requirement of a certain type. In such a case, the requirement will simply be notified by call-off order, on the pre-agreed terms. Sustainability criteria will have to be built into the original agreement or subsequent contract reviews and renewals.

3.3 There may be only one available supplier, or the organisation may have negotiated a preferred supplier or sole supplier agreement with a dependable supply partner. In such a case, the buyer may simply negotiate a contract with the preferred or designated supplier: sustainability criteria will be negotiated into the contract.

3.4 The organisation may send an 'enquiry' or 'request' to one or more shortlisted suppliers, also called a request for quotation (RFQ) or 'request for proposal' (RFP). This will set out the details of the requirement, including: the quantity and description of goods or services required, the required place and date of delivery, the buyer's standard terms and conditions of business, and a list of criteria for selecting the winning bidder (including standards the successful tenderer will need to achieve *or* work towards). Suppliers will be invited to submit a proposal and/or price for the job, which will be evaluated on a competitive basis.

3.5 A full competitive bidding or tendering process may be required for contracts over a certain value threshold – and is compulsory in the public sector on this basis. Lysons & Farrington define tendering as 'a purchasing procedure whereby potential suppliers are invited to make a firm and unequivocal offer of the price and terms on which they will supply specified goods or services which, on acceptance, shall be the basis of the subsequent contract'.

Good practice tender process

3.6 A best-practice tender procedure would have the following steps. Note that the fair and ethical administration of tenders is itself an issue of economic and social sustainability.

- Preparation of detailed specifications and draft contract documents by the procurement department (as discussed in Chapter 5). Once the tender procedure is in motion, there is little room for re-negotiation and adjustment of specifications. Attention must be given to accurate specification of the requirement, including sustainability criteria, so that the tender evaluator's task will be simply to (a) check that tenders received comply with the requirements, and (b) choose the lowest price (or best value) bid.
- Determination of a realistic timetable for the tender process, allowing reasonable time for responses at each stage, especially for suppliers with few bid preparation resources
- Issue of invitations to tender. In the case of selective tendering, this would be by means of an invitation to bid or request for quotation (RFQ) sent to shortlisted suppliers. In the case of open

tendering, it would be by means of a public advertisement, with invitations to bid issued to suppliers who respond to the advertisement within the stated time frame. Specifications (including all sustainability criteria) should be issued to each potential supplier in identical terms and by the same date. It should also be made clear to all tenderers that they are to comply strictly with the timetable for submission.

- Submission of completed tenders or bids by potential suppliers.
- Opening of tenders on the appointed date. Tenders received after this date should be returned un-opened. The tenders received should be logged, with the main details of each listed on an analysis sheet for ease of comparison.
- Analysis of each tender, according to stated objective criteria, with a view to shortlisting the best offers.
- Tender clarification and verification of supplier information (eg using site visits and capability or sustainability audits) for shortlisted suppliers. This is an opportunity to check that shortlisted suppliers understand all relevant codes of practice and standards specified by the tender documentation.
- Selection of the best offer, usually on a lowest-price, best value or 'economic advantage' basis. Any non-economic criteria used in the contract award decision (such as environmental or social sustainability or innovation) should be clearly notified in the invitation to tender, together with the weightings to be allocated to those criteria.
- Post-tender negotiation, where required and permitted. If post-tender negotiation is to be carried out, the invitation to tender must state clearly that the buyer will not be bound to accept the lowest price quoted, and that post-tender negotiation may be entered into, if necessary to qualify or clarify tenders, or to discuss potential improvements or adjustments to suppliers' offers.
- Award of the contract and/or establishment of the commercial relationship.
- The giving of feedback, on request, to unsuccessful tenderers, to support sustainability development and improvement.

Developing a request for quotation or invitation to tender

3.7 The development of request and tender documentation should be led by procurement, but should also involve key internal stakeholders, in order to ensure continued buy-in to the balancing of sustainability considerations with value and other priorities – and to promote a consistent message to the market and existing suppliers.

3.8 The weighting criteria and evaluation methodology (particularly in regard to non-price criteria) should also be communicated to bidders from the outset, so that the importance of sustainability requirements (among other aspects of the tender) is clearly understood.

Weighted evaluation criteria for supplier selection

3.9 Examples of non-cost criteria for supplier appraisal and selection are given in Table 6.1.

Table 6.1 *Examples of non-cost tender assessment criteria*

ECONOMIC	SOCIAL/ETHICAL	ENVIRONMENTAL
Financial • Competitive whole life cost • Financial stability • Resource efficiency • Cost transparency and fair pricing **Operational** • Production or service capacity • Process capability • Managerial expertise • Risk management • Supply chain management **Technological** • Innovation capability • Technology leverage • Compatible information systems	**CSR** • Demonstrated compliance with law and regulation • CSR and sustainability policies • Accreditation to relevant standard (or willingness to work towards standard accreditation) • Use of SMS and diverse suppliers or subcontractors • Commitment to transparency and improvement **Workforce practices** • Evidence that workers know their rights and responsibilities at work • Presence of independent trade unions or management-worker committees addressing pay, hours and conditions • Monitoring of sub-supplier practices and conditions • Participation in multi-stakeholder education and change initiatives	**Environmental impacts** • Environmental policies • Environment management systems (ISO 14001) • Lifecycle impacts of materials, products, packaging and processes • Green design, production and innovation capability • Transport energy and emissions • Reverse logistics, re-use and recycling • Environmental risk management • Willingness to 'green'

3.10 Tenders will be scored against each stated criterion, taking into account the weighting (or relative importance) given to each. Cost and non-cost criteria may be scored separately, weighted and combined to give an overall score. As an example, the tender documentation may state that the contract award decision will be based on:

- *Technical quality*: 50%, to be evaluated on the technical specification
- *Lowest price*: 30%
- *Sustainability performance*: 20%, to be evaluated on information requested from tenderers (including declarations on respecting the ILO Core Conventions).

3.11 The overall weighting allocated to sustainability considerations, relative to other criteria (such as technical quality and price) should reflect:

- The contribution of sustainability to the price or value for money assessment (taking into account whole life costs, eco-efficiencies and the 'monetisation' or quantification of benefits such as risk minimisation and reputational defence)
- The significance of sustainability impacts, and scope for improvement
- The potential to influence the market through the procurement.

For example, a higher overall sustainability weighting should be applied for procurements with high sustainability risk and impact, and with considerable scope for improvement. (We will discuss the analyses underpinning such assessments in Chapter 8.)

3.12 In addition, the buyer may need to decide on the relative weightings of specific sustainability considerations.

- Weightings will depend on the nature of the purchase and supply chain. For example, contracts involving frequent deliveries may emphasise the reduction of environmental transport impacts; contracts for business equipment may emphasise energy efficiency, end-of-life disposal, or the labour conditions in manufacturing plants; and contracts for agricultural produce may emphasise fair trade pricing and supportive demand management.
- Weightings might offer higher scores for suppliers able to demonstrate a consistent track record of

measuring and managing sustainability impacts, compared to suppliers that are only able to indicate what steps they have taken to reduce their impacts (without measurement or benchmarking) – which might score higher, in turn, than those that only offer unsubstantiated future intentions.

3.13 Robust weighted criteria allow for more consistent scoring and comparison of bids, as it enables the evaluators more effectively to differentiate between bids on the basis of relevance, quality and commitment.

- Robust environmental management systems – perhaps including certification under ISO 14001 environmental standards, Eco-Management and Audit Scheme (EMAS) or equivalents
- Compliance with environmental protection and emissions law in the country of operation.

Receipt and evaluation of tenders

3.14 Tenders should be evaluated against the specific, objective award criteria set out in the initial invitation to tender. Normally, the successful tender will be the one with the lowest price, or representing the best economic value over the lifetime of the purchase.

3.15 However, as we have seen, there may need to be further discussion and analysis among the evaluation team, to decide whether and how effectively each bid meets the requirements. Even amongst tenders that do meet the basic requirement, there may be considerable variety in the product and total solution 'package' being offered. One solution may be more attractive than another (innovative, environmentally friendly, risk-reducing, showing potential for sustainable business development) – even if price tells against it. Non-price criteria will have to be reviewed with particular care (and more details sought, if required), if suppliers have not been pre-qualified for sustainability.

3.16 For some vulnerable supply chains, high-impact sustainability issues or high-priority categories of spend, pre-qualification and tender processes may be insufficiently robust to offer sustainability assurance. **Site visits or environmental audits** may be used, once suppliers have been shortlisted at the tender evaluation stage, to gain assurance as to a supplier's conditions, practices and systems. Off-site interviews with workers and ex-workers may also be required, to ensure that they can speak freely.

3.17 This may be part of a wider supplier audit, site visit or capability survey: a visit to the supplier's premises by a cross-functional appraisal team (eg with experts on purchasing, quality, engineering and sustainability) which shares responsibility for the decision to approve or reject the supplier.

Recognition of trade unions and collective bargaining arrangements

3.18 Sustainable relationships between suppliers and their workers, including the payment of living wages, are part of supply chain risk management: reducing the likelihood of industrial disputes (with impact on delivery schedules); maintaining productivity and product quality; and minimising reputational risk (arising from worker exploitation, child labour and so on).

3.19 Individual (non-organised, non-represented) workers are particularly vulnerable to exploitation, especially where they are employed on a temporary or casual basis. The Responsible Purchasing Initiative *(Win/Win)* argues that buyers should encourage suppliers in developing countries, in particular, to negotiate collective bargaining agreements with independent trade unions on behalf of workers. Such agreements may:

- Help improve and monitor HR practices, through worker representation, advocacy and (if necessary) recourse to collective industrial action to protect worker rights
- Put in place fair and transparent terms and conditions (eg without discrimination on the basis of gender, race or religion)
- Support supply chain productivity and improvement. ('Negotiating with an elected workforce representative to make overtime optional, and discussing how to improve production techniques,

upgrade skills or improve health and safety, is likely to be more effective than imposing overtime on a tired workforce.')

3.20 The RPI highlights the need for buyers to gather follow-up information on prospective suppliers' industrial relations, worker representation and rights to collective bargaining, in developing country supply chains. Where post-PQQ appraisals are undertaken (eg through site visits, and interviews with local NGOs and worker representatives), it is recommended that the buyer ask questions about the following issues.

- The attitude and ethos of the supplier: whether there is evidence of leadership in improving workplace conditions (as well as the local environment and community benefits)
- The recognition of trade unions or other worker representation for the purposes of collective bargaining and consultation. If a union is present, worker representatives should not be appointed by management: membership should be freely chosen by workers. If unions are not present in the workplace, suppliers should demonstrate (a) openness to unions, where appropriate and (b) the existence of some other ongoing management process for worker consultation and negotiation (eg works committees).
- Whether workers' pay equals or exceeds the minimum income required to meet living costs (ie living wage): this is an indicator of the effectiveness of collective bargaining arrangements.

3.21 Purchasing organisations can then support sustainable working relationships and conditions (in line with the business case outlined above), by the following means.

- Giving preference in contract award to suppliers who have collective bargaining agreements with a recognised independent trade union
- Discussing with preferred suppliers the value of a modern human resource management approach, and the business case for effective dialogue between management and worker representatives
- Promoting 'quick win' improvements, such as the establishment of quality or health and safety committees – which can address immediate issues such as excessive overtime hours, and demonstrate the potential benefits of discussing production processes with workers
- Taking steps, where necessary, to support 'whistleblowing': creating confidential avenues for disclosure when breaches of workplace standards have been observed or experienced, as a 'safety valve of last resort'. ('If workers are not able to present their priority concerns to the employer, then problematic practices can develop and continue unchecked, resulting in reputational accidents waiting to happen, which will expose buyers and other supply chain partners': RPI, *Taking the Lead*.)
- Signing an international framework agreement with an international trade union. Since this topic is highlighted by the syllabus at this point (although it is not really part of the supplier selection process), we will discuss it briefly.

The use of international framework agreements

3.22 International framework agreements (IFAs) are generally negotiated between transnational enterprises and **global union federations** (GUFs) or international trade unions (such as the International Metalworkers' Federation and the International Textile, Garment and Leather Workers' Federation).

3.23 IFAs are a global instrument with the main purpose of ensuring that international labour standards are met in all of a transnational enterprise's locations and supply chains. Similar instruments include **European framework agreements** (EFAs), although these are limited to the European area and cover a broader range of topics. In most cases, the request to negotiate IFAs came from the home country trade unions and European works councils. Over 70 IFAs are currently in operation, including an agreement between garment retailer Inditex and the International Textile, Garment and Leather Workers' Federation.

3.24 The basis of an IFA is a Code of Labour Practices, formulated jointly by the International Confederation of Free Trade Unions (IFCTU) and International Trade Secretariats (which later became GUFs). The Code is regarded as a guide for unions on the rules of conduct to be applied by transnational enterprises. Unlike voluntary codes of conduct, however, IFAs are negotiated agreements representing collective bargaining at a transnational level, and often provide for the joint development of implementation and monitoring procedures.

3.25 All IFA agreements are based on the ILO Core Labour Standards, specifying that companies must undertake to respect the ILO conventions on freedom of association (Convention 87) and the right to collective bargaining (Convention 98). Most IFAs also refer to the conventions on non-discrimination against labour representatives, the abolition of forced and child labour, the prevention of discrimination in employment and equal pay for work of equal value. Some current agreements go beyond the ILO standards, and seek to ensure decent wages and working conditions, and safe and hygienic working environments.

3.26 Nearly half of the current IFAs in place require that the transnational enterprise inform its subcontractors and suppliers, and encourage them to respect the principles laid down in the IFA. A smaller number of agreements provide for measures to *ensure* that suppliers comply with the IFA, and some make compliance mandatory through the whole supply chain, with the transnational enterprise assuming full responsibility for supply chain compliance.

3.27 No legal enforcement mechanisms exist at the global level: enforcement of IFA provisions relies on trade union influence, and management willingness, to resolve complaints. It is recommended that at least one annual meeting is devoted to monitoring application of the IFA, and this may be supported by NGO monitoring and reporting.

3.28 The European Union website argues that: 'For transnational enterprises, IFAs represent a means to foster industrial peace through the deepening of dialogue with their employees and trade unions. Furthermore, transnational enterprises sign IFAs in order to promote a positive public image aimed at avoiding potentially damaging public campaigns, gaining access to capital and product markets, and building up good relations with political and economic decision-makers. Meanwhile, the GUFs view IFAs as an opportunity to engage transnational enterprises' operations in a process of private standard-setting, in order to improve the conditions of workers and trade unions worldwide.'

4 Contract award

4.1 Whatever process is used, at some point the buying organisation will have to select what it considers the optimal offer or preferred supplier, in order to finalise and award the contract.

4.2 In general, sustainability considerations should have been built in, in detail, to specification and supplier pre-qualification, so that the contract can be awarded objectively and transparently to the lowest price or best value bid.

4.3 The BSI *Sustainable Procurement Guide,* however, suggests that sustainable elements may still be captured in objective and transparent tender evaluation criteria for contract award.

- Tenders can be **risk evaluated** (including sustainability risks) and points awarded to those bids with lower-risk supply.
- Extra points may be awarded for **proposals exceeding minimum criteria** stated in the specification (with incremental points for the degree of superior performance).
- **Whole life costing** may be used to achieve a more complete picture of the total costs of purchasing a good or service – rather than purchase price alone.

Whole life costing

4.4 Whole life costing (lifecycle costing or through life costing) is one form of analysis that can be used for determining whether a project meets stated performance requirements. It is defined in the ISO 15686: 2008 standard as 'economic assessment considering all agreed projected significant and relevant cost flows over a period of analysis, expressed in monetary value. The projected costs are those needed to achieve defined levels of performance, including reliability, safety and availability'.

4.5 Whole life costing is recognised as a valuable approach to the sustainable procurement of capital assets with a long useful life.

- The buyer makes assumptions about the level of costs that will arise in each year of the asset's useful life, including the initial purchase price – but also the costs of delivery, installation and commissioning; routine maintenance and periodic overhaul; energy, labour, consumables and other running costs; time lost for breakdowns; disposal costs (which may be negative, if the asset has resale value at the end of its life) and so on.
- At the same time, the buyer attempts to quantify the benefits that will arise from the ownership of the asset – and to allocate them to each year of the asset's useful life.
- Discounted cashflow calculations are used to express costs and benefits, and therefore total costs, in today's values. (Annual costs, in today's values, can also be calculated to allow comparison of assets or proposed asset purchases, even if they have different life spans.)

4.6 The point of calculating whole life costs is to identify options that cost least (economic sustainability) over the long term – which may not be apparent from the purchase price. It enables realistic budgeting over the life of the asset; highlights, at an early stage, risks associated with the purchase; promotes cross-functional communication on economic sustainability issues; and supports the optimisation of value for money.

4.7 In some cases, as we saw in Chapter 4, sustainably preferable goods may be more expensive to purchase – but may generate savings throughout their life (eg through reduced maintenance or repair costs, greater energy efficiency, higher end-of-life value, or reduced impact-related costs). Whole life costing can therefore be applied to help justify a value for money outcome, where the good or service with the lowest sustainability impact:

- Costs the same as, or less than, that of other bids, and other qualitative criteria scores are similar
- Costs more to purchase than other bids, but results in savings over time, offsetting the greater upfront cost (eg energy-saving devices).

Contract award in the public sector

4.8 In the public sector, under the EU Public Procurement Directives, contracts over a certain value threshold (to which the directives apply) must be awarded on the basis of competitive tender, using objective award criteria. In order to ensure fair competition, and competitive value for money, buyers are generally obliged to award contracts on the basis of:

- Lowest price *or* (more commonly)
- Most economically advantageous tender (MEAT).

4.9 In relation to non-price (eg environmental and social sustainability) criteria:

- Lowest price and MEAT criteria for contract award allow issues such as resource consumption and disposal costs, for example, to be taken into account. Any social or environmental sustainability criteria used must be directly related to the performance of the contract, and appropriately weighted.
- Public bodies can specify sustainable options, provided that doing so does not unreasonably distort competition or discriminate against products or suppliers from any EU member state. It is possible, for example, to specify recycled paper or energy-efficient IT equipment. Fair Trade options can be 'welcomed' – and an authority might require caterers to supply fair trade coffee or tea products, for example, as this would not affect competition between caterers.
- EU rules do not permit preference being given to any sector of suppliers such as local suppliers, women-owned or minority-owned businesses or SMEs. It is permissible, however, to remove any *obstacles* that might be preventing such groups from competing for public business. This might be done by, for example, ensuring they are aware of where opportunities will be advertised and making

tendering documentation and procedures as simple as possible for all suppliers.
- The best opportunity to incorporate sustainability criteria is therefore at the need definition, specification and pre-qualification stages of the procurement cycle – and through post-contract negotiated improvement agreements.

Post-tender negotiation

4.10 In the private sector, buyers are free to engage in post-tender negotiation. CIPS defines post-tender negotiation as: 'negotiation after the receipt of formal tenders and before the letting of contract(s) with the suppliers(s) submitting the lowest acceptable tender(s), with a view to obtaining an improvement in price, delivery or content in circumstances which do not put other tenderers at a disadvantage or affect their confidence or trust in the competitive tendering system.'

4.11 Post-tender negotiation may offer a good opportunity, while the preferred supplier is highly motivated:
- To highlight the importance of sustainability issues and emphasise the need for commitment to sustainability improvements (where required)
- To check suppliers' understanding of codes of practice and standards to which they have agreed to adhere (or work towards) as part of their tender
- To influence the preferred supplier's forward sustainability agenda and improvement plans, in order progressively to improve whole supply chain performance
- To refine or improve the winning bid, in relation to sustainability targets (without materially changing the content of the bid in a way that would distort competition)
- To gain supplier agreement to mitigate specific sustainability risks or impacts that have been identified during the supplier pre-qualification and selection process, with defined improvement targets and monitoring measures
- To negotiate into the contract (or a separate supplier improvement plan or memorandum of understanding) any sustainability commitments that could not be delivered through the tender process.

4.12 In the European public sector, organisations have limited scope to engage in pre-bidding negotiation as part of a competitive dialogue procedure. The use of negotiated procedures is in general highly restricted, in order to favour fair, open and value-based competition for contracts.

Supplier debrief

4.13 Sustainable best practice (and, in the public sector, tender regulations) dictate that unsuccessful bidders or applicants be offered feedback on why they did not win the contract. This enhances the transparency and fairness of the process: ensuring that decisions are justifiable. It also supports sustainability by facilitating learning, improvement and skill development, and enhancing the ability of small, local and diverse suppliers to compete more effectively for contracts.

Creation of contract or relationship

4.14 A variety of sustainability considerations will be built into contract negotiation and development, or the creation or deepening of a sourcing relationship.

EXAMPLE: ORANGE

Global telecommunications provider Orange publishes the following ethical sourcing policy.

In our ethical sourcing policy we commit to:

- **Understanding our supply chains, including health and safety, environmental, labour and human rights issues**

- **Expecting responsible behaviour, as well as quality and value**
- **Working with suppliers to make improvements, where their practices fall short of our expectations**
- **Withdrawing from contracts where improvement is impossible**
- **Respecting suppliers' confidential information and running fair selection processes**
- **Making payments in accordance with our contractual commitments**

Under the ethical, social and environmental criteria, suppliers are assessed, among other things, on:

- **Compliance with relevant legislation and regulations**
- **Use of energy and other natural resources**
- **Respect for confidentiality**
- **Whether they have a civic and responsible attitude**
- **Whether they have principles for action defining their commitments and priorities**
- **Whether they have an environment policy.**

These assessments are reviewed jointly with our suppliers and lead to an improvement plan being drawn up if necessary.

4.15 For example, the sourcing process may have been leading up to a one-off purchase order; a framework agreement, call-off contract or rolling contract to fulfil requirements over a period of time; or a partnership or joint-venture agreement to pursue shared objectives and areas of interest (such as the development of 'green' brands or technologies). The type and duration of the supply relationship will depend to an extent on sustainability considerations.

- As the Kraljic matrix indicates, the type of relationship sought will depend in part on supply risk. Economically sustainable supply may dictate arms' length systems contracts, for example, for routine and leverage items – and long-term relationships or partnership for bottleneck and strategic items.
- Social and environmental sustainability may best be managed in the context of collaborative, long-term supplier relationships, because of the need for trust, continuous improvement, capability development and innovation.
- Economic and environmental sustainability may best be managed in the context of the whole life of the purchase: including issues such as whole life costs, maintenance and repair, upgrade, warranty, running costs, resource and energy consumption and end-of-life issues such as take-back and disposal.

4.16 The development of contract terms will crystallise the commitments, responsibilities and rights of both parties in regard to the full range of sustainability issues; the apportionment and transfer of costs and risks; legislation and standards that will be adhered to; how performance will be monitored and measured; what commitments are made in relation to continuous improvement; how disputes will be managed; and so on. Sustainability aspects may be built into the purchase order; standard terms and conditions of purchase; supply contracts; service level agreements; partnership agreements – and any schedules and appendices added to these documents in regard to sustainability criteria and commitments.

5 Supporting SME and diverse suppliers

5.1 Although not mentioned explicitly in the syllabus (which focuses mainly on sourcing from developing-country supply chains), the issue of supplier diversity is seen as increasingly important for the European sustainable procurement agenda. This is driven by the recognition that in the interests of sustainability *and* commercial advantage, buyers should consider increasing the accessibility of contracts to a wider supplier base.

5.2 More specifically, a sustainable procurement orientation argues that purchasers should seek to remove unnecessary barriers to participation for smaller or less established suppliers who might nevertheless:

- Have the technical capability to fulfil requirements, especially if supported through supplier development
- Be able to add value through qualities such as responsiveness, innovation and entrepreneurship,

understanding of consumer segments, and quality of service (due to eagerness to win and retain business).

5.3 In the first instance, it may be necessary for buyers to:

- Appreciate the value of **widening and developing the supply market** through increasing diversity and participation
- Consider whether **sourcing policies and practices** (such as international sourcing, the use of technical specifications, the aggregation of orders into large contracts to secure economies of scale, or the requirement for high-level quality accreditations) may act as a barrier to participation
- Appreciate the **frustration** of suppliers unable to compete for business, and facilitate access where possible (eg through advance notice of upcoming contracts, information about sourcing processes, or the giving of post-tender feedback)
- Appreciate the **ethical issues** in fair access to contracts. Appraisals, quotations and tenders cost prospective suppliers time, effort and money – and it is unethical to subject them to this cost frivolously or manipulatively: that is, if there is not a genuine, fair and open opportunity for them to win the business.

Small and medium enterprises

5.4 Small and medium enterprises (SMEs) are a significant contributor to economic activity, comprising some 99% of enterprises in the EU in 2005, and providing around 65 million jobs.

5.5 SME suppliers may have an advantage over large firms in clearly defined, small markets: it would not be worth large firms entering markets where there is no scope for economies of scale arising from mass production. Such an advantage may apply in a geographically localised market, say, or in a 'niche' market for specialist, customised or premium-quality products. In addition, the entrepreneurial nature and speed of communication in small enterprises makes them particularly well suited to innovation and invention, and they may have an advantage over larger, less flexible firms in fast-changing, high-technology markets.

5.6 On the other hand, SMEs are at a competitive disadvantage in areas such as: raising loan and share capital (because they are a greater risk); managing cashflow (being harder hit by late payment or non-payments); ability to take financial risks (including investment in research and development); and dealing with bureaucratic requirements. They are also unable to take advantages of the economies of scale which are available to larger suppliers, which may affect their ability to price competitively.

Why source from SME suppliers?

5.7 From the above discussion, you may be able to identify particular challenges for a buyer sourcing from SMEs. The buyer will need to take into account issues such as: the supplier's limited capacity to handle large-volume and aggregated contracts; the supplier's potential financial instability (due to cashflow issues and difficulties securing credit); and the ethical and business risk of a small supplier becoming overly dependent on a large customer.

5.8 In addition, there will be a key sourcing trade-off between:

- The economic advantages of dealing with large suppliers (the ability to aggregate requirements for reduced transaction costs and bulk discounts, and more competitive pricing due to economies of scale)
- The potential for 'better value' arising from dealing with SME suppliers
  - Access to a wider supply market, potentially enhancing competition (and therefore lower pricing through the market as a whole)
  - Competitive pricing due to lower administrative overheads and management costs
  - Greater responsiveness and flexibility (with shorter decision-making and approval channels)

- Innovation capability and diversity of business solutions, through the early exploitation of new technology, providing products or services in new or underdeveloped markets, or using innovation capability to differentiate themselves from established market players.
- Expertise in focused niche markets
- Willingness and ability to produce small-order, niche, bespoke and customised items (where larger suppliers may have minimum order quantities and standardised offerings)
- Higher quality specialist products, due to greater skills, originality and commitment (where the market is unattractive to larger enterprises)
- Higher commitment and levels of service (due to the value of the business to the supplier).

Barriers to access for SME suppliers

5.9 If a buyer wishes to take advantage of these sources of value, for appropriate procurements, he may be able deliberately to prioritise, or give preference to, SME suppliers in sourcing decisions. In the public sector, however, this is generally not permissible, as it represents a distortion of competition. Instead, attention is given to identifying and removing barriers to participation and competition that might prevent or deter SMEs from accessing contracts.

5.10 Here are some of the barriers to SME participation.

- Not being able to find out about opportunities. (In the public sector, for example, low-value procurements may not be widely advertised, because of falling below the EU threshold for open tendering.)
- Lacking marketing resources to raise their profile in the supply market
- Believing that the process involved in bidding will be (unnecessarily) complex and costly, and therefore being deterred from participating
- Lacking expertise in areas such as interpreting complex requirements documentation or constructing good-quality proposals or tenders
- Lacking a track record of performance, or several years of financial records, for pre-qualification (since SMEs are more likely to be recent start-ups)
- Lacking the capacity to handle large volume contracts, where the trend (in both public and private sectors) is towards aggregation of demand into fewer, larger contracts; the use of framework contracts; and a reduced supplier base.

5.11 Buyers can support, encourage and facilitate SME participation by measures such as the following.

- Publicising opportunities widely, particularly for small and low-value contracts
- Regularly 'refreshing' approved supplier lists, to include SMEs where appropriate
- Using the corporate website to make information available to potential suppliers (including 'Selling to...' or 'Doing business with...' guidance on sourcing procedures, pre-qualification requirements, buyer policies and expectations, and contacts for questions)
- Holding 'Meet the Buyer' events to discuss requirements and sourcing processes with potential suppliers
- Ensuring that sourcing procedures and pre-qualification requirements are appropriate to the size and complexity of the requirement (ie not unnecessarily onerous for small, routine purchases)
- Keeping tender and specification documents concise and jargon-free – and using outcome or performance specifications where possible (more flexibly focusing on 'what' is to be delivered, rather than 'how')
- Using a pre-qualification questionnaire to minimise the initial administrative burden on small suppliers
- Setting realistic timescales for sourcing processes
- Considering dis-aggregating contracts: making smaller contracts available to SME suppliers, eg by separating out specialist elements or new work from the main contract; or dividing large requirements into smaller lots for multi-sourcing

- Encouraging large first-tier or prime contractors to use SMEs as subcontractors, particularly where they can provide specialist or innovative products
- Publishing the names of prime contractors in upcoming contracts, to help SMEs identify subcontractor opportunities
- Ensuring that the buyer, and its main contractors, pay SME subcontractors on time – or as soon as possible. Other cashflow support may be provided by considering stage or interim payments (linked to progress or work done), or advance payments.
- Being open to consortium bids from groups of SMEs, for large procurements.

Supplier diversity and under-represented businesses

5.12 Similar considerations may apply in regard to minority-owned and women-owned businesses. Supply base diversity can:

- Support strategic alignment, by ensuring that the supply base reflects (and can respond with knowledge and insight to) the increasing diversity of the customer base
- Help build stakeholder relations and generate goodwill (eg among diversity-aware consumer groups)
- Support corporate image and reputation by demonstrating commitment to equality and inclusion
- Contribute to improved supply chain performance: a wider pool of suppliers can generate competition and innovation.

5.13 Here are some proactive approaches to improving supplier diversity.

- Removing barriers to participation in competing for contracts (as for SMEs)
- Positive action policies, whereby suppliers in certain under-represented groups are targeted to offer opportunities to compete for contracts
- Encouraging or requiring suppliers to have diversity plans in place for their supply chains

---

EXAMPLE: JOHNSON & JOHNSON

Johnson & Johnson has long been one of the world's most admired and ethical corporate brands. It also has a history of partnership with inventors, academics and suppliers, and a strong sustainable procurement policy ('Our Credo').

Johnson & Johnson follows a procurement approach that is based on Our Credo: to obtain the highest-quality products and services at a cost that represents the best possible value, while maintaining the highest ethical standards, and taking our social and environmental responsibilities seriously.

The Johnson & Johnson Family of Companies is committed to the ongoing identification of small and diverse suppliers that can add value to our businesses and help us achieve our long-term growth objectives. Small and diverse businesses not only provide economic and social vitality to the communities in which we live and work, but they add value to our companies, and help us enhance our role as a health care leader. In keeping with this commitment, our Supplier Diversity Program is designed to provide opportunities for qualified small and diverse businesses. Included in our program are:

- Certified minority-owned businesses, small and large
- Certified woman-owned businesses, small and large
- Certified Small Disadvantaged Businesses
- Small veteran-owned and service disabled veteran-owned businesses.

It is our policy to identify and include qualified businesses of these types when we buy the goods and services we need to serve the parents, patients and customers who purchase our products.

Chapter summary

- Suppliers with unsustainable practices might be able to offer very low prices. However, buyers should look beyond this in the interest of long-term supply security.
- Pre-qualification of suppliers is important to ensure that they have adequate environmental performance, supply chain practices and sustainability awareness.
- Supplier selection criteria should include sustainability performance. The fair and ethical administration of tenders is itself a sustainability issue.
- Contract award criteria should include whole life costs and sustainability.
- Encouraging SMEs and diverse suppliers is both good ethical practice and potentially valuable for buyers.

 ## Self-test questions

Numbers in brackets refer to the paragraphs where you can check your answers.

1. List elements of the supplier selection process where sustainability standards might be incorporated. (1.4)

2. What qualitative requirements may be incorporated into the criteria for pre-qualifying suppliers? (2.6)

3. How should the process of pre-qualification be handled in order to ensure sustainable procurement? (2.15)

4. Describe the steps in a best-practice tender procedure. (3.6)

5. How can buyers support sustainable working conditions in developing countries? (3.21)

6. What is an international framework agreement? (3.22)

7. Define whole life costing. (4.4)

8. List sustainability benefits that may be achieved by means of post-tender negotiation. (4.11)

9. In what circumstances may SMEs have a competitive advantage over larger firms? (5.5)

10. In what ways can buyers encourage and facilitate SMEs? (5.11)

CHAPTER 7

Sustainable Performance Measurement

Assessment criteria and indicative content

3.4 Evaluate how sustainability can be incorporated into supplier performance measurement

- Social, ethical and environmental targets
- Setting key performance indicators (KPIs) on sustainability
- Obtaining feedback from suppliers on performance measurement
- Using balanced scorecards

Section headings

1. Sustainability benchmarks and targets
2. Key performance indicators
3. The balanced scorecard
4. Collaborative performance management
5. Contract and supplier management

Introduction

In this chapter we focus on how sustainability measures can be incorporated into the framework by which supplier performance is measured and managed.

We explore various techniques for incorporating sustainability into supplier performance measurement, including the setting of targets; the use of benchmarks; development of key performance indicators (KPIs); and the use of balanced scorecards.

We emphasise the collaborative and equitable nature of performance measurement in the context of responsible procurement.

Finally, we will look briefly at an important related concept: the important phase of procurement in which the contract is *implemented* and *managed* over its life, through contract and supplier management. We will return to this theme in Chapter 10, where we consider the importance of supplier relationship and performance management in securing and developing compliance with sustainability standards – and in dealing with non-compliance and improvement issues.

1 Sustainability benchmarks and targets

Performance measurement and management

1.1 Performance measurement is, broadly, the process of developing specific, measurable indicators against which performance can be systematically tracked in order to assess progress towards the achievement of goals and objectives.

1.2 Supplier performance measurement generally implies the comparison of a supplier's current performance against:

- *Defined performance criteria* (such as KPIs or improvement agreements), to establish whether the aimed-for or agreed level of performance has been achieved
- *Previous performance,* to identify deterioration or improvement trends
- *The performance of other organisations* (suppliers, purchasing functions) or standard *benchmarks*, to identify areas where performance falls short of best practice or the practice of competitors, and where there is therefore room for improvement.

1.3 Performance measurement is vitally important in supply chain management because it supports the planning and control of operations and relationships: it is often said that 'what gets measured, gets managed'. Performance measurement is explicitly intended to lead to performance improvement and supplier development, by identifying areas in which suppliers' current performance falls short of desired, competitive or best-practice levels. It is also an important tool for communicating with stakeholders about their part in supply chain performance and sustainability, and how they are doing. Performance measures, such as KPIs, can be used to manage, motivate and reward individuals, teams and suppliers.

1.4 One of the key principles of sustainability is the need to satisfy the needs and interests of an extended group of organisational stakeholders, and this in turn implies the need to control performance. Setting clear goals and targets for sustainable procurement – and then monitoring, measuring, evaluating and reviewing progress and performance – ensures that:

- Deviations or shortfalls can be corrected, and problems identified and solved
- Potential for improvement can be identified and lessons learned for future rounds of planning
- Individuals and teams can be motivated by clear objectives and targets, and the rewards of having demonstrably and measurably achieved them (or made progress towards them)
- Executives responsible to stakeholders can give an accurate account of progress and performance and the discharge of their responsibilities
- The expense of resources can be justified by the results, and the business case for sustainable procurement confirmed (hopefully, garnering support and resource allocation for a further round of improvements).

1.5 Monitoring a supplier's sustainability performance throughout the life of a supply contract or relationship should happen alongside the monitoring of other contract requirements, such as cost, quality and service delivery standards and compliance issues.

1.6 Similar considerations, of course, relate to the measurement of *buyer-side* procurement and supply chain performance. It is important for buyers to be alert to the impact of their *own* policies, practices and performance on supply chain effectiveness, efficiency and sustainability. Improvement solutions may well focus on the measurement and adjustment of procurement performance – prior to, or alongside, that of the supply chain. (We discuss this proposition in Section 4 of this chapter.)

Yardsticks for measurement

1.7 The first key element of any performance management system (or control cycle) is the setting of indicators against which measured or assessed progress and performance can be compared: that is, measures or 'yardsticks' that will indicate (a) the targets and standards to which effort and resources will be directed; and (b) whether actual results are on track, going according to plan, or reaching the required or expected standard.

1.8 Such measures may be formulated as objectives, targets or key performance indicators, for example – which in turn may be formulated as a result of processes such as critical success factor analysis, risk analysis, the use of national or international standards, or benchmarking processes. We will discuss some of these approaches later in this chapter, and others, in more detail, in Chapter 8.

Monitoring and measurement

1.9 The term 'monitoring' is used broadly to include the measurement of performance against goals and targets, as well as other means of periodic oversight, review and evaluation. Monitoring methods include self-reporting, audits, inspections or observations, interviews and surveys, and measurements.

1.10 We will look at the monitoring of performance in detail in Chapter 9, including a variety of audit, assessment and evaluation tools.

Performance correction, adjustment and improvement planning

1.11 The third phase of the performance management cycle is the management and adjustment of performance to bring it back 'on course': solving problems, identifying and implementing improvements, and adjusting targets downwards (to be more realistic) or upwards (to set fresh challenges) where required. Chapter 10 will deal in detail with improving and developing compliance with targets and standards.

Setting sustainability targets and objectives

1.12 The BSI *Sustainable Procurement Guide* emphasises that: 'one of the biggest challenges to sustainable procurement lies in understanding what impact your actions and your suppliers' actions will have. Understanding **what to measure** and **how to measure** it is key... To make sustainable procurement measures meaningful, they need to be used in the context of achieving your stated sustainability objectives, which should be aligned with (and contribute to) your higher-level organisational corporate sustainability goals.'

1.13 Once the key areas of focus for a sustainability policy have been identified (by processes covered in detail in Chapter 8), the team can articulate specific objectives and targets, expressing exactly what the policy is designed to achieve – and how progress and performance will be measured.

- An *objective* is defined by ISO 14001 as a 'policy statement of intended action which may or may not be quantified' (for example: to develop reverse logistics, re-use and recycling capability through the supply chain).
- A *target* is 'a specific, measurable action to achieve the objective' (eg to increase the proportion of recycled materials used by 10% from the previous year).
- An *indicator* is 'a measure or other expression of information about performance, performance influencers or conditions' (eg proportion of recycled materials per unit of production).

1.14 A sustainable procurement policy should not set too many objectives, as this will dilute focus and spread resources too 'thin'. Ten to twelve key objectives (subject to periodic review) may be sufficient for any one strategic planning period.

1.15 The procurement function will therefore generally be working towards pre-determined functional sustainable performance targets, set as part of the organisation's sustainability or CSR policy. It is the responsibility of procurement officers to translate those targets that are relevant to specific procurement processes or categories into specific supplier requirements and performance targets, both:

- Within the specification, tender and contracting process and
- Through the life of the contract, through contract and supplier management processes.

1.16 The various influences on supplier performance and improvement targets can therefore be depicted as in Figure 7.1.

Figure 7.1 *Development of supplier sustainability requirements, measures and targets*

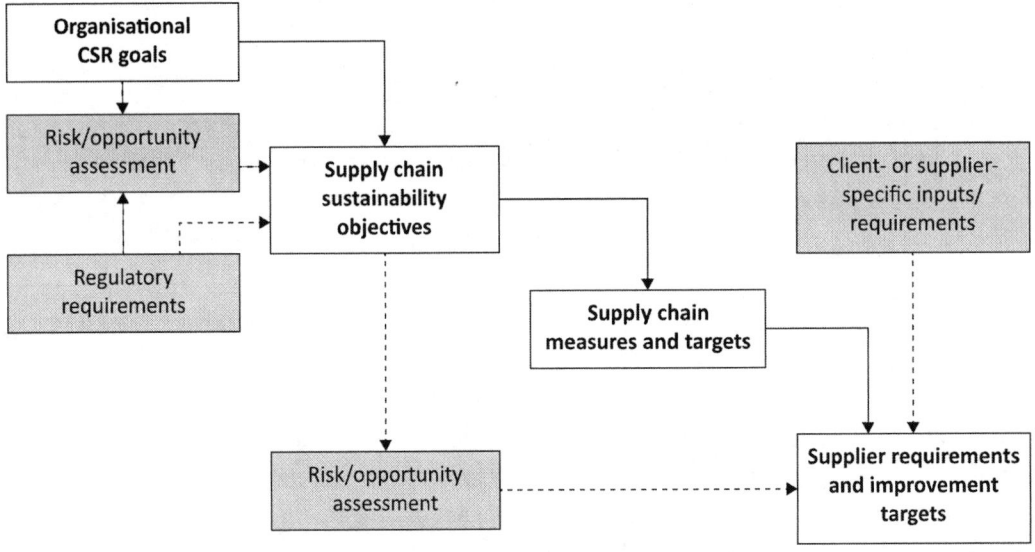

Source: BSI *Sustainable Procurement Guide*

1.17 In Chapter 6 we looked at ways in which social, ethical and environmental criteria could be built into contract specifications and contract terms. However, the British Standards Institution (*Sustainable Procurement Guide)* notes that 'not all supplier sustainability requirements may be delivered by the tender and captured in the resulting contract'. For example, sustainability requirements may relate to:

- Longer-term aspirational sustainability objectives of the organisation, which will require ongoing incremental improvements to work towards (in order to avoid unfairly discriminating against, or burdening, developing suppliers)
- Emerging environmental issues that are scientifically not well understood at the time of the specification or contract
- Issues which emerge as a result of ongoing risk assessment processes, stakeholder consultation or legislative changes.

1.18 The buying organisation may therefore seek to negotiate performance or improvement targets with suppliers, to be adhered to on a voluntary basis (eg as part of a continuous improvement agreement, supplier development programme or adherence to promoted sustainability guidelines). Suppliers are not obligated to deliver on any sustainability measures or improvement targets not explicitly written into the contract – but may be persuaded to 'buy in' to the long-term benefits of sustainability initiatives.

2 Key performance indicators

2.1 An 'indicator' is a 'signal' that alerts you to key factors in a situation: in performance measurement terms, how things are going, and where you are 'up to' in relation to your goals and targets.

2.2 Key performance indicators (KPIs) are clear qualitative or quantitative statements which define adequate or desired performance in key areas (critical success factors), and against which progress and performance can be measured. The important point about KPIs is that they state performance goals in a way that is capable of direct, detailed, consistent measurement at operational level, using available data collection systems. KPIs are monitored, reviewed and reported on at regular intervals, to ensure that the organisation or project is 'on track' in relation to its most important 'yardsticks' of success.

2.3 Sustainability may be addressed through KPIs by approaches such as the following.

- Setting specific targets or actions that the supplier is required to attain within a prescribed timeframe (eg achieving accreditation under ISO14001, or recognising a trade union)
- Requiring a supplier progressively to improve its sustainability performance over a given period (eg achieving 30% product eco-labelling or FairTrade certification by Year 2 of the contract, to rise to 40% in Year 4)
- Requiring particular supply chain initiatives (eg reporting on the origin and certification of products)
- Requiring suppliers and contractors to provide annual reports on their sustainability progress, initiatives and innovations

Developing KPIs

2.4 Effective performance measures and objectives are often described by the acronym 'SMART'.

- **Specific:** clear and well-defined statement of precisely what the desired outcomes or deliverables are, so that the parties to the contract know what they are committing to and accountable for.
- **Measurable:** susceptible to monitoring, review and measurement (ideally in quantitative or numerical terms) so that both parties can meaningfully assess progress and achievement.
- **Attainable:** achievable and realistic, given the time and resources available – even if the aim is to be 'stretching' or to stimulate improvement, attainment of the required level of performance must be possible!
- **Relevant:** performance measures should be relevant to, and aligned with, the strategic objectives of the organisation; the policies and objectives of the procurement function; the critical success factors of the organisation and supply chain; and the business need.
- **Time-bounded:** given defined timescales and deadlines for completion (or review) – ie not 'open ended'.

2.5 Some versions of the SMART model substitute, or add, the following.

- **Stretching:** performance measures may deliberately be made challenging enough to motivate suppliers and stimulate committed performance, learning, development and improvement (eg as part of supplier development or continuous improvement agreements)
- **Sustainable** (or Responsible): KPIs should take into account potential impacts on key stakeholders, in the light of the unit's (and organisation's) ethical responsibilities towards them
- **Agreed:** incorporated in a contract, agreement or charter (formal or informal), in order to secure joint commitment and accountability.
- **Rewarded:** attainment of KPIs may be linked to positive incentives or rewards of some kind, as part of the performance management and supplier motivation process.

2.6 A simple, generic process for developing KPIs is summarised in Figure 7.2.

Figure 7.2 *Developing key performance indicators*

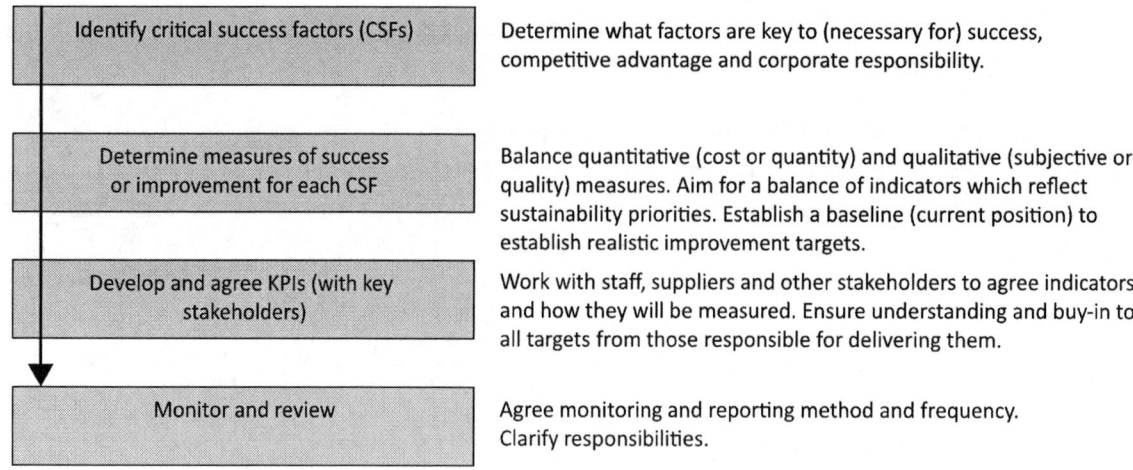

Identify critical success factors (CSFs)	Determine what factors are key to (necessary for) success, competitive advantage and corporate responsibility.
Determine measures of success or improvement for each CSF	Balance quantitative (cost or quantity) and qualitative (subjective or quality) measures. Aim for a balance of indicators which reflect sustainability priorities. Establish a baseline (current position) to establish realistic improvement targets.
Develop and agree KPIs (with key stakeholders)	Work with staff, suppliers and other stakeholders to agree indicators and how they will be measured. Ensure understanding and buy-in to all targets from those responsible for delivering them.
Monitor and review	Agree monitoring and reporting method and frequency. Clarify responsibilities.

2.7 You don't want to specify too many KPIs for a given contract: only those that are indicative measures of performance in areas necessary to achieve critical success factors. Otherwise, it will be too complicated and costly to monitor and measure performance – and the supplier may find the pursuit of multiple KPIs too complex and onerous. Eight to ten well-formulated KPIs may be realistic for any given planning and control period.

2.8 Effective communication is essential in KPI development. The buyer will need to be able to explain to the supplier exactly what performance standard is expected. It may issue recent history trend data (if available), with a written explanation of key issues and requirements. For complex high-value new-buy contracts, for which the effort is justified, buyers should involve suppliers in the joint development of KPIs – rather than simply negotiating their agreement with KPIs already formulated. Suppliers may be able to contribute valuable expertise and experience to the process, and consultation creates a better likelihood of 'buy-in' or commitment to jointly-developed KPIs.

Advantages and disadvantages of using sustainability KPIs

2.9 There are a number of benefits of developing KPIs as performance measures for sustainability.

- Increased and improved (results-focused) communication on sustainability performance and issues
- Motivation to achieve or surpass the specified performance level (particularly with KPI-linked incentives, rewards or penalties). Motivation is in any case stronger where there are clear targets to aim for.
- Support for collaborative buyer-supplier relations, by enabling integrated or two-way performance measurement (with KPIs on both sides of the relationship, as discussed later in this chapter)
- The ability directly to compare year on year performance, to identify improvement or deterioration trends
- Focus on key results areas (critical success factors) such as cost management, reputational protection and environmental compliance
- Clearly defined shared goals, facilitating cross-functional and cross-organisational teamwork and relationships.

2.10 Setting KPIs for *supplier* sustainability performance, in particular, may be beneficial in the following ways.

- Setting clear performance criteria and expectations for compliance and improvement
- Managing sustainability-related risk
- Supporting contract management and supplier motivation
- Identifying high-performing suppliers for inclusion on approved or preferred supplier lists (which in turn supports efficient buying by user departments)

- Identifying high-performing suppliers with potential for closer partnership relations
- Providing feedback for learning and continuous improvement in the buyer-supplier relationship – both for the supplier, and for the purchasing department.

2.11 It is worth noting that KPIs can have some disadvantages as well. The pursuit of individual KPIs can lead to some dysfunctional or sub-optimal behaviour: cutting corners on quality or service to achieve efficiency targets, say, or units focusing on their own targets at the expense of cross-functional collaboration and co-ordination. Targets will have to be carefully set with these potential problems in mind. KPIs should be limited in number; focused on critical success factors, to maximise their relevance and leverage potential; and vertically and horizontally aligned.

Types of performance measure for sustainability

2.12 The BSI suggests that sustainability measures can typically be categorised as follows.

- **Management measures**, reflecting procurement practices (measures of 'inputs' rather than measures of 'outcomes'). Examples include: percentage of contracts awarded based on whole life costing criteria; percentage of contracts with sustainability criteria included; number of supply chain staff trained in sustainable procurement; or percentage of audits carried out for high-risk supply chains
- **Operational measures**, more focused on the target outcomes of sustainability initiatives. Examples include: percentage reduction in waste sent to landfill, reduction in GHG emissions, or percentage of suppliers meeting labour standards.
- **Environmental condition measures**, which are not typically used at the supply chain level, but can be used to inform strategy development. Examples include: average wages and benefits paid to labour; percentage of labour forces represented by trade unions; or levels of motor vehicle emissions.

Sample KPIs for sustainability

2.13 Suggesting KPIs for sustainable procurement is potentially a fertile area for exam questions. Table 7.1 offers some sample suggestions for KPIs in each of the Triple Bottom Line areas. Bear in mind that these are generic: more specific KPIs may be appropriate in particular industry sectors and business types, according to their sustainability priorities and current levels of performance.

Table 7.1 *Example KPIs for sustainability*

	EXAMPLE PROCUREMENT KPIS	EXAMPLE SUPPLIER KPIS
Economic performance	• Cost (eg procurement costs as a percentage of spend) or cost savings (annual cost savings as a percentage of spend) • Productivity (eg cost per procurement cycle, time taken per procurement cycle) • Supplier leverage (eg percentage of suppliers providing 80% or more of annual spend) • Customer satisfaction (eg percentage of deliveries received on time in full)	• Price (eg basic purchase price, value of cost reductions) • Quality or conformance (eg reject, error or wastage rates) • Delivery (eg percentage of on time in full deliveries) • Service and relationship (eg promptness in dealing with enquiries and problems) • Innovation capability (eg number of innovations proposed or implemented) • Overall performance (eg benchmarking against other suppliers)

Continued . . .

	EXAMPLE PROCUREMENT KPIS	EXAMPLE SUPPLIER KPIS
Environmental performance	• Percentage reduction in energy, water purchase • Percentage reduction in supplier (or logistics or procurement) GHG emissions • Percentage reduction in supplier water and energy usage • Percentage purchase of recycled materials • Percentage of vehicle fleet which is hybrid • Volume of waste to landfill (buyer and supplier) • Percentage of spend with suppliers who report on environmental impacts, or operate EMS.	• Percentage reduction in energy, water and other resource use • Percentage reduction in waste to landfill, pollution, GHG emissions etc • Percentage of recycled materials used • Progress towards accreditation of EMS (under ISO 14001) • Attainment of environmental benchmark standards • Green innovations proposed or implemented • Sustainable management of land and practices (eg forestry, agriculture) • Reporting on environmental impact
Social and ethical performance	• Diversity and equal opportunity among procurement staff • Training and development opportunities (and percentage of take-up) • Compliance with workplace law and standards, ethical sourcing and trading standards • Reduction in health and safety incidents, grievance proceedings etc • Supplier diversity (number of women-owned, minority-owned, small suppliers) • Percentage supply chain monitored and managed for compliance • Supply chain compliance (eg year on year reduction in incidents of non-compliance)	• Diversity and equal opportunity among supplier staff • Minimum working conditions and wages for staff • Compliance with human and labour rights law and standards • Year on year improvements in health and safety record • Percentage supply chain monitored and managed for compliance • Percentage products tested on animals (and adherence to animal welfare standards) • Progress towards sustainability management system or development of CSR policy

2.14 The report *Measurement of Sustainable Procurement* (Action Sustainability, 2009) advocates a 'smart KPI approach', in which different methodologies are used to measure economic, social and environmental indicators. For each dimension of the Triple Bottom Line, there are likely to be:

- A small number of generic, corporate-level indicators (which should be applied to all procurements) – eg reducing energy consumption, reducing the use of non-renewable resources, or setting minimum labour standards for all suppliers
- A larger number of KPIs specific to the sustainability priorities related to each particular procurement (depending on supply chain vulnerabilities, relevant environmental issues, supply market labour conditions and so on).

Benchmarking

2.15 A useful definition of benchmarking is: 'Measuring your performance against that of best-in-class companies, determining how the best-in-class achieve these performance levels and using the information as a basis for your own company's targets, strategies and implementation' (Lawrence S Pryor). The aim is to learn both where performance needs to be improved and how it can be improved, by comparison with excellent practitioners.

2.16 Benchmarking can be used to analyse any aspect of organisational performance, including environmental and social sustainability, or sustainability management. Benchmarked performance targets and quality standards are likely to be realistic (since other organisations have achieved them), yet challenging (since the benchmarking organisation hasn't yet achieved them). At the same time, benchmarking helpfully stimulates more research and feedback-seeking into customer needs and wants, and generates new ideas and insights outside the box of the organisation's accustomed ways of thinking and doing things.

2.17 Bendell, Boulter & Kelly distinguish four types of benchmarking, which can be applied to sustainability benchmarking.

- *Internal benchmarking:* comparison with high-performing units in the same organisation. For example, a divisional purchasing function might be benchmarked against a sustainability 'centre of excellence' in another division.
- *Competitor benchmarking:* comparison with high-performing competitors for whom sustainability is a source of competitive advantage.
- *Functional benchmarking:* comparison with another, high-performing organisation. For example, an electronics manufacturer might benchmark its procurement against that of a construction company known for excellent waste management.
- *Generic benchmarking:* comparison of business processes across functional and industry boundaries. The benchmark may be set by the example of CSR and sustainability leaders (as featured in sustainability rankings and awards), or may be formalised in sustainability standards (such as those discussed in Chapter 3).

2.18 Where an organisation wants to carry out its own sustainability benchmarking, the process may be something like Figure 7.3.

Figure 7.3 *The benchmarking process*

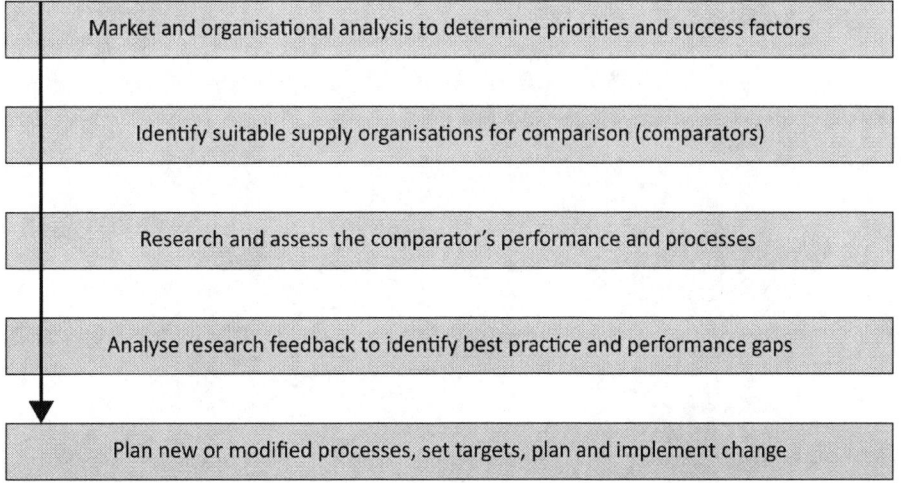

Market and organisational analysis to determine priorities and success factors

Identify suitable supply organisations for comparison (comparators)

Research and assess the comparator's performance and processes

Analyse research feedback to identify best practice and performance gaps

Plan new or modified processes, set targets, plan and implement change

The flexible framework

2.19 Among the key recommendations of the UK Sustainable Procurement National Action Plan was the building of capacity by introducing a **flexible framework** to enable public sector organisations:

- To undertake a detailed review and appraisal of their procurement capabilities, against clear benchmarks
- To identify priority areas for change
- To plan improvements
- To measure ongoing progress, using a five-stage monitoring tool
- To 'locate' all organisations within a benchmark standard: encouraging lower-end organisations to get started – while still challenging those at the higher end.

2.20 The framework identifies five key themes, presenting the key behavioural and operational change programmes that need to be delivered for sustainable procurement.

- People
- Policy, strategy and communication
- Procurement process
- Engaging suppliers
- Measurement and results

Table 7.2 *The flexible framework summary*

	LEVEL 1: FOUNDATION	LEVEL 2: EMBED	LEVEL 3: PRACTICE	LEVEL 4: ENHANCE	LEVEL 5: LEAD
People	SP champion identified. Key procurement staff have received basic training in SP principles. SP is included in key staff induction programmes.	All procurement staff have received basic training in SP principles. Key staff have received advanced training in SP principles.	Target refresher training on latest SP principles. Performance objectives and appraisal include SP factors. Simple incentive programmes in place.	SP included in competencies and selection criteria. Sustainable procurement included as part of employee induction programme.	Achievements publicised, used to attract proc. professionals. Internal and external awards. Focus on benefits achieved. Good practice shared with other organisations.
Policy, strategy and communication	Agree overarching sustainability objectives. Simple SP policy in place, endorsed by CEO. Communicate to staff and key suppliers.	Review and enhance SP policy: consider supplier engagement. Check alignment. Communicate to staff, suppliers and key stakeholders.	Augment SP policy > strategy covering risk, process integration, marketing, supplier engagement, measurement and review process. CEO endorsed.	Review and enhance SP strategy: recognise potential of new technologies. Try to link strategy to EMS and include in overall corporate strategy.	Strategy reviewed regularly, external scrutiny, linked to EMS. SP strategy recognised by leaders, communicated widely. Detailed review undertaken to determine future priorities.
Procurement process	Expenditure analysis undertaken, key sust. impacts identified. Key contracts start to include general sust. criteria. Contracts awarded on the basis of VFM, not lowest price.	Detailed expenditure analysis undertaken, key sustainability risks assessed and used for prioritisation. Sustainability considered at early stage in procurement of most contracts. Whole life cost analysis adopted.	All contracts assessed for general sustainability risks and management actions identified. Risks managed through all stages of procurement process. Target to improve sustainability agreed with key suppliers.	Detailed sustainability risks assessed for high impact contracts. Project/ contract sustainability governance in place. A lifecycle approach to cost/impact assessment applied.	Lifecycle analysis undertaken for key commodity areas. KPIs agreed with key suppliers. Progress rewarded/penalised. Barriers removed. Best practice shared with other organisations.
Engaging suppliers	Key supplier spend analysis undertaken and high impact suppliers identified. Key suppliers targeted for engagement and views on procurement policy sought.	Detailed supplier spend analysis undertaken. General programme of supplier engagement initiatives, with senior management involvement.	Targeted supplier engagement programme in place, for continual improvement. Two-way communication between procurer and supplier, with incentives. Supply chains mapped for key spend areas.	Key suppliers targeted for intensive development. Sustainability audits, supply chain improvement progs in place. Achievements recorded. CEO involved in supplier engagement prog.	Suppliers recognised as essential to delivery of SP strategy. CEO engages with suppliers. Best practice shared. Suppliers recognise they must continually improve sustainability profile.
Measurement and results	Key sustainability impacts of procurement activity have been identified.	Detailed appraisal of sustainability impacts undertaken. Measures implemented to manage identified high risk impact areas.	Sustainability measures refined from general departmental measures to include individual procurers. Linked to development objectives.	Measures integrated into a balanced scorecard approach. Comparison made with peer organisations. Benefit statements produced.	Measures used to drive strategy direction. Progress formally benchmarked. Benefits from SP clearly evidenced. Independent audit reports in public domain.

2.21 It defines five levels of performance in each of these themes, against which organisations can review and appraise their procurement capabilities, and plan an improvement route against recommended time-frames.

- Stage 1   Foundation
- Stage 2   Embedded
- Stage 3   Practice
- Stage 4   Enhanced
- Stage 5   Leadership

2.22 We include the benchmark criteria, just as an example: Table 7.2. (We use the abbreviation SP to mean sustainable procurement.) You may like to carry out an informal 'benchmarking' exercise, by locating your own organisation on the flexible framework, and identifying the next step for improvement in each area.

3   The balanced scorecard

3.1 As we noted earlier, one of the key factors in achieving horizontal alignment of strategy is having common, and consistently applied, targets, objectives and performance measures across the organisation.

3.2 A problem with traditional performance measurement techniques is that whilst any particular key performance indicator (KPI) can be aligned to an overall business objective, its achievement might very well be at the expense of another part of the business. For example, there might be an overall business objective to reduce costs, in pursuit of which procurement may source from low-cost suppliers. It has fulfilled its objective – but possibly at the expense of the quality, sustainability and reputation management objectives of other functions, or of the business as a whole.

3.3 The BSI *Sustainable Procurement Guide* cites the report *Accounting for Sustainability* (2007) which found that 'reporting of sustainability performance is inconsistent and often overcomplicated and inaccessible' and suggests that: 'Leading organisations are now working hard to understand how best to measure and report sustainability performance to give a more balanced and complete picture of overall company performance. This means ensuring that broader and longer-term sustainability considerations are integrated and connected with traditional accounting measures.'

Triple Bottom Line accounting

3.4 One of the earliest and most respected advocates of corporate sustainability is John Elkington. In 1987, he co-founded SustainAbility, a strategic consultancy, research and advocacy organisation, 'offering a range of services and undertaking advocacy in order to create financial value at the same time as addressing environmental, social and governance issues in an integrated manner'.

3.5 Elkington was looking for a new language to express what was seen as an inevitable expansion of the environmental agenda to embrace wider sustainability concerns. In 1994, he coined the term **triple bottom line** (TBL).

3.6 Based on the accounting concept of 'the bottom line' (profit), the term was designed to engage business leaders, raising awareness that corporate activity not only adds economic value, but can potentially also add environmental and social value – and, more importantly, create environmental and social costs (previously regarded as 'externalities', not accounted for in the performance measurement of organisations). Traditionally, these have been borne financially by governments and experientially by communities. In TBL thinking, businesses which cause costly social and environmental impacts should share (or at least recognise) these costs.

3.7 The triple bottom line (also called TBL, 3BL, and later 'People, Profit, Planet') recognises the need for businesses to measure their performance not just by how well they further the interests of their primary stakeholders (shareholders) through profitability (the 'economic bottom line'), but also by how well they further or protect the interests of their secondary stakeholders (including wider society), in relation to social and environmental sustainability. TBL accounting means expanding the traditional reporting framework of a company to take into account ecological and social performance, in addition to financial performance.

The balanced scorecard

3.8 The balanced scorecard model was developed in 1990 by Robert Kaplan and David Norton (*The Balanced Scorecard: Translating A Strategy into Action*). They argued that traditional financial objectives and measures are insufficient to control organisations effectively. Organisations need other parameters and perspectives, in order to avoid the problem of 'short-termism', which arises when managers are judged by criteria which do not measure the long-term, complex effects of their decisions.

3.9 Bengt Karlof & Frederik H Lovingsson (*An A–Z of Management Concepts and Models*) suggest that: 'Few can withstand the simple and obvious logic underlying balanced scorecard: namely, that there are factors other than the financial which are important to control and follow up and that it can be a good idea to establish which factors these in fact are.' The main thrust of this argument is obviously strongly in tune with the concept of sustainability and the triple bottom line: the idea that organisations need to measure their performance not just on financial or economic criteria, but also on their environmental and social impacts and contributions.

Four key perspectives

3.10 Kaplan and Norton proposed four key perspectives for a balanced scorecard (sometimes called a balanced business scorecard or BBS): Figure 7.4.

- *Financial.* Are we creating value for our shareholders? (In relation to sustainable procurement, this might include cost savings, contribution to profit, shareholder value from reputational strength and so on.)
- *Customer.* Are we creating value for our customers? Who are our target customers, and what do they value? How are we doing on measures such as customer satisfaction, customer retention and market share? (In relation to sustainable procurement, customer value might be defined and measured by sustainable product, service and brand attributes.)
- *Internal business processes.* What must we excel at? What are the critical success factors (CSFs) for our business? How efficient and effective are our processes in achieving them? (In relation to sustainable procurement, this might most obviously include environmental management systems, and the management of both internal and external supply chains.)
- *Innovation and organisational learning.* How can we continue to improve and create value? What gaps are there between our aspirations and our current capabilities? What do we need to do better? How strong are our resources for innovation and improvement: skills, information systems, organisation structure and so on? (These questions can obviously be related directly to the development of sustainable procurement capability.)

Figure 7.4 *The balanced scorecard*

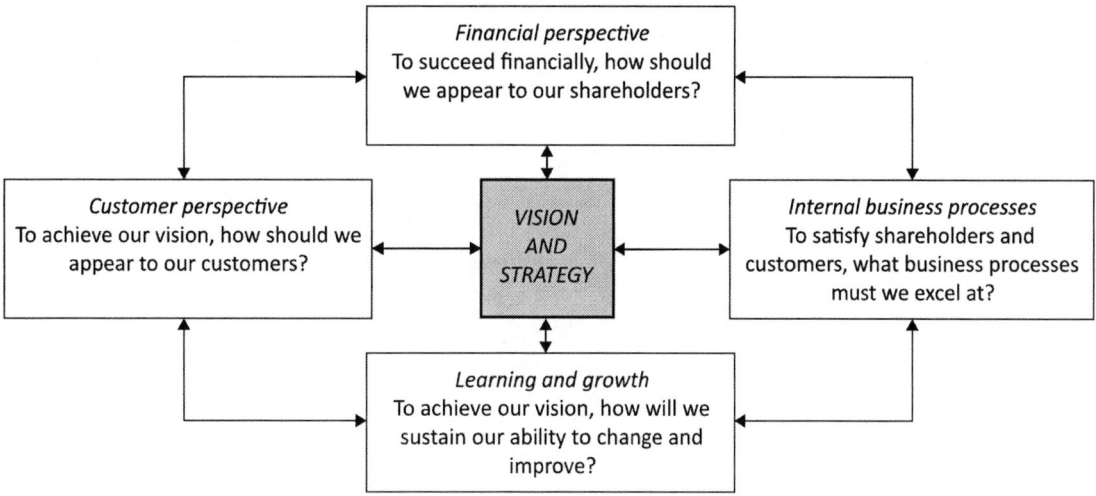

3.11 The scorecard has been designed to balance decision-making by focusing on the interrelationship between the differing competitive pressures facing the organisation and stimulating continuous improvement. The 'balance' of the balanced scorecard is thus between: financial and non-financial performance measures; short-term and long-term perspectives; and internal and external focus.

3.12 Working with a balanced scorecard requires describing, for each 'perspective':

- The organisation's long-term goals
- The success factors established to achieve those goals
- The key activities which must be carried out to achieve those success factors
- The key performance indicators which can be used to monitor progress.

3.13 Once the strategic-level scorecard has been developed, focusing on a dozen or so specific objectives, it must be cascaded through the organisation, in the form of business unit and functional plans. (The procurement function may extend this further, to develop joint scorecard measures for supplier and supply chain performance.)

Incorporating sustainability in scorecards

3.14 Some authors have argued that sustainability can be integrated within the balanced scorecard simply by adding a fifth box to Figure 7.4, labelled 'sustainability perspective'. However, this goes against the principle of the balanced scorecard in that it would make sustainability a separate issue, not allowing for integration across the four categories.

3.15 A more integrated approach to a sustainable scorecard embeds the balanced scorecard within the 'triple bottom line': Figure 7.5. For each of the three main areas of sustainability, there are four categories of indicators of organisational performance.

Figure 7.5 *Sustainability and the balanced scorecard*

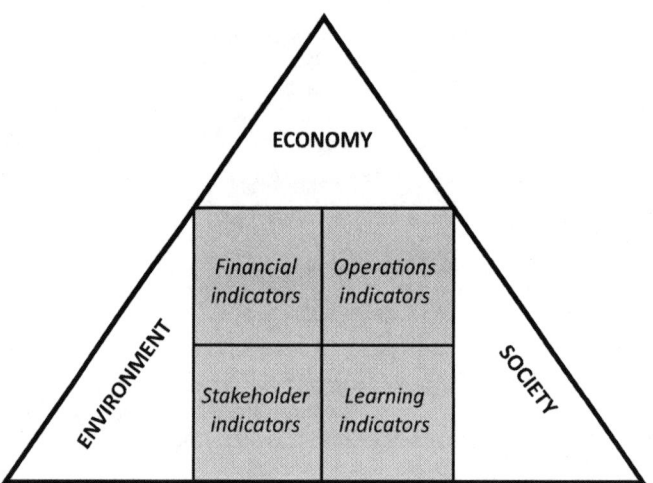

3.16 Blackburn (*Sustainability Handbook*) has identified an alternative set of balanced scorecard measures specifically adapted for the area of sustainability, and built around key stakeholder groups.

- Employee objectives: build the best global team in our industry
- Financial (investor or lender) objectives: delivering significant shareholder return
- Supply chain (customer or supplier) objectives: create sustainable win-win supply chain relationships
- Citizenship (community or government) objectives: improve lives in local and global communities.

3.17 He proposes this as an 'alignment tool', as well as a more sustainability-focused approach to performance measurement, because: 'To the extent possible, each group proposing strategic sustainability objectives and goals should present their information in the same format and under the same overarching strategic categories used for the companywide strategic plan. This will help show how the sustainability initiatives align with the business objectives.'

3.18 You should be able to see how procurement-specific objectives could be set for each of the stakeholder objectives proposed in Blackburn's model. Here are some examples.

- *Employee*: attract, develop and retain procurement talent to achieve current and future results
- *Financial*: improve cost efficiency by achieving targets for inventory turns and costs of supplies
- *Supply chain*: consistently evaluate and meet agreed internal customer requirements; contribute to the development of innovative products and services to meet external customer needs; pursue policies for sustainable and ethical supply chain relationships and development
- *Citizenship*: contribute to the reduction of waste and achieve targeted improved efficiencies in energy and packaging use; gain certification for fair trading.

4 Collaborative performance management

4.1 A sustainable supply chain management orientation explicitly recognises the **shared responsibility** for sustainability: the responsibility of suppliers to implement good workplace and environmental practices – and the responsibility of buyers to encourage and support such practices by suppliers. Throughout this Course Book, we have emphasised the extent to which some common buying practices – such as opportunistic switching, urgent or varied orders, and price squeezing – can militate *against* sustainable practices by suppliers.

4.2 The syllabus therefore highlights the need for buyers to:

- Measure their own performance and practices against sustainability criteria

- Consider the impacts of their performance and practices on sustainability further down the supply chain
- Gather feedback from suppliers on the impacts of buying practices, in the local cultural, economic and environmental context
- Consider how strategic suppliers regard them as a customer (eg using the supplier preferencing model) to ensure that they maintain positive customer status and attractiveness, in order to protect security of supply and service levels. 'A buyer should avoid making such high ethical demands (compared with the value of the business) that the supplier puts them into the Nuisance box' (Responsible Purchasing Initiative, *Win-Win*).

4.3 It is also important to recognise that performance measurement and management itself can be a responsible purchasing or sustainability issue.

- Overly onerous requirements and targets may discriminate against small, diverse and developing-country suppliers, disadvantaging them in accessing contracts.
- KPIs and improvement targets may be unrealistic, failing to take into account cultural, economic and environmental constraints on suppliers (particularly in developing supply markets).
- Overly onerous requirements (especially with an emphasis on compliance rather than improvement) may be counter-productive in securing sustainability, by leading suppliers to falsify reporting on sustainability indicators, or to cut corners in other areas.
- Performance measurement and appraisal may be perceived as a paternalistic or coercive use of power in the supply chain, forcing suppliers into sub-optimal or unsustainable solutions which are ill-adapted to the context and needs of local stakeholders.
- Performance appraisals may be *conducted* in an insensitive manner: disrupting production, causing inconvenience, raising stakeholder conflict (eg where auditors seek the views of workers, against the wishes of management) and so on.

4.4 It is therefore important, as highlighted by the syllabus, for the organisation also to seek feedback from suppliers as to the impact of the performance measurement and appraisal process.

4.5 As we have emphasised in our discussion of KPI development, feedback from suppliers will in any case support the development of relevant and attainable performance measures. Consultation with suppliers can:

- Check shared understanding of sustainability issues and measures
- Highlight relevant workplace and environmental issues (especially if other local stakeholders are also involved)
- Capture local (culturally relevant and stakeholder aware) ideas and suggestions for the improvement of social and environmental performance
- Elicit important information on how the buying organisation can (or will need to) support and facilitate improvements (eg through changing its own buying practices or investing in supplier development).

Joint performance appraisal

4.6 Joint performance appraisal (JPA) is a relational, collaborative approach to performance measurement and management, in which the buyer assesses the supplier's performance – *and* the supplier assesses the buyer's performance. The objective of this approach is to:

- Recognise the impact of buyer-side processes and behaviours (such as adversarial supply relationships, price-focused competition, late changes to requirements or late payments) on the performance, efficiency and sustainability of the supply chain
- Identify problems within the buyer-supplier relationship that may impair the performance of either party, with a view to collaborative problem resolution
- Support long-term value-adding relationships, by ensuring mutual advantage and the equitable sharing of relationship risks and rewards

7

- Encourage collaboration on continuous measurable improvements in supply chain performance and relationship satisfaction.

4.7 Joint appraisal measures are typically based on the following themes.

- Shared mutual objectives
- Compatible benefits to both parties
- Agreed problem-solving methods
- Shared risks, according to who is best equipped to manage them
- Continuous measurable improvements
- Proactively managed relationship

4.8 Clearly, JPA is likely to be most appropriate in the context of collaborative (rather than short-term, adversarial or competitive) contracts and supply chain models, since a high level of trust and openness is required for suppliers to respond honestly and constructively to requests for appraisal feedback on the buyer's relationship performance!

4.9 A well-supported JPA process is time consuming, and should typically be confined to strategic supply relationships. Some effort should also be put into auditing the effectiveness of the process itself. Cross-functional buyer-side and supplier-side teams may review the process on a periodic basis:

- To assess tangible benefits gained from the system. Where appropriate, these can be cascaded as best practice considerations.
- To assess any concerns with the process (eg potential bias due to dominating personalities, or barriers to honesty for fear of reprisals)
- To generate suggestions for further development of the appraisal system.

360-degree feedback

4.10 The concept of 360-degree feedback (or multi-source appraisal) was originally pioneered for use in individual performance appraisals. The individual is rated by a range of selected internal and external stakeholders in their performance (eg managers, direct reports and team members, peers, and customers or suppliers), alongside self-appraisal reporting.

4.11 The same principles of multi-source feedback can be used in joint performance appraisal, in order to:

- Provide the appraised party with an opportunity to learn how multiple stakeholders and contact touch points perceive them, leading to increased self-awareness
- Encourage self-development of both buyer and supplier
- Support a more open relationship culture, in which giving and receiving constructive developmental feedback becomes the accepted norm
- Increase the communication interface between supply chain organisations
- Provide a powerful catalyst for continuous improvement and innovative supply network thinking.

Complementary buyer/supplier scorecards

4.12 The Responsible Purchasing Initiative (*Win-Win*) argues that a complementary approach to rewarding good performance (based on an integrated balanced scorecard for both buyers and suppliers) effectively recognises the shared responsibility of both parties for sustainability.

4.13 The *Win-Win* report suggests an example of aligned buyer-supplier scorecard components: Table 7.3.

Table 7.3 *Complementary buyer and supplier scorecards for rewarding good performance*

SUSTAINABLE COMPONENT OF BUYER SCORECARD		SUSTAINABLE COMPONENT OF SUPPLIER SCORECARD	
DESIRED BEHAVIOUR	INDICATORS	DESIRED BEHAVIOUR	INDICATORS
Choice of, and loyalty to, suppliers who demonstrate commitment and actions to improve working conditions	% of business through suppliers scoring well on this indicator	Championing better jobs for workers, good labour standards and having a positive impact in the community. Actively working to a plan to improve standard	Staff turnover at production sites. Good HRM systems. Good labour standards audit results. Sharing good practice with other suppliers
Retaining suppliers who are willing to work through labour standards problems. Exiting from suppliers who have demonstrated no commitment to improving working conditions	% of suppliers who have acknowledged issue and made improvements. % of suppliers making no progress who have been de-listed	Taking pride in steps taken to demonstrate improved working conditions at all times, including when issues arise.	Sites with initiatives such as active trade union representation. Existing recognition agreements and collective bargaining agreements. Ratio of insecure to contracted workers (differentiated by gender). Analysis of working hours
Loyalty to suppliers with long relationship with production sites	Average length of relationship with individual production sites	Stable relationships with own suppliers and contractors	Average length of relationship with individual production sites. Open dialogue on labour standards in subcontracting sites
		Transparent about supply chain and production	Shared list of all sources of supply, including subcontractors and homeworkers
		Open dialogue on labour conditions	Level of willingness to discuss issues such as pressures on working hours and pay
Commitment to a critical path which allows sufficient planning and production time	No of deviations from critical path. No of late changes in orders	Constructive feedback on how processes can be adapted to meet business as well as minimum social objectives	Quality of relationship between buyer and supplier, gauged by 360% feedback
Contributing to enabling environment for improved labour standards in the supply chain	Willingness to work collaboratively. Number of active collaborative projects with NGOs, trade unions etc	Contributing to an enabling environment for improved labour standards on site	Level of willingness to work collaboratively to bring about sustainable labour standards improvements on site
Demonstrating ongoing commitment to learning about sustainable procurement	Relevant personal development objectives, training attended etc		
Ethics integrated into core business process	Number of contracts with ethical criteria for supplier selection	Evidence that supplier uses buyer ethical scorecard for procurement from next tier	Selection of suppliers with good social performance
Contributing to and enabling environment for improved labour standards within the supply chain	Detailed appraisal of sustainability impacts undertaken. Measures implemented to manage identified high risk impact areas.	Sustainability measures refined from general departmental measures to include individual procurers. Linked to development objectives.	Measures integrated into a balanced scorecard approach. Comparison made with peer organisations. Benefit statements produced.

(Source: RPI, 'Win-Win: Achieving Sustainable Procurement with the Developing World)

7

Obtaining supplier commitment

4.14 It may be comparatively easy to secure the *compliance* of most suppliers with sustainability policies – unless they have significant bargaining power in the buyer-supplier relationship – through mechanisms such as: information (widely disseminating the policy via contract managers, the corporate website or extranet, in contract terms and conditions, at supplier conferences and meetings, and so on); the use of contract incentives, penalties and sanctions in regard to adherence to the policy; and making continued business contingent on adherence to the policy.

4.15 If the buying organisation wants the extra benefits of commitment, flexibility, innovation, proactive problem-solving, continuous improvement and co-operation – over and above what is expressly required by the policy, and contracts under it – they will have to make it worth the supplier's while. A range of incentives may be used.

- Contingency payments (eg part of the payment is linked to sustainability measures)
- Sustainability key performance indicators (KPIs) or improvement targets linked to recognition and rewards: extension of the contract or the promise of further business; inclusion on the approved or preferred supplier list; publicised supplier awards and endorsements; financial bonuses (eg for extra units of productivity); and so on.
- Revenue, profit or gain sharing (eg allocating the supplier an agreed percentage or flat fee bonus for cost savings arising for reduced resource usage). Where supplier improvements create added value, revenue or profit for the buyer, the 'gain' is shared: a 'win-win' outcome.
- The promise of long-term business agreements, increased business, or guaranteed or fixed order levels, allowing the planning of investments and improvements by the supplier
- Opportunities for innovation: the contract gives the provider the chance to implement or devise new solutions that will develop their business and reputation
- The offer of development support (eg training or technology sharing).

5 Contract and supplier management

5.1 Contracts for the supply of goods or services may be much more complex, and longer in duration, than a simple purchase order. Once contracts are signed, therefore, it is not as simple as saying: 'The supplier will now do that'. There will be obligations to be followed up on either side. If contingencies arise, the contract may (or may not) lay down what happens next. If the supplier's performance falls short in any way, there will be a variety of options for pursuing the matter. Circumstances and requirements may change (for example, as new sustainability issues emerge, or as continuous improvements are sought), and contract terms may have to be adjusted accordingly.

5.2 This is an ongoing process through the life of the contract. **Contract management** is the process designed to ensure that both parties to a contract meet their obligations, and that the intended outcomes of a contract are delivered. It also involves building and maintaining a good working relationship between the buyer and the supplier, continuing through the life of a contract.

5.3 The term 'contract management' suggests that the focus of attention is on the performance of particular contracts. The term 'relationship management' is often used to describe the management of an ongoing relationship with a supplier, beyond the performance of individual transactions.

5.4 The process of supplier performance measurement, using KPIs, should therefore be seen within a wider process of:

- *Risk management*: collaborating with users and suppliers to identify potential sustainability risks or barriers to sustainability performance, so that they can be managed or mitigated
- *Continuous improvement planning*. Buyer and supplier may work collaboratively over the life of

the contract to set year-on-year improvement targets, solve performance issues, identify emerging opportunities and so on. The contract may need to be revised to reflect new targets and agreements – or may make a general provision for improvement planning.

- *Supplier motivation*: incentives and rewards for performance, added value, suggestions or improvements on sustainability. These may take the form of contract extension, preferred supplier status, supplier awards or gain-sharing, for example. Sanctions and penalties may also be used for non-compliance, and will form part of a performance management process.
- *Performance management*: problem-solving and corrective action in the event of progress or performance shortfalls; pursuing dispute resolution procedures (as set out in the contract); pursuing remedies to mitigate loss or damage as a result of breach of contract or non-compliance.

5.5   We will discuss supplier and relationship management further in Chapter 10.

Allowing for new developments and targets

5.6   It is worth highlighting the need for flexibility in the purchase contract or relationship agreement, to allow for new developments in sustainable procurement, and ongoing targets for improvement, to be incorporated over time.

5.7   New sustainability issues, risks or opportunities may emerge, which buyer or supplier (or both) may wish to take account of in the supply contract or relationship. For example, one or both parties may introduce or revise CSR or sustainability policies. New technologies or alternative resources may be developed, offering solutions to sustainability challenges. Provisions for periodic contract review and the negotiation of adjusted terms should be built into contracts and service level agreements. The willingness of a supplier to agree to such flexibility may be another important consideration in contract award.

5.8   The buyer or supplier (or both) may wish to establish commitments and targets for continuous improvement – and related supplier development – in sustainability performance, within defined planning and review periods (eg year on year).

- Specific year-on-year improvement targets may be agreed at the contract stage: eg annual percentage reductions in carbon emissions or waste to landfill, or attainment of ISO 14001 over a defined period.
- Alternatively, commitment to continuous improvement may be embedded in the initial contract. Details of moving targets (and the commitment of resources to support them) can then be negotiated and formulated in separate continuous improvement agreements for each planning period. This approach may respond more flexibly to emerging sustainability issues, the pace of innovation, resource availability and so on.

7

Chapter summary

- Buyers should monitor the sustainability performance of their suppliers, using defined benchmarks and targets.
- Effective KPIs should be SMART: specific; measurable; attainable; relevant; time-bounded.
- Broad approaches to the assessment of sustainability performance include the triple bottom line and the balanced scorecard.
- Sustainability is a responsibility shared between buyers and suppliers. This can be formalised in a system of joint performance appraisal.
- Contract and supplier management is an ongoing process throughout the term of a supply contract.

Self-test questions

Numbers in brackets refer to the paragraphs where you can check your answers.

1   What are the objectives of measuring suppliers' performance? (1.4)

2   Distinguish between quantitative and qualitative approaches to supplier monitoring. (1.9)

3   List the steps in developing KPIs for performance measurement. (Figure 7.2)

4   List benefits of developing KPIs as performance measures for sustainability. (2.9, 2.10)

5   Give examples of KPIs for sustainability. (Table 7.1)

6   What are the three elements of the 'triple bottom line'? (3.7)

7   Explain how performance measurement can itself be an issue of responsible purchasing. (4.3)

8   What are the objectives of joint performance appraisal? (4.6)

9   What is meant by 360-degree feedback? (4.10)

10   Define contract management. (5.2)

CHAPTER 8

Managing Supply Chain Complexity

Assessment criteria and indicative content

 4.1 Analyse how the levels of complexity in supply chains impact on compliance with standards for sustainability

- Mapping supply chains
- The use of subcontractors by suppliers
- Portfolio analysis that measures sustainability risk and importance to the organisation
- Portfolio analysis that measures sustainability risk and scope for improvement

Section headings

1   Supply chain complexity
2   Supply chain mapping
3   Managing for risk and vulnerability
4   Portfolio analysis
5   Other tools of analysis
6   Supply chain visibility

Introduction

This chapter begins a sequence covering the final syllabus section, which broadly concerns the management of compliance with sustainability standards through the supply chain.

In Chapter 7 we discussed the various standards, targets and key performance indicators that could be set for both buyer-side and supplier-side performance. In Chapter 9 we will look at how performance and progress can be monitored and measured against those 'desired behaviours' and indicators. And in Chapter 10 we will explore how non-compliance or performance gaps can be dealt with, in the context of sustainable supply chain relationships.

Meanwhile, in this chapter, we set the context for compliance management, by highlighting the complexity of supply chains, and how supply chain complexity adds extra layers of risk and challenge to the management of sustainability standards. We then go on to cover the indicative syllabus content which relates to various tools for analysing supply chains, with a specific view to identifying and prioritising key areas of risk and leverage for sustainability management.

1   Supply chain complexity

1.1   A supply chain is defined as 'a network of organisations, people, activities, information and resources involved in moving a product or service in a physical or virtual manner from supplier to customer.' (Responsible Purchasing Initiative, *Taking the Lead*)

1.2   A supply chain 'encompasses all organisations and activities associated with the flow and transformation of goods from the raw materials stage, through to the end user, as well as the associated information flows. Material and information flow both up and down the supply chain' (Robert B Handfield & Ernest L Nichols, *Supply Chain Redesign)*

1.3   Part or all of an inter-business supply chain may in fact be brought within the control of a single holding company. Large oil companies, for example, typically have control over all the main stages of exploration, production, refining and retailing. In most cases, however, supply chains are controlled through supply contracts and collaborative relationships between separate, autonomous entities.

1.4   Supply chain complexity is a key area of vulnerability for sustainable procurement for the following reasons.

- Increasingly complex international supply chains include components sourced in numerous countries, assembled in others, with sales and customer services in yet others – often, according to which suppliers can offer the most competitive price at a given time.
- 'The trend towards the transfer of operational management to others (eg tier-one suppliers, category managers, outsource providers or agents) reduces transparency and distances the buying organisation from the market and what is happening in its own supply chain' (RPI, *ibid)*.
- Where supply chain complexity increases *and* transparency decreases, the risks are magnified.

1.5   CIPS affirms that 'ethical supply chain management is one of the greatest challenges facing organisations. It is becoming unacceptable for organisations to be unaware of how the workers involved in making their products or supplying their services are treated. The global nature of trade often leads to complexity within the supply chain; this alone can make ethical trading a daunting task in itself' (Practice Guide on CSR).

1.6   Throughout this Course Book, we have highlighted the fact that sustainable procurement issues and principles apply from the farthest upstream end of the supply chain onwards. The challenge is to monitor, identify and manage sustainability risks 'back' through the tiers of the supply chain (suppliers' suppliers) – right back to the extraction or production of raw materials and commodities, if necessary.

1.7   This is a major challenge for procurement professionals, because, as the syllabus highlights:

- Supply chains are increasingly complex: it is not always possible for a buying organisation to identify where purchased items 'ultimately' come from, or through whose hands they pass, and
- It is costly, time-consuming and potentially unsustainable for the buying organisation to monitor and control all tiers and members of the extended supply chain.

1.8   Buyers must therefore seek:

- To **understand their supply chains**, and the ways in which supply chain complexity creates risk and vulnerability
- To **increase the end-to-end visibility of their supply chains**, in order to be able to identify points of risk and vulnerability
- To **identify high-risk or high-leverage points** in the supply chain, in order to prioritise managerial time and resources for sustainability monitoring and control. A CSR or ethical procurement orientation (seeking to protect corporate reputation and supply continuity) may prioritise on the basis of *risk:* focusing on areas of exposure or vulnerability. A Fair Trade or affirmative procurement orientation

(seeking proactively to ameliorate social and environmental conditions in supply markets) may prioritise on the basis of *leverage:* focusing on areas with maximum scope and potential for improvement.

- To engage in **vulnerability and risk assessment**, focusing not just on potential impacts on the organisation – but potential impacts *by* the organisation on vulnerable social, economic or environmental resources in the market or supply chain.

International supply chains

1.9 Supply chains are increasingly lengthy in a *geographical* sense, for reasons discussed at length in Chapter 2. Internationalised or globalised supply chains add complexity because of a number of factors.

- Physical distance may separate many members of supply chains, creating (a) logistical complexity (with impacts on sustainable demand management and transport impacts) and (b) difficulties for supplier appraisal and selection, and sustainability monitoring, auditing and compliance management – especially in developing countries where there may be a lack of ICT and transport infrastructure.
- Legal and cultural differences may create barriers to the management of compliance with standards. Local governments may fail to enforce statutory protections for the workers or environment, for example. There may be economic barriers to compliance with onerous supplier requirements, or cultural barriers (eg to compliance with equal opportunity standards in patriarchal cultures). These differences may not be well understood by an opportunistic global buyer.

Tiered supply chains

1.10 Supply chains are increasingly lengthy in a *configuration* sense, because of competitive pressures for specialisation, and the development of supplier tiering. A manufacturer may see strategic advantage in outsourcing all activities other than final finishing, sales and service: its direct procurement relationship may be (in simplified terms) with a single supplier or tier of suppliers. Each supplier in the first tier would have an extensive role to fulfil in the manufacture of the final product, making use of 'second-tier' suppliers: Figure 8.1

Figure 8.1 *Tiered supply chain*

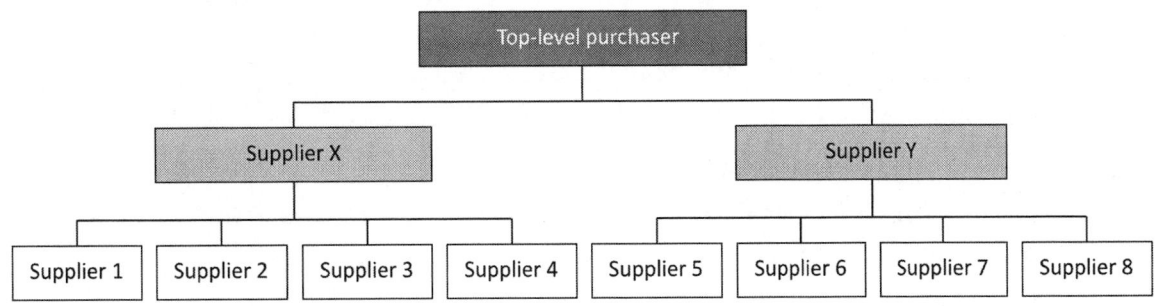

1.11 An organisation might adopt a deliberate policy of tiering its suppliers, so as to reduce the number of first-tier suppliers: the 'supplier base' with which it has to deal directly. This may be part of a process of supplier rationalisation or supply chain re-structuring, for example. The organisation deals directly only with its first-tier suppliers: second-tier suppliers deal with a first-tier supplier. First-tier suppliers are often expected to collaborate with the top-level purchaser to add value (making improvements and eliminating wastes) throughout the supply chain, and to pursue innovation in products and processes. With only a small number of first-tier supplier relationships, the top-level purchaser can focus on developing these as a long-term, collaborative supply partnerships.

1.12 However, there may be a number of layers between the top-level purchaser and the 'bottom tiers' of the supply chain (commodity producers, raw material extractors). These may be the very tiers which represent the most vulnerable workers and producers, and the most direct environmental impacts – and therefore the greatest vulnerability to adverse impacts, exploitation and sustainability risk.

1.13 As an example (cited by the BSI *Sustainable Procurement Guide*), Nokia recognised sustainability concerns regarding poor practices in its supply chain for primary metals. Some of the specialised metals used in electronic products are mined in relatively few places and have great commercial value, and are therefore vulnerable to exploitation. Nokia recognised that there may be anything between four and eight layers of suppliers between a typical consumer electronics company and mining activity: Figure 8.2.

Figure 8.2 *Primary metals supply chain for a mobile phone product*

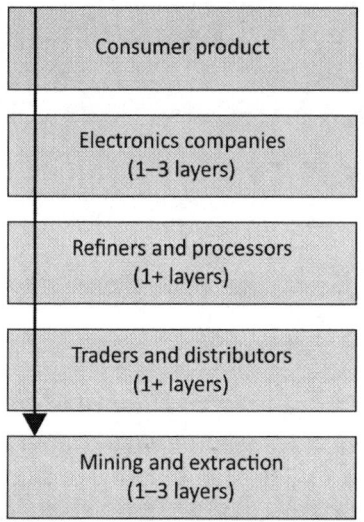

1.14 Nokia has thus recognised the need:

- To improve transparency and support verification of metals supply chains
- To ensure suppliers meet rigorous health and safety, environmental and labour standards (which it also requires suppliers to apply to *their* suppliers)
- To implement on-site visits to review standards, for key high-risk contracts
- To work with suppliers and provide training and support to help them implement and improve standards
- To support industry-level initiatives, conducting research into the key sustainability challenges in the supply of metals, the ability to trace sources of metals used in electronic products, and the industry's ability to influence conditions.

Tiered supply chains

1.15 The use of subcontractors by suppliers generally adds a layer of complexity and risk, because it creates a situation in which the buying organisation:

- Does not have a direct contractual relationship with the contractor carrying out work on its behalf, which would enable it directly to enforce standards and codes of practice
- May not have an opportunity to pre-qualify or approve the subcontractor (in regard to quality and/or sustainability requirements)
- May not even be aware of the identity (or existence) of such contractors.

1.16 The main contractor will remain liable for any failures on the part of the subcontractor, but the risk may still be unacceptable to the buyer. In legal terms, the general rule is that a contract can be assigned or subcontracted unless it is evident that a supplier was specifically chosen for its unique qualities (and it would therefore not fulfil the buyer's intentions to have the work done by another party).

1.17 A subcontracting and assignment clause may be used in the supply contract to prevent subcontracting without prior written consent of the buyer. However, outsourcing and subcontracting is a fact of modern business life, as long-term and short-term approaches to increasing capacity and managing specialisation. They are also broadly supportive of economic sustainability, since they enable small, specialist contractors and subcontractors to access parts of large contracts and projects. Pressure will, however, be put on the buying organisation to increase the visibility of the supply chain and identify areas of vulnerability.

Supply networks

1.18 Even a tiered supply chain model offers a simplified picture. In reality, each organisation in the supply chain has multiple other relationships with its own customers, suppliers, industry contacts, partners and advisers – and even competitors (in trade associations or industry think tanks, say) – any and all of whom may also be connected with each other.

1.19 Many writers now argue, therefore, that a more appropriate metaphor for the supply process is not a chain, but a network or web – which allows a more complex set of interrelated relationships and transactions to be depicted. Martin Christopher describes the supply network as 'a confederation of mutually complementary competencies and capabilities which compete as an integrated supply chain against other supply chains'.

1.20 Seeing the supply chain as a network is helpful for a number of reasons.

- It is a more strategic model for mapping and analysing supply chain relationships, and therefore for seeking to exploit synergies and improve performance in innovative ways.
- It raises the possibility of a wider range of collaborations (eg supplier associations, buying consortia or strategic alliances) which may offer mutual advantages – and perhaps alter the balance of power in supply relationships (eg increasing the buying power of small buyers by participation in a buying consortium, or increasing the capacity of small suppliers by collaboration in a consortium bid).
- It recognises the potential of 'extended enterprises' and virtual organisations: extending the strategic capability of the firm through the collective resources and performance of network contributors – and extending the strategic importance of sourcing and supplier management activities as a way of accessing those contributions.

The internal supply chain

1.21 It is worth noting that the complexity of *internal* supply chains and relationships may also impact on compliance with sustainability standards. For example:

- There may be lack of clear accountability for the development and enforcement of sustainability standards within an organisation or project structure
- Procurement activities may be devolved to 'part-time purchasers' in user departments, who may not be trained in the principles of responsible purchasing, or be fully aware of sustainable procurement policies and practices. They may, in particular, be driven by functional and operational needs (eg for urgent orders or last-minute changes) which may have a detrimental effect on vulnerable suppliers.

2 Supply chain mapping

2.1 One of the key techniques for managing the sustainability risks arising from supply chain complexity is to map or chart the configuration of the supply chain, in order to identify potential areas of vulnerability.

2.2 Supply chain mapping is a diagrammatic representation of the configuration of a supply chain, including its key participants, flows (of materials, products, information and finance) and relationships. A simplified generic example, in a construction setting, might be as shown in Figure 8.3.

Figure 8.3 *Supply chain map for a construction supply chain*

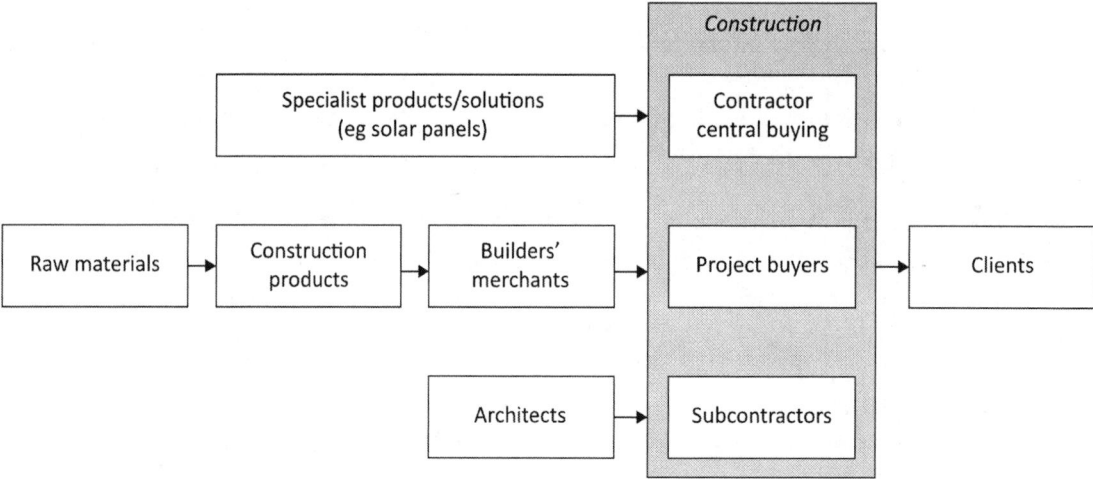

2.3 For each participant in the supply chain (as shown here), the mapping team would then add information such as: key tasks, with average lead times for each; costs, added value and profit; labour requirements (indicating labour-intensive stages of production, where worker exploitation may occur); environmental impacts (such as energy or water usage or waste generation); and so on.

2.4 Buyers may need to work with internal stakeholders, suppliers, trade associations and other expert stakeholders to build up a comprehensive supply chain map for complex supply chains.

2.5 Supply chain mapping is a tool of analysis and communication, enabling managers to identify:

- Strong and weak linkages in the sustainability chain (eg due to poor relationships; lack of communication; unknown or un-certified sub-suppliers; or supply chain members without sustainability, CSR and ethical policies in place) – which may require improvement and development
- Potential areas of sustainability, compliance or reputational risk (eg due to strong association with high-risk supply chain partners; sustainability risks affecting particular organisation types or stages of the supply process) – for which auditing or further assurance may be required
- Potential areas of opportunity or strength, arising from network connections or partners with strong capability, resources or reputation for sustainability
- Potential areas of weakness and opportunities to improve environmental and social performance – where further support and development may be required, or which offer 'quick wins'
- Areas of inefficiency in the supply chain (eg unnecessary transport, processes, or an overly large supply base) which erode economic and/or environmental sustainability. Maps may add elements such as time (eg indicating waiting and idle time) and inventory build up, for the identification of wastes.
- Potential efficiencies (eg for variety reduction, supply base rationalisation or process alignment)
- The breakdown of costs, added value, resource and energy usage, and environmental impacts (among other key sustainability factors) at each stage of the supply chain

- Areas in which improved information or resource flows are required for the development of innovation and sustainability (eg feedback from downstream members to support demand and define value for sustainable products)
- Weaknesses in reverse logistics, or lack of a closed loop supply chain, which may need to be addressed for sustainability (eg for take-back and recycling or disposal obligations)
- Areas in which the organisation may need to move from a 'chain' to a 'network' as the dominant metaphor for supply, in order to develop a wider range of collaborations for sustainability (eg with NGO partners)

2.6 Issues highlighted by the map can be further investigated. If you are interested in this area, you might like to download the *CIPS Good Practice Guide on Supply Chain Mapping*.

3 Managing for risk and vulnerability

3.1 As we have emphasised throughout this Course Book, a pragmatic view of sustainable procurement suggests that it is, essentially, a form of risk management. It is designed to minimise:

- The risk of the **buying organisation** having to curtail or cease its activities owing to supply failure or disruption, resource scarcity or cost, breakdown in stakeholder relationships, or withdrawal of the organisation's licence to operate (eg because of reputational damage)
- The risk of loss or damage to **stakeholders**, and vulnerable social, economic and environmental resources, both in the present and in the future.

3.2 We have emphasised the importance of the identification and assessment of risk and vulnerability (points of weakness that lead to risk) in prioritising areas for sustainable procurement focus: identifying high-risk supply items, supply chains, suppliers and sustainability issues and performance gaps. This is an ongoing challenge for the purchasing profession, because risk and vulnerability are highly fluid, dynamic and complex. New risks are constantly emerging – and risks change their severity and priority as circumstances change. As we have seen in this chapter, globalised, multi-tiered supply chains also create particular points of vulnerability – and challenges in monitoring and managing risk.

3.3 You may already have covered risk management in detail in your studies for *Managing Risk in Supply Chains*. We will outline some key points here, since we have not had the opportunity to do so elsewhere in this Course Book.

The risk management process

3.4 Risk management may be defined as 'the process whereby organisations methodically address the risks attaching to their activities with the goal of achieving sustained benefit within each activity and across the portfolio of all activities' (Institute of Risk Management).

3.5 As we saw in Chapter 4, the process of risk management can be portrayed as a cycle. For convenience, we reproduce the diagram here: Figure 8.4.

Figure 8.4 *The risk management cycle*

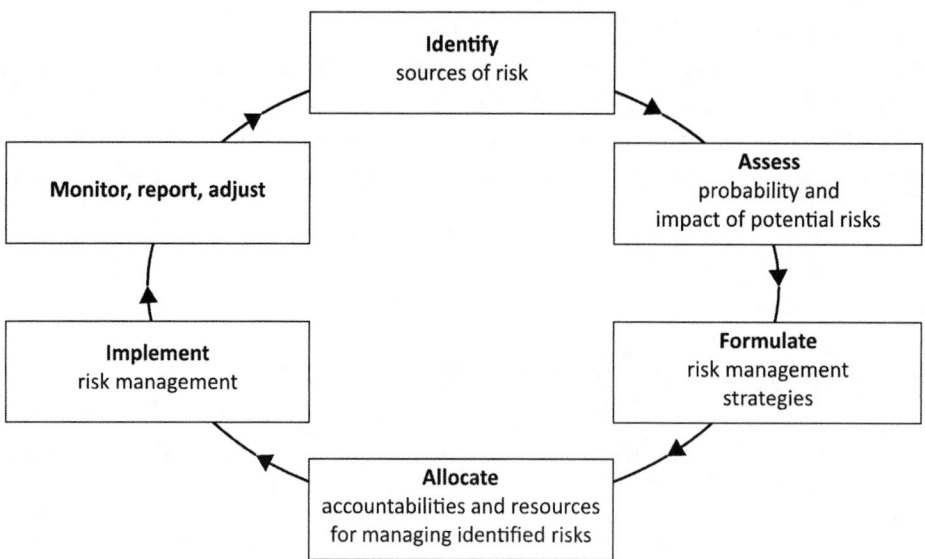

3.6   **Risk identification** is the process of seeking to identify potential problems or areas of uncertainty: in other words, asking 'what could go wrong?' This may be done by techniques such as the following.

- Environmental scanning and corporate appraisal (PESTLE and SWOT analysis)
- Formal risk analysis exercises
- Monitoring risk events in benchmark organisations
- Critical incident investigations and process audits
- Consulting with key stakeholders and industry experts
- Employing third-party risk management consultants

It should be an ongoing process, as the organisation's sustainability risk profile may continually change, presenting new risks or turning slight risks into potential crises (eg if they attract media or NGO scrutiny). A comprehensive list of identified risks should be compiled (eg in a sustainability risk register).

3.7   **Risk assessment or evaluation** is the appraisal of the probability and significance of identified potential risk events: in other words, asking 'how likely is it and how bad could it be?' Risk is often quantified using the basic formula: *Risk = Likelihood × Impact.*

- *Risk likelihood* is the probability of occurrence, given the nature of the risk and current risk management practices. This may be expressed as a number between 0 (no chance) and 1 (certainty) or as a percentage (100% = certainty), a score (1–10) or a rating (Low–Medium–High). The more likely the risk event is to occur, the higher the overall level of risk, and the higher priority risk management will be.
- *Risk impact* is the likely cost to the organisation or the likely level of impact on its ability to fulfil its objectives. The severity of impacts may be quantified (eg in terms of estimated cost or loss), scored (1–10), or rated (Low–Medium–High). Even if assessed as improbable, high-impact events should be the subject of detailed contingency planning, so that the organisation can respond effectively to the event if it occurs.

3.8   Quantifying the risk allows an organisation to prioritise planning and resources to meet the most severe risks, and to set defined risk thresholds at which action on an issue will be triggered. **Risk management strategies** ('what can we do about it?') are often classified as the Four Ts.

- *Tolerate* (or accept) the risk: if the assessed likelihood or impact of the risk is negligible
- *Transfer* or spread the risk: eg by taking out insurance cover, or not putting all supply eggs in one basket – or using contract terms to ensure that the costs of risk events will be borne by (or shared with) supply chain partners

- *Terminate* (or avoid) the risk: if the risk associated with a particular activity is too great, and cannot be reduced, the activity should not be undertaken. So, for example, suppliers may be rejected on the basis of poor labour management or environmental standards in high-visibility areas.
- *Treat* (or mitigate) the risk: take active steps to manage the risk in such a way as to reduce or minimise its likelihood or potential impact, or both. This may involve measures such as: safety procedures, maintenance schedules, internal governance controls, supplier monitoring, codes of conduct, supplier sustainability policies and standards, rigorous supplier certification or pre-qualification, critical incident reporting and analysis, stakeholder feedback gathering, contingency and recovery planning (eg alternative sources of supply), third-party auditing, subjecting sourcing strategies to third-party review; and so on.

3.9   In any case, the organisation will need to make **contingency plans** in regard to high-impact risks: alternative courses of action, alternative sources of supply, workarounds and fall-back positions ('What will we do if...?').

3.10   **Monitoring, reporting and review** ('What happened and what can we learn?') is an important part of risk management, in order to:

- Ascertain whether the organisation's risk profile or exposure is changing, and identify newly emerging or escalating sustainability-related risks
- Give assurance that the organisation's risk management processes are effective, by demonstrating effective avoidance or mitigation of risks. (This may be important in supporting investment in innovation, for example – as well as being a responsible orientation to stakeholder concerns.)
- Indicate where risk management processes need improvement, or where lessons can be learned from critical incidents.

4   Portfolio analysis

4.1   As we saw in Chapter 1, one of the key early processes in sustainable procurement is the **prioritisation** of areas of procurement or spend, so that sustainability efforts can be focused where they have the greatest leverage, impact and return on investment. There are various ways of categorising and prioritising an organisation's procurement requirements or 'portfolio'.

The Kraljic matrix

4.2   Peter Kraljic drew up a matrix model to help organisations classify their procurement portfolios according to two dimensions: **supply risk** (including factors such as sourcing difficulty, and buyer vulnerability to supply or supplier failure) and **purchase value** (including factors such as the profit potential of the item, and the importance of the purchase to the business).

4.3   Rating risk and purchase value as either high or low, the Kraljic matrix offers four quadrants: Figure 8.5.

Figure 8.5 *The Kraljic purchasing portfolio matrix*

Complexity of the supply market

	Low		High	
High	**Procurement focus** Leverage items	**Time horizon** Varied, typically 12-24 months	**Procurement focus** Strategic items	**Time horizon** Up to 10 years; governed by long-term strategic impact (risk and contract mix)
	Key performance criteria Cost/price and materials flow management	**Items purchased** Mix of commodities and specified materials	**Key performance criteria** Long-term availability	**Items purchased** Scarce and/or high-value materials
Importance of the item	**Typical sources** Multiple suppliers, chiefly local	**Supply** Abundant	**Typical sources** Established global suppliers	**Supply** Natural scarcity
	Procurement focus Non-critical items	**Time horizon** Limited: normally 12 months or less	**Procurement focus** Bottleneck items	**Time horizon** Variable, depending on availability vs short-term flexibility trade-offs
	Key performance criteria Functional efficiency	**Items purchased** Commodities, some specified materials	**Key performance criteria** Cost management and reliable short-term sourcing	**Items purchased** Mainly specified materials
Low	**Typical sources** Established local suppliers	**Supply** Abundant	**Typical sources** Global, predominantly new suppliers with new technology	**Supply** Production-based scarcity

4.4 Taking the quadrants one by one:

- For *non-critical or routine items* (such as common stationery supplies), the focus will be on reducing transaction costs. Arm's length approaches such as blanket ordering and e-procurement solutions will provide routine efficiency. Quick wins on environmental and social sustainability may be available at relatively low cost, eg through stipulating green, recycled, low-energy consumption or Fair Trade items. (The National Procurement Action Plan, for example, features a list of such quick wins.)
- For *bottleneck items* (such as proprietary spare parts or specialised consultancy services, which could cause operational delays if unavailable), the buyer's priority will be ensuring control over the continuity and security of supply. This may suggest approaches such as negotiating medium-term or long-term contracts with suppliers, which may also be an opportunity to secure cost and other sustainability improvements.
- For *leverage items* (such as local produce bought by a major supermarket), the buyer's priority will be to use its dominance to secure best prices and terms, on a transactional basis. This may mean taking advantage of competitive pricing; standardising specifications to make supplier switching easier; and using competitive bidding and/or buying consortia to secure the best deals. However, attention will still have to be paid to sustainability issues such as ethical trading and whole life costs of purchases.
- For *strategic items* (such as key subassemblies bought by a car manufacturer, or Intel processors bought by laptop manufacturers), there is likely to be mutual dependency and investment, and the focus will be on the total cost, security and competitiveness of supply. There will therefore be a need to develop long-term, mutually beneficial strategic relationships – with opportunities for supplier development, co-investment and innovation for sustainability.

4.5 Kraljic highlighted supply risks such as resource depletion and raw materials scarcity, political turbulence, government intervention in supply markets, intensified competition and accelerating technology change –

all of which are sustainability issues. However, some writers argue that the Kraljic matrix, with its focus on general operational risk, does not sufficiently highlight sustainability risk. They further argue that some of its quadrants recommend adversarial procurement approaches which may be considered 'inappropriate' in a responsible purchasing context: potentially resulting in worker exploitation or environmental 'corner cutting' in pursuit of low price.

Sustainability risk and scope for improvement

4.6 An alternative approach (recommended by the RPI) is therefore to map the procurement portfolio on two slightly different dimensions.

- **Sustainability risk**: likelihood of non-compliance with the organisation's sustainability or CSR objectives, national law and/or relevant international standards (eg using the ILO's country reports, which indicate the level of enforcement of labour laws)
- **Importance to the organisation** (of sustainability compliance or non-compliance) in terms of reputational risk exposure, corporate values and so on.

4.7 This is effectively a likelihood vs impact risk assessment in regard to sustainability. The Responsible Purchasing Initiative depicts the matrix as follows: Figure 8.6.

Figure 8.6 *Sustainability risk v importance to organisation matrix*

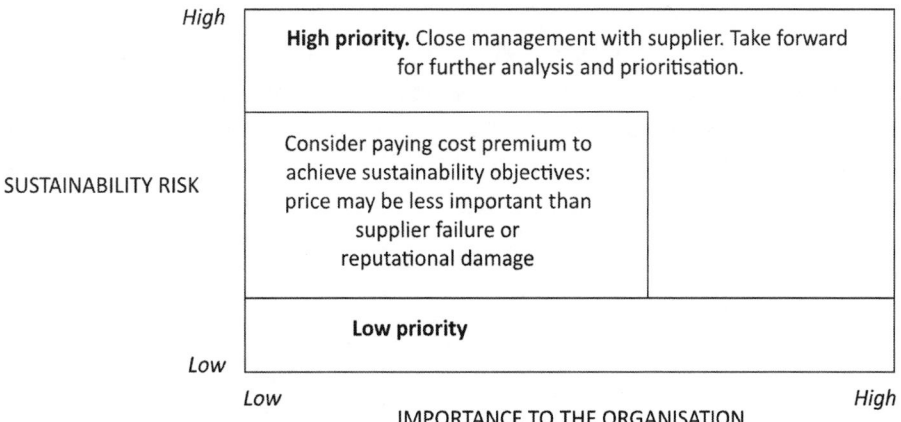

Sustainability risk and scope for improvement

4.8 High-priority procurements or categories can be *further* classified according to potential **leverage**, or scope for improvement of social or environmental performance: that is, areas in which there is *scope for the organisation to do more* in terms of reducing residual sustainability risks or impacts. Such an analysis may take into account factors such as the following.

- The inherent unsustainability of a given purchase or category, or potential for better alternatives and innovations
- Key contracts that may be coming up for renewal
- Actions that are realistically possible to bring about change (and their degree of cost and difficulty)
- The expertise of staff in particular categories of social and environmental issues.

4.9 The 'sustainability risk vs scope for improvement' assessment matrix recommended by the RPI is shown in Figure 8.7.

Figure 8.7 *Sustainability risk vs scope for improvement*

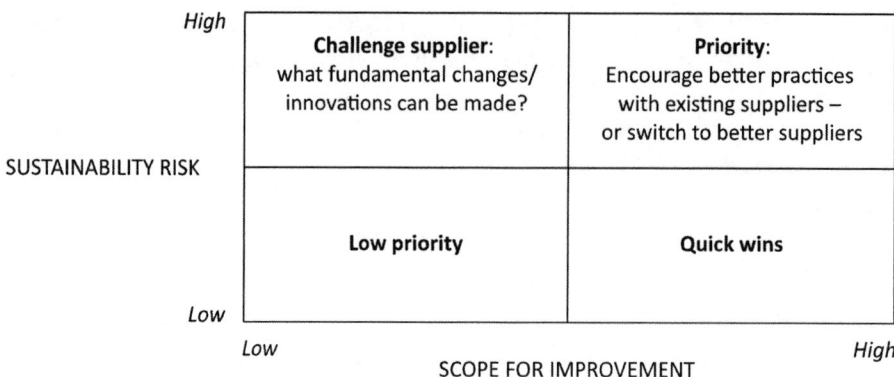

4.10 This approach enables resources to be focused on the risks and impacts where most difference can be made – and hence greater benefits achieved. It also creates a momentum for change, by supporting 'quick wins': raising the profile and business case for sustainability, and co-opting stakeholders to support sustainability initiatives. The RPI argues that 'in developing countries with poor working conditions, there is frequently considerable scope for improvement'.

Influence and scope for improvement

4.11 A third dimension may be added for further analysis, in the form of areas in which the organisation has *influence to bring about sustainability improvements* in the supply chain or market. This analysis will take into account the organisation's size, corporate profile and status, value as a customer and existing supplier (and network) relationships. The 'influence vs scope for improvement matrix' recommended by the RPI is shown in Figure 8.8.

Figure 8.8 *Influence vs scope for improvement matrix*

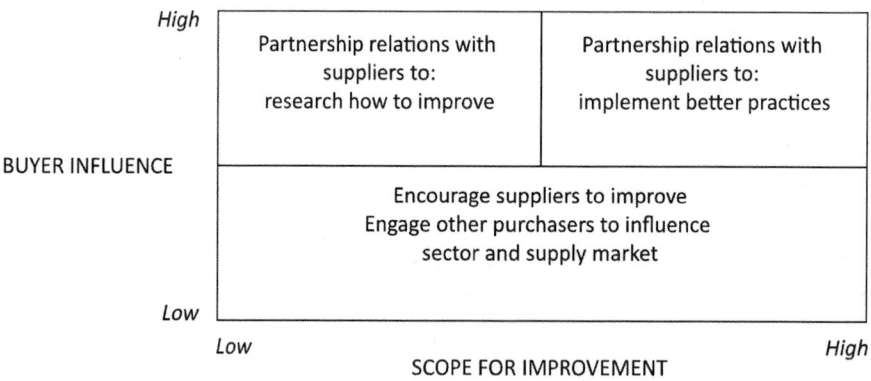

4.12 One factor in assessing influence will be the value of the buying organisation as a customer to the supply market, or particular suppliers. This is often assessed using the **supplier preferencing model** or supplier attitude matrix: Figure 8.9.

Figure 8.9 *The supplier preferencing model*

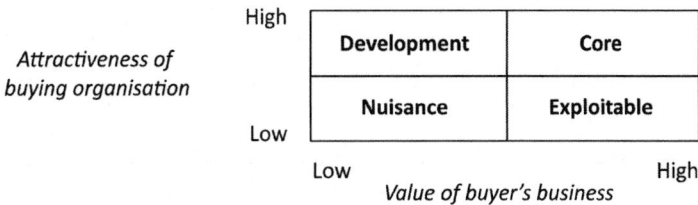

4.13 Looking at each quadrant in turn:

- **Nuisance customers** are neither attractive nor important to suppliers, creating low potential to drive sustainability issues with suppliers.
- **Exploitable customers** offer large volumes of business, which compensates for lack of attractiveness. Suppliers will typically fulfil the terms of the supply contract – but not go out of their way. Sustainability improvements will have to be incentivised and compensated, but there is potential to increase influence if the buyer can improve its attractiveness and the relationship with the supplier.
- **Development customers** are attractive, despite currently low levels of business. The supplier may see potential to grow the account, and may court extra business by 'going the extra mile': this may create good receptivity to sustainability requests.
- **Core customers** are highly desirable and valuable for suppliers, who will want to establish long-term, mutually profitable relationships with them if possible. Suppliers are likely to be very open to sustainability requests, creating a strong capacity to drive sustainability objectives and influence the supply market.

Sustainability impact scoring

4.14 Some procurements will obviously have greater sustainability impacts than others. Procurements involving labour-intensive production in low-cost countries, for example, may have significant impacts on working conditions, forced labour and community welfare. Complex manufactured items such as office equipment may have significant impacts in terms of energy usage, operating emissions and end-of-life disposal. Buyers will need to identify which procurements are likely to have the most significant sustainability impacts, so that mitigating measures can be appropriately targeted.

4.15 One simple method is to allocate a **sustainability impact score** to identified high-value, complex procurements, and then use relative scores to determine priorities. A **sustainability impact scoring chart** is shown in Table 8.1. Procurements with a score close to 21 should be the focus of attention, as reflecting high risk, influence, importance to the organisation and scope for improvement. (*Source:* Government of Western Australia Department of Finance *Sustainable Procurement Practice Guidelines*)

8

Table 8.1 *Sustainability impact scoring chart*

CRITERIA/QUESTION	RATING/SCORE
Does the procurement have a significant environmental or social impact or risk?	3 High – significant impact or risk 2 Medium – some impact or risk 1 Low – little or no impact or risk
What degree of influence does the buyer have in the supply market?	3 High – high level of influence 2 Medium – moderate level of influence 1 Low – minimal influence
Does the supply market have a proven sustainable procurement capability?	3 High – strong and proven capability 2 Medium – moderate capability 1 Low – little or no capability
Does the procurement align with or support the buyer's strategic and sustainability goals?	3 High – strong alignment 2 Medium – some alignment 1 Low – little or no alignment
How much effort and cost will be required to implement and contract-manage sustainability requirements?	3 High – little effort or resources required 2 Medium – moderate effort or resources required 1 Low – significant effort or resources required
How difficult will it be to encourage end users to change current practices?	3 High – little effort or resources required 2 Medium – moderate effort or resources required 1 Low – significant effort or resources required
What is the availability of sustainability expertise to undertake the procurement?	3 High – suitable expertise exists and is available 2 Medium – some expertise exists and may be available 1 Low – in-house expertise does not exist

4.16 All the above portfolio analyses may be combined and summarised in a **sustainability priority assessment**. A template for such an assessment may look something like Table 8.2. *(Source:* Government of Western Australia, Department of Finance: *Sustainable Procurement Practice Guidelines,* July 2011)

Table 8.2 *Sustainability priority assessment*

SUSTAINABILITY IMPACT	OPPORTUNITY TO INFLUENCE MARKET	SCOPE TO IMPROVE	PRIORITY	SUSTAINABILITY OBJECTIVE
Energy use	Medium	High	High	Reduce energy consumption during product use
Toxic waste	Medium	Low	Low-medium	Decrease content of identified toxic substances in product

5   Other tools of analysis

SWOT analysis

5.1 SWOT (strengths, weaknesses, opportunities, threats) analysis is a technique of corporate appraisal, used to assess the *internal* resources of an organisation (or procurement function or supply chain) to cope with and/or capitalise on factors in the *external* environment in which it operates.

5.2 In assessing the potential for conflict around sustainable procurement, for example, a multi-disciplinary sustainability team may work together to appraise a comprehensive list of both internal and external factors. SWOT analysis may also be used to identify issues around the implementation of particular sustainable procurement proposals, such as local sourcing or ISO14001 certification of suppliers.

5.3 Internal appraisal of strengths and weaknesses may cover aspects such as: the availability of physical and financial resources; the current product and service portfolio; human resources; the efficiency and effectiveness of functions, operations and systems; organisation structures; distinctive competencies; and measures or enablers already in place for sustainable procurement (if any).

5.4 Opportunities and threats are factors in the external environment that may emerge to impact on the business, such as those discussed at length in Chapters 1 and 2 in relation to sustainability. Blackburn (*Sustainability Handbook*) suggests a checklist of identified sustainability issues and trends (such as those covered in Chapter 2), against which each can be rated as:

- A *business risk or threat*: legal, financial, reputational, competitive or operational; and/or
- A *business opportunity*: innovation, sales, productivity, reputation, employee relations, risk reduction, licence to operate.

5.5 Figure 8.10 shows a SWOT analysis for a particular sustainability issue, drawn from Blackburn. You might like to have a go at drawing up a SWOT grid for a particular sustainability proposal, such as supplier ethical monitoring, or local sourcing.

Figure 8.10 *SWOT analysis*

Issue	*Strength*	*Weakness*	*Opportunity*	*Threat*	*Possible objectives*
Supplier labour practices in developing nations	1. Some suppliers are certified 2. Monitoring of key first-tier suppliers	1. Practices of some suppliers are unknown 2. Monitoring programmes not well developed	1. Customers attracted by certified CSR 2. More stable work force, more reliable supply	1. Risk to reputation 2. Labour unrest may interrupt supply	Develop and implement monitoring program at high-risk sites; benchmark to identify best practice

Stakeholder mapping

5.6 Stakeholder 'mapping' is a tool for categorising and prioritising stakeholders in a project or supply chain, and identifying appropriate strategies to manage them. This is likely to be important in a responsible purchasing programme, where stakeholder consultation and influencing is a key practice.

5.7 The most used tool for stakeholder mapping is Aubrey L Mendelow's power/interest matrix: Figure 8.11. You should be familiar with this from your study of other units.

Figure 8.11 *Mendelow's power/interest matrix*

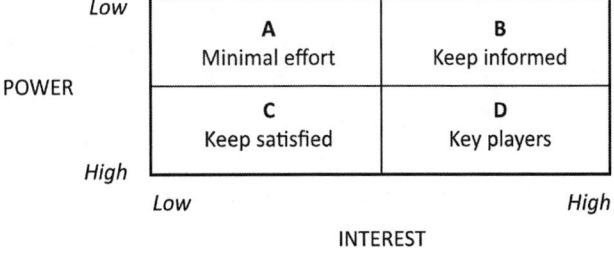

	Low	
	A Minimal effort	**B** Keep informed
POWER	**C** Keep satisfied	**D** Key players
	High	
	Low INTEREST	High

5.8 The purpose of the Mendelow matrix is basically to prioritise stakeholders according to their importance, measured in terms of (a) their power to influence the organisation and its plans and (b) their interest in doing so, or the strength of their motivation to do so. This can support sustainable procurement in the following ways.

- Identifying the stakeholders whose needs and expectations will define sustainable value and shape the sustainability agenda and priorities of the organisation (eg green consumers, influential NGOs and government)
- Identifying the stakeholders whose interests will be most affected by an organisational decision or action, and towards whom the organisation may therefore recognise some moral or legal obligations (eg communities impacted by environmental damage or the withdrawal of services)
- Identifying the stakeholders who will need to be informed, consulted or actively involved in the design and implementation of sustainable procurement policies and programmes (as suggested by the quadrants of the Mendelow matrix)
- Prioritising stakeholder interests, so that resources are not diluted or wasted by trying to 'be all things to all people' (which would be economically unsustainable).

5.9 Supporters (in various groups) need to be encouraged and kept 'on side'; opponents need to be persuaded of the merits of the agenda (or 'converted'); adversaries have to be marginalised or discredited, to reduce their influence for resistance. One of the key principles of sustainability, however, is that the needs of voiceless stakeholders (including the environment and disempowered workers) must also receive attention, despite their relative powerlessness.

Force field analysis

5.10 Force field analysis (Kurt Lewin) is a technique for identifying forces for and against change, in order to diagnose some of the change management problems that will need to be addressed, and some of the resources and dynamics available to support it. It is thus particularly useful for analysing potential points of conflict within the organisation or supply chain, in relation to sustainable procurement in general – or particular proposals and initiatives.

5.11 At any time in an organisation there exist both forces for change (pushing towards a preferred state) and forces for maintaining the *status quo* (pushing back towards the way things are). At any given moment, the interplay of these forces determines the current state of the organisation (where the forces balance each other out, creating a temporary equilibrium) and the pace and direction of change (if one set of forces is stronger than the other).

- *Driving forces* (for change) encourage people to give up old ways of doing things and to try new behaviours. Examples include: the frustration or unpleasantness caused by customer complaints or inefficient processes; new technology becoming available; or influence and support from a powerful individual or group.
- *Restraining forces* (against change) support the *status quo*. Examples include: shortage of resources; opposition from influencers or cultural values; already installed technology and established systems; managerial preoccupation with day-to-day matters and so on.

5.12 Force field analysis suggests a method of visualising or mapping the forces for and against change using directional arrows, the thickness of which represents the strength of each force. Let's use the introduction of a sustainable procurement policy for a particular organisation as our example – since this is just the sort of thing you might be asked to draft in an exam: Figure 8.12.

Figure 8.12 *Force field analysis*

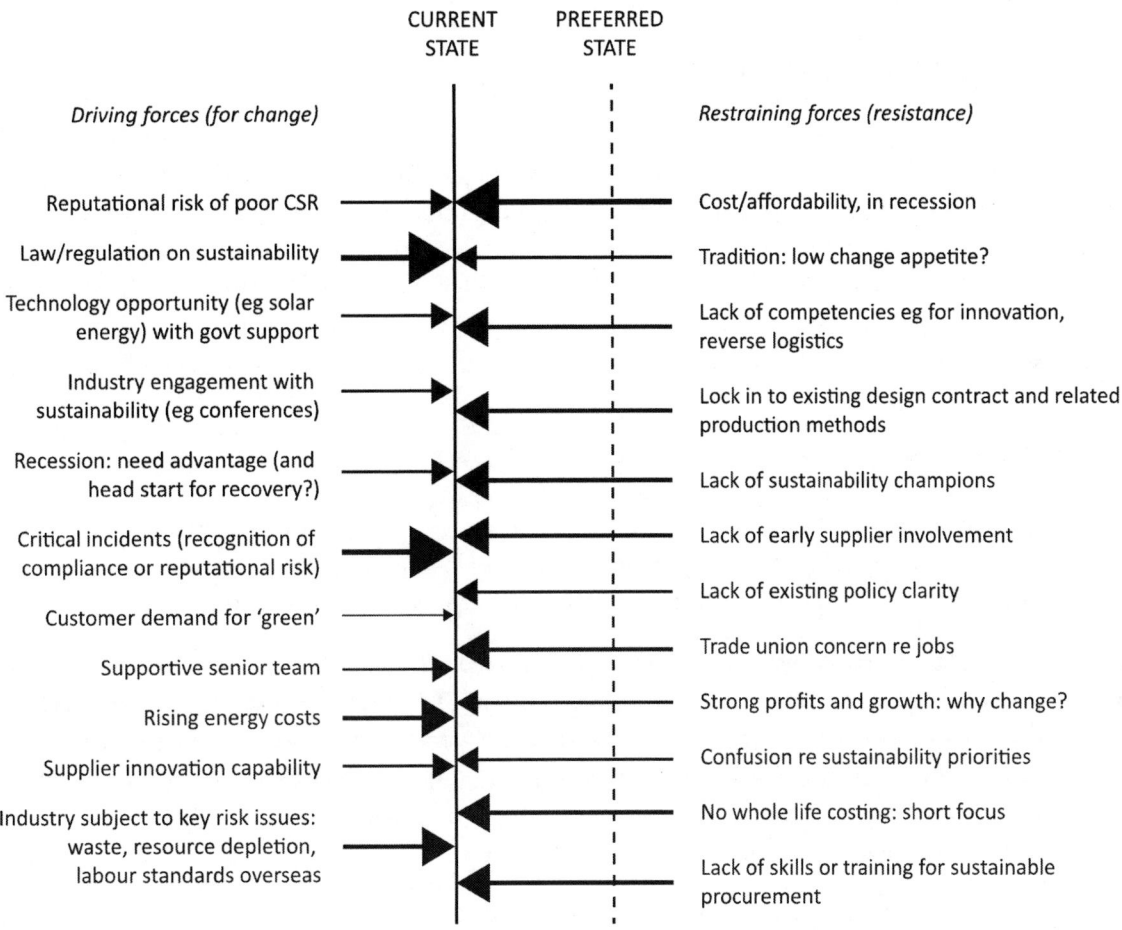

5.13 The force field model suggests that to implement change, managers should first understand the forces for and against change, and the strength of each. One simple technique is to give a numerical value to each force, on a scale of 0 (neutral) to 4 (strong). If the totals on each side are the same, the *status quo* will be maintained. (You might like to add some scores to the forces in our example – and see whether you think the introduction of sustainable procurement is currently viable or not.)

5.14 Managers can then select change management strategies and styles which concentrate either on strengthening driving forces ('adding forces in the desired direction'), or weakening restraining forces ('diminishing the opposing forces'), or both.

- Driving forces can be strengthened by emphasising the needs and benefits of the change (eg reputational risk from poor CSR); developing people to cope with change (eg buyer training and supplier development); co-opting the support of influencers (including customers, by gathering feedback, say); embedding new values in mission and value statements; and so on.
- Restraining forces can be weakened by participation (involving resistors in diagnosing and solving the problems); education and communication (persuading resistors of the risks and importance of the issues); coercion (applying policy power to silence resistors); or negotiation (offering concessions to buy resistors off).

5.15 Using the numerically-scored technique on our example in Figure 8.12, for example, we might decide on a programme of negotiation with the trade unions (to weaken one of the stronger restraining forces). This might add +1 to the score for 'cost' – but reduce trade union concern by –3. We would need to reinforce customer demand for green products (perhaps partnering with NGOs), to strengthen this factor by +2. Procurement staff could be shown that sustainable procurement gives them more opportunities for development, creating a new driving force of +2. And so on. This would add to the total 'driving' score and lower the 'restraining' score – giving preference to change.

6 Supply chain visibility

6.1 In *Supply Management's* special issue on embedding sustainable procurement (27 August 2009), the chair of the Commission for a Sustainable London 2012, Shaun McCarthy, notes that the most asked question on sustainable procurement is: 'How far down the supply chain should we go?'

6.2 The key factor in deciding how far down the supply chain you need to investigate will be exposure to risk.

EXAMPLE: THE SPORTSWEAR INDUSTRY

'The sportswear industry has suffered badly with international news coverage of poor labour conditions and excessive profiteering, which affected the sales and stock values of global brands [such as Adidas and Nike] significantly.

A major sportswear manufacturer told me: "We know where every garment we sell is manufactured and under what labour conditions. We know where every metre of fabric that goes into every garment is made and under what conditions. We don't yet know where every fibre comes from to make up the material – but we are working on it."

The issue of fibres is mostly about cotton. This product accounts for 25% of the world's pesticides and has a significant impact on ground and air pollution. In some countries, cotton is picked by forced labour. Man-made fibres have their own problems related to the energy intensity of manufacture, safety and toxic waste. Put these factors together and you have a major reputation risk for the industry, so it becomes necessary to trace every fibre. Organisations with less risk related to clothing may only choose to go back to the point of manufacture; others may not address the issue at all. A robust risk analysis is needed to develop the right solution.'

Managing end-to-end supply chain activity

6.3 An article in *Supply Management* ('Responsible Technology', 7 July 2005) emphasised that for many organisations fighting for survival with limited resources in an extremely competitive economic environment, pursuing ethical monitoring of the supply chain is likely to be seen as an unattainable luxury. However, it also makes the following points.

- It is possible to **prioritise** items and supply chains for investment in monitoring, on the basis of reputational risk assessment [and other techniques, discussed in this chapter]. We have just used the example of the sportswear industry, in which public scrutiny is so rigorous that supply chains are risk-assessed right back to the source of fibres. Less 'sensitive' purchases or industries would not require 'drilling down' so far; and supplier assurances and certifications would be sufficient.
- Methods of **accessing information** on suppliers are becoming increasingly sophisticated... 'In previous eras, checking basic facts about suppliers in the market would have taken days or weeks: now with the right tools, it can be done in seconds [using information technology]'. This also reduces the environmental impact of monitoring activity: eg carbon footprint of travel for the purpose of site visits.
- Procurement professionals can tap into the **experience and expertise** of organisations which have already developed strategies to identify where there may be problems in the supply chain: for example, through third party auditing or risk assessment, and collaboration with multi-stakeholder groups 'on the ground'.

6.4 Meanwhile, it is important to remember that sustainability impacts also extend *downstream* in the supply chain, to customers and customers' customers – all the way to the end users of products and services. The challenge is therefore, increasingly, to manage how products are transported, delivered, advertised, sold (eg via retail outlets), used, returned and/or disposed of. These aspects all reflect back on the producer – and in some cases (such as the disposal of electronic and electrical waste products) are the legal responsibility of the producer.

- Are products transported to distribution outlets or customers in such a way as to minimise environmental impacts and carbon footprint?
- Are products responsibly and accurately labelled: eg with 'eco' standards claims; safety warnings; responsible storage, usage and disposal instructions; and so on?
- Are outsourced services delivered as responsibly as the contracting organisation would wish? How can the procurement function manage the outsourcing contract to support this?
- Are products advertised truthfully, priced affordably and sold on terms which support social responsibility and ethical objectives? How can the organisation educate and influence downstream intermediaries to support this?
- Are products designed to be disassembled, recycled, re-used and/or safely disposed of at end-of-life?
- Does the organisation have recovery (reverse logistics), recycling and disposal capability?

6.5 Managing this challenge requires whole life sustainability planning and downstream partnerships.

Lifecycle management

6.6 Whole life sustainability planning is based on analysis of the sustainability impacts of a product or service over its total life-span.

6.7 The lifecycle of a product may be defined in different ways.

- Marketers define product lifecycle (PLC) in terms of sales volume and profitability over time, with phases of: introduction, growth, maturity, saturation, decline and withdrawal. The model is arguably of little relevance to sustainable procurement, other than suggesting opportunities (and perhaps a business case) for introducing more sustainable products and services to the portfolio (in order to have a flow of new products entering profitable maturity), or for 'refreshing' declining brands with sustainable attributes, or for sustainable disposal of withdrawn products.
- More relevant might be a product lifecycle model which surveys each stage of a product's progress through various processes: supply of materials, conversion (manufacturing, assembly, processing), storage and distribution, sale, installation, consumption, maintenance, decommissioning and end-of-life disposal. Using such a model, both purchased products (inputs) and end products (outputs) can be examined – ideally at specification or design stage – to identify their economic, environmental and social impacts, risks and benefits at each stage. At what stage of the lifecycle is most energy used, or emissions or wastes created? At what stages can sustainability benefits and 'quick wins' be secured most readily? At what stages can specific measures (such as recycling) be applied? Will downstream, internal or upstream management create the best leverage?

EXAMPLE: MARKS & SPENCER

Under its Plan A CSR measures, M & S conducts lifecycle assessments of a range of its retail products and their packaging. It found that some 70% of all energy used in the total life of a clothing garment was accounted for by washing in consumers' homes. In order to apply leverage to the objective of lowering energy consumption (supporting reduced carbon footprint), M & S is manufacturing own-brand clothes that can be washed at lower temperatures, as well as educating customers to wash more energy-efficiently, and engaging them in Plan A pledges to make these changes.

Supply chain management

6.8 Lysons and Farrington define **supplier management** as: 'That aspect of purchasing or procurement which is concerned with rationalising the supplier base and selecting, co-ordinating, appraising the performance of and developing the potential of suppliers, and where appropriate, building long-term collaborative relationships'. CIPS defines it more simply as: 'Managing the supplier in order to extract additional value and benefits as a result of the relationship'.

6.9 Where supplier management focuses on the firm's suppliers and supplier relationships, the term **supply chain management** is generally used for a more holistic and integrated approach, focusing on processes and relationships across the whole supply chain.

6.10 Supply chain management has been defined as:

- 'The management of upstream and downstream relationships with suppliers and customers to deliver superior customer value at less cost to the supply chain as a whole' (Martin Christopher)
- 'The integration and management of supply chain organisations and activities through co-operative organisational relationships, effective business processes, and high levels of information sharing to create high-performing value systems that provide member organisations a sustainable competitive advantage' (Handfield & Nichols)

6.11 SCM consists primarily of building collaborative relationships across the supply chain, so that the whole chain works together to add value for the end customer in a profitable and sustainable way. Christopher *et al* (*Relationship Marketing*) argue that, these days:

'The real competitive struggle is not between individual companies, but between their supply chains or networks... What makes a supply chain or network unique is the way the relationships and interfaces in the chain or network are managed. In this sense, a major source of differentiation comes from the quality of relationships that one business enjoys, compared to its competitors.'

6.12 The following are some benefits of an SCM approach to sustainable procurement.

- Reduced costs, by eliminating waste activities and implementing cost reduction programmes throughout the supply chain. ('Often there are many activities that do not create value involved in trade between two companies. Jointly locating and eliminating these activities, as well as developing co-operative goals and guidelines for the future, can focus resources on real improvements and development possibilities': Birgit Dam Jespersen & Tage Skjott-Larsen)
- Improved responsiveness to sustainability issues and drivers (by focusing the whole business process on customer sustainability in an integrated way)
- Access to complementary resources and capabilities (eg joint investment in research and development, technology-sharing and ideas-sharing and so on)
- Enhanced sustainability performance (eg through collaborative sustainability management, increased supply chain communication, continuous improvement programmes and improved supplier motivation)
- Faster lead times for product development and delivery (so that new and modified products can be offered in response to changing customer demand and sustainability opportunities)
- Better control over sustainability performance and risks at lower tiers of the supply chain (since reputational risk may arise from suppliers' suppliers).

6.13 However, it is important (in exams, as in real life) to be realistic about the benefits claimed for SCM – and to analyse whether it is relevant, possible or beneficial for a particular organisation. It is not for everyone! For one thing, it requires considerable investment, internal support and supplier willingness – any or all of which may not be available. It also involves focusing on closer relationships with a smaller number of suppliers, and this may be risky (if the relationships don't work out, for example, or if the firm becomes dependent on a supplier which later has sustainability problems).

6.14 We will look further at issues of supply chain visibility and supply chain management in Chapters 9 and 10.

Chapter summary

- As supply chains have become more complex, it has become more difficult for buyers to ensure good sustainability practices at every link of the chain.
- A key technique is to map the configuration of a supply chain in order to identify potential areas of vulnerability.
- A pragmatic view of sustainable procurement is that it is a form of risk management. A systematic approach is provided by the risk management cycle in Figure 8.4.
- Sustainability efforts should be focused where they can do most good. It helps to use a tool of prioritisation, such as the Kraljic matrix. This can be adapted so as to make it specifically aimed at sustainability.
- Other tools of strategic analysis can also be applied to sustainability: SWOT analysis, stakeholder mapping and force field analysis are examples.
- Supply chain management has become increasingly important as buyers have sought to improve transparency and visibility along the entire supply chain.

Self-test questions

Numbers in brackets refer to the paragraphs where you can check your answers.

1   Why is supply chain complexity a key area of vulnerability in relation to sustainability? (1.4)

2   Why does the use of subcontractors increase the risk borne by buyers? (1.15)

3   What are the benefits of supply chain mapping? (2.5)

4   List the stages in the risk management cycle. (Figure 8.4)

5   What are the Four Ts of risk management? (3.8)

6   Sketch the procurement portfolio model developed by the RPI. (Figure 8.6)

7   What are the four quadrants of the supplier preferencing model? (4.13)

8   What is meant by stakeholder mapping? (5.6)

9   Explain the driving forces and restraining forces in Lewin's model of force field analysis. (5.11)

10   Define supplier management. (6.8)

CHAPTER 9

Managing Supply Chain Compliance

Assessment criteria and indicative content

 4.2 Evaluate how indicators of desired behaviours can support compliance with standards for sustainability in supply chains

- Monitoring performance
- Feedback from suppliers on purchasing processes that help achieve compliance to standards for sustainability
- Subjecting sourcing strategies to independent review
- Accountability for achieving social, ethical and environmental standards

 4.3 Evaluate the capabilities of third party organisations to promote compliance with standards for sustainability in supply chains

- Sourcing third parties for auditing services
- Assessing the competence of third party organisations for the provision of audit services
- The difficulties with duplications of codes and audits

Section headings

1 Monitoring sustainability performance
2 Supply chain audits
3 Third party auditing
4 Maintaining accountability

Introduction

In terms of the sustainable procurement process, this chapter follows on from Chapter 7, where we discussed the development of sustainability performance measures or 'indicators of desired behaviours', to explore how those indicators can be *used* to support compliance with sustainability standards.

In this chapter, therefore, we focus on the monitoring, measurement and evaluation of *performance* against agreed indicators of desired or acceptable standards, and of *progress* against agreed indicators of improvement. We look at processes for subjecting the policies and practices of the *buying organisation* to review, as well as for monitoring and assessing the performance of *suppliers*.

Following the syllabus, we focus on audits as a tool of compliance management, and explore the use of third-party organisations to audit supply chain compliance.

1 Monitoring sustainability performance

1.1 The term 'monitoring' is used broadly to include the measurement of performance against goals and targets, as well as other means of periodic oversight, review and evaluation. Monitoring methods include self-reporting, audits, inspections or observations, interviews and surveys, and measurements. The focus, criteria and methodology of monitoring may be either quantitative or qualitative.

- *Quantitative:* based on numerical or statistical measurement. Examples in sustainability monitoring may include: the tracking of air pollution concentrations or the quantity of carbon emissions; the percentage of purchased products made of recycled materials; the number of discrimination complaints or employee accidents; or the percentage of supplier workforces on formal contracts, earning agreed living wage levels and so on.
- *Qualitative:* based on informed (though inevitably subjective) judgement, and focusing on qualitative aspects of sustainable procurement such as equity, non-discrimination, worker wellbeing and satisfaction and so on.

1.2 Blackburn *(The Sustainability Handbook)* highlights a number of difficulties with monitoring in general.

- Qualitative monitoring, being subjective, can lead to doubt and conflict, potentially eroding support for sustainability initiatives.
- Quantitative measurements are not always easy to make, and there may be problems with data integrity: different definitions of items to be measured (eg 'hazardous waste'); untrained observers or analysts; or bugs in reporting software.
- Monitoring systems may not gather or manage information frequently enough, with a view to regular reporting, feedback, problem identification and tracking, lesson learning and improvement planning.
- Monitoring systems may gather information *too* frequently, creating onerous costs, 'audit fatigue', resentment at the perception of 'micro-management' and distrust, and information overload.
- Where computerised data systems are used, there is a risk of ineffectiveness due to poor system design; irrelevance to the organisation's specific sustainability issues and management systems; data build up, overload and obsolescence; lack of user training ('rubbish in, rubbish out'); and waste of resources.

1.3 It may be useful to note that 'measurement' and 'assessment' ('what is being achieved?') are not the same as 'evaluation' – which implies value judgements about whether the measured or assessed level of progress or performance is good or bad, adequate or inadequate, to be continued and encouraged or corrected.

Supplier performance evaluation or vendor rating

1.4 There is a wide range of feedback mechanisms for gathering data on supplier sustainability performance, and comparing them against relevant performance measures. Here are some examples.

- The gathering of feedback from internal and external customers, employees and other stakeholders, using market research, employee interviews and attitude surveys, focus groups, complaint procedures, survey questionnaires and project reviews
- The gathering of social and environmental performance information through observation (eg on site visits), interviews (eg with employees and suppliers), testing (eg inspections), and analysis of documentation, transaction records and management reports (eg inspection reports, complaint and dispute records, incident and accident report forms and so on)
- Formal sustainability audits, reviews or vendor rating exercises: reviewing sustainability performance against benchmark standards, KPIs and improvement targets, and feeding back the information for learning needs analysis and improvement planning
- Contract management, continually monitoring or periodically reviewing compliance with contract terms, policies and codes of practice

- Regular meetings between buyer-side and supplier-side representatives (or project or account managers) to review general progress or specific issues
- The use of third-party consultants and auditors to monitor compliance with sustainability standards and benchmarks (eg monitoring overseas suppliers' workforce practices or environmental performance). This will be discussed in detail in Section 3 of this chapter.

Accessing sustainability information about suppliers

1.5 In addition to suppliers' published annual reports and accounts, and voluntary sustainability reports (where available), there are also a number of secondary sources of information for assessing the sustainability performance of suppliers.

- Sustainability Indices, such as the Dow Jones Sustainability Index
- Awards and directories: eg the Chartered Association of Certified Accountants (ACCA) awards for sustainability reporting, and various Top Ethical Brand and Most Admired Company listings
- The Supplier Ethical Data Exchange (Sedex): a web-based not-for-profit organisation for companies wanting to monitor and improve ethical performance in their supply chains – including founding members such as Waitrose, Tesco and Marks & Spencer. Members can view supplier data, run reports on their supply chains, report on their own activities, or input data to self assessment questionnaires, depending on membership category.
- Public environmental reports posted under the EMAS standard
- Case studies and reports posted on the websites of relevant standards organisations and NGOs.

Gathering supplier feedback on procurement processes

1.6 As we emphasised in Chapter 7, performance and compliance measurement is a collaborative process, since supplier non-compliance with standards may well be driven by buying practices, such as cancellation of orders, last-minute changes to volume requirements, failure to use formal contracts, and adversarial price squeezing.

1.7 The Responsible Purchasing Initiative *(Buying Matters)* emphasises that: 'Feedback from suppliers – without the fear of retribution – about the impact of purchasing and supply management practices would provide useful information to companies and help buyers to improve.' Such feedback enables learning from instances of non-compliance, and the development of new ways of working which support compliance better.

1.8 Identifying indicators and collecting information that highlight 'supplier distress' (eg solvency and liquidity ratios, industrial disputes, accidents, wage levels, overtime hours, or worker turnover) might indicate particularly damaging practices.

1.9 Feedback should also be sought from suppliers (and other internal and external stakeholders) on the impact of sustainable procurement policies and provisions. Such feedback may indicate where requirements are overly onerous or costly to apply, or culturally insensitive.

Subjecting sourcing strategies to independent review

1.10 Another way in which buying policy and practice can benefit from feedback is to subject the organisation's sourcing strategies to independent review and scrutiny. Independent challenge and/or endorsement of strategies by qualified third parties (such as relevant NGOs or multi-stakeholder organisations):

- Provides a stronger mandate for change among internal stakeholders
- Helps to build trust and confidence
- Improves the organisation's accountability for procurement

1.11 There may also be periodic independent reviews of the *effectiveness* of sourcing strategy, as part of the procurement audit process.

2 Supply chain audits

2.1 One major way in which sustainability monitoring may be accomplished is by appointing auditors to perform a **systematic review** of an operation, site or function: collecting, assessing and reporting on resources, processes, performance, risks and opportunities. This may be done as part of a portfolio of reviews: periodic reporting, checklist inspections, stakeholder surveys and so on.

2.2 An audit can be described (British Standards Institution, *Sustainable Procurement Guide)* as: 'a process to assess a supplier's systems, processes and business practices, to establish the validity and reliability of information provided to the customer organisation. From a sustainable procurement perspective, supply chain audits are used to verify if the supplier organisations are consistently meeting (or are capable of meeting) stated environmental, social and economic requirements, which would normally be set out in the tender process and incorporated in the contract conditions).

2.3 Auditing may take place:

- As part of **supplier selection**, once prospective suppliers are shortlisted at the tender evaluation stage, to verify information provided on pre-qualification questionnaires (for purchases with significant social or environmental concerns – as determined by the kinds of analysis explored in Chapter 8)
- As part of **ongoing contract and supplier management**, to verify compliance with agreed standards and targets for improvement. (A decision will have to be made which supply chains to audit, and how far down a supply chain to audit, and again, these decisions will be made on the basis of perceived risk, the importance of sustainability to the organisation, scope for improvement and other factors discussed in Chapter 8).

Types of audit

2.4 Blackburn identifies several different types of audit relevant to sustainability monitoring.

- **Compliance audits:** assessing conformance to law and regulations (eg health and safety regulations), and requirements for government permits and licences (eg waste disposal licences)
- **Internal standards audits:** assessing how well the buying organisation meets requirements it has developed for itself (such as sustainable procurement principles)
- **External standards audits:** assessing conformance with an outside standard to which the organisation subscribes (eg the ILO standards, Fair Trade standards or ETI Base Code)
- **A management systems audit:** assessing the organisation's adherence to processes described in an internal management standard (eg a sustainable procurement policy) or an external one (eg ISO 14001 or SA 8000). This is a type of process audit. More generally, for example, an audit may look at the implementation, effectiveness and efficiency of performance management or procurement processes.
- **Risk or best practice assessments:** assessing potential liabilities and risks, or seeking high-standard approaches that can be shared with others (which may be the focus of a purchasing audit, for example)
- **Productivity assessments:** assessing opportunities to improve efficiency (eg via energy conservation, waste reduction, material substitution or process change). Tools such as Six Sigma, which you may have encountered elsewhere in your studies, can be used to identify and develop such opportunities. A similar approach might be a value for money audit or cost-benefit audit.

2.5 We might add some more specific categories of audit.

- **Supplier and supply chain audits** focus on the capabilities, capacity, resources, skills, systems, processes, management and performance of suppliers.
- **Environmental (or 'green') audits** focus on an organisation's capabilities, resources, skills, systems, processes and management in support of environmental objectives; the environmental impacts of operations; and areas of environmental (and related compliance and reputational) risk
- **Social audits** focus on an organisation's performance and processes in regard to human and labour rights and community impacts
- **Statutory audits** are a legal requirement for corporate governance. Private sector companies above a certain size must appoint an independent external auditor to review their financial systems, accounts and records and must report to shareholders on whether the accounts show a true and fair view. Similar audits are conducted on public sector bodies by the Audit Commission and the National Audit Office.

2.6 Audits may be undertaken by staff of the purchasing organisation or by a third party (eg NGOs or commercial audit companies).

- **Internal audits** are conducted by the organisation's own staff, in the form of self-assessments (reviews of an operation conducted by its own personnel) or independent internal assessments (undertaken by a separate internal auditing group, outside the operation being reviewed). This approach is relatively inexpensive, encourages internal 'ownership' of compliance issues, and has the advantage of the assessors' familiarity with the activities, personnel and organisational context. However, it may be subject to influence from the operation's management, or limited in its perspectives. Self-assessment auditors, in particular, may lack technical skills or training for the task.
- **External audits** are conducted by consultants or other independent entities outside the organisation. This approach is more expensive, potentially disruptive and subject to suspicion and resistance from subjects. However, it is useful for adding objectivity, fresh viewpoints, cross-functional and best practice perspectives and credibility (arising from perceived independence). Specially qualified external auditors are usually required for formal certifications eg under ISO, EMAS and certain Fair Trade standards. We will discuss this further in Section 3 of this chapter.

2.7 A combination of approaches may elicit more reliable, objective and well-rounded information.

Purchasing management audit

2.8 A purchasing management audit is 'a comprehensive, systematic, independent and periodic examination of a company's purchasing environment, objectives and tactics to identify problems and opportunities and to facilitate the development of appropriate action plans' (EE Scheuing, *Purchasing Management*).

2.9 Purchasing management audits have four main purposes.

- To verify the extent to which procurement policies (including sustainable procurement) are being adhered to
- To ensure that procedures and methods conform to best working practice
- To monitor and measure the extent to which resources are used efficiently and effectively
- To assist in the detection of fraud

Supplier audit

2.10 The scope of a supplier audit or capability survey (eg for the purpose of supplier appraisal, approval or ongoing vendor rating) generally includes: a capability assessment, a review of the supplier's management systems, assessment of how they assure quality or sustainability, and how compatible they are with the buyer's systems and working practices. More focused **environmental or social audits** may focus on the supplier's labour, environmental and ethical management standards, processes and performance – ideally enabling drilling down to the suppliers' supply chain.

2.11 Qualified independent auditors will usually be required to conduct supplier certifications under external quality, environmental and social responsibility management standards. Buyers may have to rely on external certifications, or on audit assessments provided by suppliers themselves. However, where suppliers have agreed to comply with the buyer's sustainable procurement principles or other standards, the buyer should be able to agree to conduct periodic site visits, audits and assessments. Again, these may involve the use of third-party assessors where appropriate (eg in the auditing of overseas suppliers or contractors). In the interests of relationship sustainability, however, audits should not be excessively frequent, onerous or disruptive.

2.12 Supplier audits may be carried out initially via self-administered supplier questionnaires. Where a contact requires particular social or environmental standards to be met, for example, purchasers may simply:

- Check the supplier's understanding of the desired standard (with reference to available standard documentation)
- Provide suppliers with self-assessment workbooks, compliance checklists and explanatory guides to compliance. Such an approach may be helpful when national laws or international standards are unfamiliar to either party.

2.13 However, self assessments are generally supplemented with visits to supplier premises on a regular cycle (for high priority or high risk suppliers or purchases, for which the cost can be justified). The idea of site visits is to look at the supplier's operations – in this context, with a particular focus on sustainability issues – and discuss any shortcomings that are identified, with a view to achieving improvements by the time of the next visit. Operations can be observed, outputs sampled, and workers (and ex-workers) interviewed (ideally, off site, in places and conditions where they are free to speak honestly).

2.14 Site visits are an important source of information on such matters as: equipment, operations, working practices and processes, production capacity, human resources, management and technical capabilities, working conditions and so on. Multi-functional site visit teams are often used to provide the expertise required for a broad-ranging assessment.

2.15 The legitimacy of observation, document-checking and checklist-based approaches to social audits has been challenged, with the increasing recognition that suppliers may seek to 'cover up' human and labour rights abuses in order to 'tick the right boxes' for compliant status. More forensic assessments, including off-site worker interviews, may be required to detect instances of child or forced labour, wages below minimum level, faked records of wages and working hours, and so on.

Environmental (green) and sustainability audits

2.16 An environmental audit is the inspection of a company to assess the environmental impact of its activities, or of a particular product or process, as the basis for managerial decision-making. For example, the audit of a manufactured product may look at the impact of production (including energy use and the extraction of raw materials used in manufacture), usage (which may cause pollution and other hazards), and disposal (potential for recycling, and whether waste causes pollution).

2.17 An environmental review would normally start with the identification of areas of a site to be assessed: external areas (such as vehicle access, waste storage and drainage areas) and internal areas (offices, process areas). A checklist of environmental issues (wastes, emissions, hazardous substances, energy consumption) can then be assessed for each area, using observation, interviews and review of documentation and records: waste management documentation, Integrated Pollution Control (IPC) authorisations, discharge consents from water companies and so on. An assessment report will be communicated to key stakeholders, and a register of impacts drawn up, as the focus for problem-solving, risk assessment and management, and ongoing improvement planning.

2.18 The Envirowise agency, a government-funded business consultancy focusing on environmental sustainability, recommends audit tools similar to those used in supplier audits.

- An audit checklist (to structure the audit and ensure completeness)
- Self-administered questionnaires (to cover matters of fact)
- Interviews (to test staff awareness of issues and policies)
- Discussion (for briefing, consultation and clarification)
- Reporting on findings, highlighting areas for decision-making and action

2.19 Environmental audits may be general eg in the case of supplier appraisal or vendor rating, or as a first step in developing an environmental management system – or in gaining accreditation for such a system, under standards such as ISO 14001 and EMAS (discussed in Chapter 3). Alternatively, they may focus on particular areas.

- A *waste audit*, for example, is concerned with waste production and handling – as the first step in waste minimisation programmes. The focus will be on safe, environmentally friendly and cost-efficient handling, storage and disposal (including transport and disposal by contractors). Quantities and origins of waste will be identified with a view to reduction. Waste management record-keeping processes, and documentation compliance (eg waste management licences) should also be checked.
- A *water audit* is concerned with water use and waste water production. A 'mass balance' can be derived, identifying inward and outward water volumes: discrepancies may indicate leakage, for example. Areas of high water usage or wastage can be investigated for reduction.

SWOT analysis

2.20 Audit information can be used for strategic planning. One useful tool in this respect is a SWOT analysis (strengths, weaknesses, opportunities, threats). As we saw in Chapter 8, SWOT analysis is a strategic planning technique, used to assess the internal resources and capabilities of a supplier (or indeed the buying organisation or the purchasing function) to cope with and/or capitalise on factors in its external environment. In the present context:

- Strengths and weaknesses are internal aspects of the supplier that enhance or limit its ability to perform sustainably. Internal appraisal may cover physical and financial resources; the product and service portfolio; human resources; the efficiency and effectiveness of functions, operations and systems; organisation structure; and distinctive competencies.
- Opportunities and threats are sustainability issues and factors in the external environment that may emerge to impact on the business. What potential do they offer to either enhance or erode competitive advantage, profitability or sustainability?

2.21 Internal and external factors can be mapped in a SWOT grid: Figure 9.1.

Figure 9.1 *SWOT analysis*

INTERNAL	**Strengths** New technology Environmental management system Stable, high quality staff Strong brand reputation	**Weaknesses** Low capability for design and innovation Poor financial and governance controls High use of non-renewable resources
EXTERNAL	**Opportunities** E-procurement Green consumer preferences Tax breaks for regional development	**Threats** Non-renewable resource issues Risk of scrutiny re governance Pressure to innovate

2.22 SWOT is used to identify areas where there may be sustainability risks and/or potential for mitigation and development. The buyer may need to:

- Plan to build on strengths and/or minimise weaknesses – in order to be able to capitalise on the identified opportunities (or create new ones) and to cope better with the identified threats.
- Plan to convert threats into opportunities – by developing the strengths (and contingency plans) to counter threats more effectively than competitors, and by being prepared to learn from them.

Benefits and drawbacks of the audit approach

2.23 Blackburn argues that a systematic audit process may be beneficial in various ways.

- Providing a new, fresh assessment of gaps in compliance, risk control or efficiency – which regular internal monitoring may not allow
- Adding credibility to a performance report – or to the presentation of a business case for sustainable procurement
- Certifying conformance to an ISO or other recognised standard (particularly if the audit is carried out by independent third-party assessors)
- Improving the quality of other review processes
- Demonstrating transparency in the face of suspected impropriety, reducing the risk of escalating legal and reputational cost later.

2.24 However, there are some drawbacks of auditing.

- The time-consuming and expensive nature of the audit process
- The limitations of audit information. Audits only offer a 'snapshot' of practice during the period when the auditor is on site – and the quality of information depends on factors such as the competence of the auditor, the relevance and flexibility of the audit checklist (if this approach is used), and the willingness of the supplier to be transparent (leaving aside the risk of deliberately falsified information eg on wage records and working hours).
- The risk that auditing itself drives dishonesty, as suppliers are tempted to provide the 'right' answers to audit questions – falsifying records, forcing or coaching workers to lie in audit interviews, or bribing auditors – rather than risk the loss of business for non-compliance.
- The risk of counter-productive reactions by buyers. Social audits of suppliers, for example, can be counter-productive if the results are used to justify withdrawal of business from a non-compliant supplier – which may impact on vulnerable workers and producers, and erode the supplier's resources and motivation for improvement.
- The risk of serious legal and moral compromise, if compliance issues or threats to people (or the environment) are identified by the audit, and management does nothing
- The risk of 'analysis paralysis': gathering more performance information as a substitute for managing performance
- Potential damage to morale, motivation and supplier relationships, due to a perceived lack of trust, a perceived disincentive to proactive initiative and action, or suppliers' being made to pay for audits and improvements (without support or co-investment from the buyer requiring the audit – or even, in some cases, a guaranteed order).
- Over-reliance on auditing, fostering a compliance mentality (only doing what the audit recommends) and a bias for inaction ('no point doing anything now, in case the auditors tell us it's wrong'), and eroding the capacity for critical self-analysis and initiative for improvement

2.25 The BSI *Sustainable Procurement Guide* sums up the drawbacks from the point of view of workers and business: Table 9.1.

Table 9.1 *Limitations of supply chain social audits*

FROM A WORKER'S PERSPECTIVE	FROM A BUSINESS PERSPECTIVE
Auditors focus on visible 'working conditions' rather than the broader 'employment conditions' (contract status, performance targets, assumptions on overtime) which often matter more to workers.	Audits do not provide assurance even against the worst forms of exploitation because of poor audit skills and methodology, and increasing levels of fraud.
Typically, 80% of corrective actions relate to health and safety concerns; very few relate to issues such as freedom of association, a living wage, discrimination or harsh treatment.	Audits add direct costs (particularly with parallel or duplicate audits, and the need to protect commercial confidentiality)
Many workers are not covered by audits, as they are not formal employees.	Audits add indirect costs, taking up to 80% of the time of ethical trade personnel.

2.26 Research findings by Oxfam International *(Better Jobs in Better Supply Chains,* 2010) suggest that: 'Audits have delivered some significant benefits. They have helped companies to map their supply chains, gain greater visibility of issues in the workplace, identify and deal with extreme forms of abuse, and make the workplaces safer and more hygienic. But on the negative side, commercial audits in particular have delivered limited change for workers, do not provide reliable assurance about standards and add significant cost to the supply chain.'

2.27 'On balance,' says Blackburn, 'auditing by qualified experts, done at frequencies based on risk, can be a good thing for a company, providing an honest understanding of problems and prompting constructive change. This kind of auditing should be an important part of any sustainability program.'

2.28 Owing to the limitations of auditing, reliance solely on audit data is not advisable. Other processes (such as the involvement of trade unions or independent workers' organisations) should be put in place to lead to sustainable improvement in conditions. The RPI *(Win-Win)* argues that 'There has been an over-emphasis on audits in the past. A more cost-effective allocation of resources would be to build up worker awareness of their rights, and establish an effective worker-management dialogue mechanism'.

2.29 There has therefore been a trend towards going 'beyond auditing', with buying organisations focusing on what they need to do to help suppliers develop and improve their social and environmental performance. In other words, the focus is shifting from merely ascertaining compliance or non-compliance, to supporting systemic change which assures compliance. We will discuss these approaches in Chapter 10.

3 Third party auditing

The use of third party auditing services

3.1 Feedback on supplier performance may be sought from local organisations or multi-stakeholder coalitions, in regard to labour and environmental performance at supplier sites, in order to avoid potential distortion of the facts by self-interested suppliers.

3.2 In some cases, the buying organisation may formally employ a third-party organisation, such as an NGO or commercial audit company, to provide one-off or periodic supplier auditing services, particularly where:

- The buying organisation is geographically distant from the supplier, as is increasingly the case in international and global sourcing
- The buying organisation is unfamiliar with the cultural, environmental, economic and technological factors affecting the supplier, and/or the issues affecting workers and producers in the supply market
- The buyer desires to have an independent mandate or endorsement for corrective action to enforce compliance, as an additional (and potentially less aversive) source of influence with the supply market.

3.3 Independent third-party audit may also be a requirement for certification under international standards, such as ISO 14001, for which an organisation has its environmental management system (EMS) certified by an external assessor. Third-party recognition can help to provide assurance (and reputational value) to shareholders, customers, industry regulators and the general public.

3.4 To ensure and demonstrate consistency in the maintenance of standards, third-party certifying bodies can be accredited (eg by the UK Accreditation Service, UKAS), with consistency achieved internationally via the International Accreditation Forum (IAF). Even so, a 2003 survey found that nearly half of the sample of ISO 14001-certified companies, consultancies and certification providers felt that certification bodies were, in general, not sufficiently competent.

Sourcing third-party auditors

3.5 In many ways, the sourcing of third-party audit services is no different from the sourcing of other professional services. Guidelines developed by a number of audit bodies recommend the following general process.

- **Planning**
  - Determine specific audit requirements, referring to relevant standards or consulting expert third-party organisations where required
  - Identify the attributes and competencies necessary in the auditor
  - Decide how to evaluate prospective audit firms (eg on price, technical qualifications, 'local' expertise)
  - Review relevant requirements (eg for auditor accreditation for standards certification)
  - Consider a multi-year agreement (saving on sourcing costs, enabling increasing familiarity and trust etc)
  - Establish an audit timetable and work schedule.
- **Sourcing the market**
  - Conduct directory, register and web searches for listings of potential providers
  - Seek recommendations and endorsements from past and existing clients of the audit organisation
  - Appraise the capabilities, track record and geographic coverage of short-listed providers
- **Communicating requirements**
  - Prepare a brief or statement of requirement, including administrative information, time requirements, work and reporting requirements
  - Issue requests for quotation, requests for proposal or invitation to tender to shortlisted providers – and conduct bidders' conference, negotiation or competitive tender as appropriate
  - Consider collaboration with existing clients of an audit organisation, with similar sustainability requirements, to share the costs of audit and remediation actions
- **Evaluate proposals** according to criteria such as: adequacy and relevance of the proposal; qualifications of staff assigned to the engagement; size and location of the firm; range of activities performed by the firm; audit protocols used by the firm; additional services offered (eg supplier development); information and reporting capabilities and so on
- **Develop a written agreement** (contract or engagement letter): clearly document expectations in regard to audit scope, objective and purpose; deadlines and timetable; cost; report format; and so on.

Assessing the competencies of third-party auditors

3.6 The competence of the third-party auditor (and the confidence of the buying organisation in that competence) is crucial, if the buyer intends to rely on documentation from the audit to manage sustainability risk. The RPI *(Win-Win)* emphasises that: 'Purchasers must check that individual auditors have appropriate competencies – and sensitivity to the confidentiality of workers' statements'.

3.7 Competencies for auditors include the following.

- Demonstrated experience in designing systematic and effective audit programmes for organisations of the relevant type in the relevant supply market
- Detailed awareness of the requirements of relevant corporate, national and international standards against which compliance is being verified
- Awareness of relevant social, ethical, labour and environmental issues, standard industry practices, local customs and legal frameworks in the relevant supply market and country of operation. Commercial audit organisations should ideally have access to a network of local auditors to cover international sites.
- Ability to understand relevant company and worker documentation, and its implications (eg contracts, wage records, training records, health and safety records, working hours and overtime logs, and records of complaints and grievances raised by workers)
- Interviewing, with particular skills in identifying attempts to hide or falsify data, signs of 'coaching' of workers and so on
- Investigative competencies in order to corroborate evidence
- Sensitivity to the need to ensure confidentiality of information and the anonymity of workers, when dealing with sensitive matters such as forced labour and human rights, and the risk of retaliation against 'whistle blowers'
- Cross-cultural communication competencies, supporting the ability to interview a wide cross-section of workers and management
- Team leadership and teamworking competencies, to work in cross-functional audit teams
- Professional integrity (especially in environments where corruption is rife and attempts may be made to bribe auditors to give positive findings)
- Well developed and integrated information systems, ideally including web-based solutions for real-time access to audit status, audit results and supply chain trends
- Demonstrated capability in preparing, agreeing and communicating corrective action plans, as the output of the audit process: explaining the requirement improvements and timetable to non-compliant suppliers and sites
- Rapid response capabilities, in order to provide audits in the wake of critical incidents
- Willingness and capability to provide collaborative, integrated audits for multiple clients, in order to share the costs of audit and remediation efforts

3.8 Auditing companies and lead auditors for standards certification (eg ISO 14001 or SA 8000) may be specially qualified and accredited by appropriate bodies. For example, Social Accountability Accreditation Services (SAAS) is an independent, not-for-profit organisation which accredits auditing companies for the SA8000 standard, as well as the Business Social Compliance Initiative and other, more specific, social standards bodies

3.9 Appropriate agencies may also offer registers, directories and referral services for audit providers. For example, the Institute of Environmental Management and Assessment (IEMA) operates an internationally recognised Environmental Auditors Register and referral service. The database can be searched to find appropriately qualified auditors to undertake specific environmental auditing and EMS-related projects.

3.10 It is also worth noting that audit services themselves require monitoring and evaluation by the buyer – especially during the first year of a new auditor's contract, or during the audit of a particular unit or supplier that is unique, complex, strategic or high-risk. There should also be review meetings after the completion of audits, to discuss draft reports and corrective action plans.

Duplication of codes and audits

3.11 The proliferation of standards and monitoring systems, particularly at the corporate level, has resulted in multiple audits of some suppliers, which – as we have already mentioned – can be time consuming, costly, inefficient and confusing. There have therefore been a number of initiatives to promote collaboration and the sharing of audit data.

- The Supplier Data Exchange (Sedex) is a not-for-profit association that enables suppliers to share ethical information and audit data about their production sites with customers.
- Achilles Global is a commercial organisation which collates and validates supplier information for purchasing organisations. It offers a range of supplier identification, qualification, evaluation and monitoring services, specifically covering sustainability requirements – and enabling the sharing of supplier data with buyers in a given sector. Together with major buyers, it has also developed the Achilles Carbon Reduction Programme CEMARS (Certified Emissions Management and Reduction Scheme) for suppliers to measure, manage and report carbon footprint.
- E-TASC (Electronics: Tool for Accountable Supply Chains) is an example of an industry-specific initiative: a web-based system for ICT companies to conduct basic risk assessment of prospective suppliers, supported by more in-depth self-assessment by suppliers using a web-based questionnaire (on ethics, labour rights and health and safety, as well as environmental management).
- The Global Social Compliance Programme (GSCP) is an initiative set up to allow consensus-building on best practice in labour standards and environmental protection in supply chains. This is designed to provide a single, clear, consistent standard for suppliers – and to allow contract management processes to focus on identifying and correcting root causes of non-compliance. GSCP does not undertake accreditation or certification activities: it is designed to provide a reference framework – rather than another duplicate monitoring initiative.
- The British Social Compliance Initiative (an initiative of the Foreign Trade Association) has developed a Code of Conduct based on ILO conventions and the UN Global Compact. Supplier performance is audited by independent SAAS-accredited audit companies, and the BSCI database contains information about audit results which are shared exclusively between members. 'The database avoids multiple auditing of the same suppliers and helps to track non-compliances found in audits, while indicating where capacity-building for suppliers is needed'.

3.12 Since suppliers with prior experience of international marketing may already have been audited by previous or existing customers, the first step may be for buyers to seek access to recent audit results (eg through Sedex).

4   Maintaining accountability

Accountability for achieving social, ethical and environmental standards

4.1 Accountability is a 'macro' issue in the sense that, in order to support sustainable development and procurement, buying organisations must be accountable for the impact of their actions, both directly in terms of what they do (eg ethical and responsible procurement) and indirectly in terms of what happens in the supply chain on their behalf.

4.2 Accountability is also an organisational issue. If sustainable procurement is to gain traction in an organisation culture and practice, it is critically important to make procurement functions, and individual buyers, accountable for delivering social, ethical and environmental performance, alongside other business needs and objectives.

4.3 The Responsible Purchasing Initiative (*Taking the Lead)* emphasises that: 'Without accountability, confusion and ineffective implementation is likely. Single accountability makes it clear that buyers are responsible for leading the implementation of more responsible practices, and for reconciling these with other sourcing priorities... Buyers are responsible for working with suppliers to achieve agreed standards, in a manner which is corporately agreed and supports the achievement of expected standards.'

4.4 The organisation's sustainability policy or related deployment guidelines should clearly allocate responsibilities (and accountabilities) for implementation – and for the ongoing management of the policy. Depending on the size and structure of the organisation, and how sustainability is 'set up' within it, specific areas of responsibility may be allocated to:

- A corporate-level sustainability leader, steering committee or team, with responsibility for the authorisation, review and co-ordination of functional sustainability policies, and for resource allocation and consultancy to sustainability initiatives and projects. The RPI *(Taking the Lead)* argues that a key success factor for sustainability is for senior managers to take ownership of responsible purchasing, since they have the cross-functional authority to reconcile differing organisational priorities and co-ordinate sourcing efforts in pursuit of over-arching sustainability goals.
- A senior sustainability 'champion' within the procurement function, with responsibility for developing and co-ordinating sustainability-related activity within the function; representing the function on sustainability issues (eg on sustainability committees or project teams); and acting as a hub for communication and reporting on sustainability issues. This role may include responsibility for supplier management, staff training, document development, performance monitoring and so on – or these responsibilities may be delegated to other individuals within the procurement team.
- The Chief Procurement Officer, Purchasing Manager or other head of the function, with responsibility to support the sustainability policy in various ways: allocating resources, authorising training, steering changes to systems and procedures, sponsoring implementation projects, and integrating sustainability measures into job specifications, recruitment, team objectives, performance management and reward – and so on.
- Members of the procurement team, who may be appointed as sustainability representatives, supervisors, consultants or stakeholder managers, as the policy is cascaded down to procurement departments, part-time buyers in user departments, cross-functional project teams and supply networks. These roles may be generalist, or specialised on the basis of sustainability issues (eg ethics, diversity, climate change or waste reduction), categories of spend or vendor groups.

4.5 Meanwhile, all members of the procurement team have the general responsibility of implementing and adhering to the sustainability policy in all areas of procurement activity: incorporating principles and practices into specifications, terms of trade, supplier contracts, contract reviews, supplier selection and appraisal criteria, supplier development programmes and so on.

4.6 The important thing is to ensure that there is clear allocation of responsibility of all key activities and issues to appropriate stakeholders and individuals, with no overlaps or gaps; matched to the capability and authority of the individuals or teams concerned; and without creating a separate 'layer' of responsibility or accountability which might frustrate or distract people. Clear accountability and leadership also helps to support integrity (alignment of words and actions) and trust.

Sustainability reporting

4.7 This area is not really mentioned in the syllabus, although it could be argued that it is connected to the process of performance measurement and management. However, it is an important area, so we will briefly touch on some key points here – just in case.

4.8 There are a number of reasons for advocating transparency in sustainability reporting.

- Blackburn *(The Sustainability Handbook)* argues that 'shining a light on performance can produce the heat of accountability, which heightens the likelihood of constructive change'. Sustainability reports spur change because they invite scrutiny, and reaction to performance, from stakeholders.
- Sustainability reports highlight issues, drivers and gaps in performance, creating an impetus for

improvement planning and risk management – and enabling the resolution of problems before they escalate.

- The process of preparing reports encourages stakeholder communication on sustainability issues, and educates employees on the issues.
- Examples of good practice may emerge, for use as benchmarks, or as the focus of recognition and reward – reinforcing and motivating improvement.
- Transparency builds stakeholder trust and an organisational reputation for honesty, which may be beneficial in gaining support, resources, reputational capital, goodwill and resilience in the face of PR crises.

4.9 Sustainability reporting may also be a compliance issue. Financial reporting has been a statutory requirement for many years. In the UK, law implementing the EU Accounts Modernisation Directive (AMD) now requires large companies to include a Business Review in their annual reports, including information about the effectiveness of the organisation's sustainability policies, and, where appropriate, an analysis of KPIs related to employee, supplier and environmental matters and social and community issues. Some countries also have detailed pollutant-disclosure laws (eg toxic release inventory reporting in the US), 'right to know' laws, or national registers of environmental emissions.

4.10 There have also been a number of voluntary sustainability reporting initiatives. The EMAS standard (discussed in Chapter 3), for example, requires participating companies to produce a public, externally verified environmental statement, covering environmental policies, programmes, management systems, goals, performance results, and significant environmental impacts and their effects. Another major voluntary framework is the Global Reporting Initiative or GRI, discussed further below.

4.11 An important point to note is the emphasis on **transparency** – not just 'reporting'. In a 2003 survey of NGOs, reported by Blackburn, less than half of the respondents considered corporate sustainability reports 'believable'. The most effective way to improve credibility was said to be to acknowledge non-compliance, poor performance and significant problems – not just to state policies or boast achievements.

Barriers to sustainability reporting

4.12 Blackburn suggests reasons why many companies do not implement transparent sustainability reporting – and what can be done to overcome the barriers: Table 9.2. This framework might be used within the buying organisation – or to encourage supply chain partners to become more transparent in their reporting.

Table 9.2 *Supporting transparent sustainability reporting*

BARRIERS TO REPORTING	WAYS OF OVERCOMING BARRIERS
Embarrassment about performance	Begin with transparency in internal reports
No competitive advantage, if competitors aren't reporting	Draw attention to broad multi-stakeholder support for transparency programmes
Protection of confidentiality	Sell the business case for transparency
Concern about legal liability	Emphasise communicable wins
Concern about negative PR, stakeholder or media responses	Demonstrate resilience of transparent firms: eg Shell, Nike, Johnson & Johnson
Failure to recognise, understand or give priority to the issue	Educate internal stakeholders and demonstrate risks of non-transparency
Belief that cost and effort would be excessive	Reduce costs: start small (scope, frequency), use readily available data and resources, audit internally, combine with other audits or use NGO volunteers

The Global Reporting Initiative

4.13 The GRI was started in 1997 by the Coalition for Environmentally Responsible Economies (CERES) and UNEP, with the aim of promoting reporting on economic, environmental and social performance by all organisations. The Sustainability Reporting Guidelines are applicable across sectors and industries, with sector supplements for specific industries and reporting entities.

4.14 Reporting entities are asked to provide information on strategy, organisational profile, governance, stakeholder engagement, and commitments and management approach on sustainability matters. In addition, specific KPIs are listed across the triple bottom line dimensions, and reporters are required to use those indicators that are material to their stakeholders and decision-making. Blackburn argues that 'although the use of GRI is no substitute for actual dialogue between a company and its own stakeholders, it does offer a perspective even broader than dialogue can produce, helping report writers anticipate issues their own customers, investors and employees may raise in the future.'

4.15 Some 460 organisations are listed as using the guidelines systematically and in full. The number and percentage of companies engaged in GRI reporting – and in sustainability reporting in general – is therefore very small. However, Blackburn identifies a number of drivers in its favour. Some major investment analysts are urging publicly traded companies to prepare GRI reports, for example, to support analysis of underlying risks, liabilities and advantages from corporate activities. Activist shareholders are also pressing for GRI reporting at shareholder meetings.

4.16 As befits a global family of market-leading toy brands – a sector under a high degree of scrutiny, due to child safety issues – Mattel Inc has been a leader in transparent CSR, sustainability and governance reporting.

- In 1997, it developed a set of Global Manufacturing Principles (GMP), focused on ensuring the safe and fair treatment of employees in its own and contractor factories. Compliance is independently monitored.
- In 2003, it issued its first GRI report, to publicly assess the success of the GMP and commit to improvements.
- In 2003, it also rolled out a Code of Ethical Conduct for all employees.
- In 2004, it issued a public Corporate Responsibility Report: the first to be issued by a toy company. Its website includes public statements on ethics, corporate governance, good corporate citizenship, strategic sustainability initiatives and core values.
- In 2007, it created the post of Vice President of Corporate Responsibility, to take charge of developing and implementing worldwide programmes to underscore Mattel's commitment to business integrity, reporting directly to the CEO.

Chapter summary

- Suppliers (and potential suppliers) should be monitored in respect of their sustainability performance by means of both qualitative and quantitative approaches.
- A supplier audit is a systematic review of a supplier's systems, processes and business practices. Auditing may take place as part of supplier selection and also as part of ongoing contract and supplier management.
- An environmental audit is the inspection of a company to assess the environmental impact of its activities, or of a particular product process, as the basis for managerial decision-making.
- In some cases, a buyer may employ an independent third party organisation to conduct supplier audits. Often, such organisations will have been accredited (eg by the UK Accreditation Service).
- Buying organisations are accountable for the environmental impact of their actions. Their sustainability policies should allocate clear responsibilities for implementation. This should be backed up by transparency in sustainability reporting.

 ## Self-test questions

Numbers in brackets refer to the paragraphs where you can check your answers.

1   List possible difficulties in monitoring sustainability performance. (1.2)

2   List possible sources of information on the sustainability performance of suppliers. (1.5)

3   What are the different types of audit that may be relevant to sustainability monitoring? (2.4)

4   What are the purposes of a purchasing management audit? (2.9)

5   What are the benefits of a systematic audit process? (2.23)

6   In what circumstances might a buyer use third party auditing services? (3.2)

7   List the competencies required of third party auditors. (3.7)

8   List reasons why transparency in sustainability reporting is desirable. (4.8)

9   List possible barriers to such transparency. (Table 9.2)

CHAPTER 10

Improving and Developing Compliance

Assessment criteria and indicative content

 4.3 Critically assess how relationships with suppliers should deal with infringements of standards for sustainability

- Raising awareness of standards
- Involving workers in workplace matters
- Creating corrective action plans and supplier development programmes
- Escalating problems and exit arrangements

Section headings

1. Supplier relationship management
2. Corrective action planning
3. Continuous improvement planning
4. Supplier development programmes
5. Problem-solving and exit arrangements

Introduction

In this chapter we complete the sustainable procurement – and compliance management – cycle by exploring a range of approaches and actions to manage non-compliance, or infringement of sustainability standards.

The syllabus sets this discussion in the context of 'relationships with suppliers', so we begin by highlighting the importance of supplier relationship management in sustainability.

We then go on to consider two basic approaches which may be used to deal with non-compliance. The first response to identified infringement of standards, and the typical output of supplier compliance audits, is the preparation of a corrective action plan: putting in place time-bounded, resourced measures to address the causes of the infringement. The second is a broader approach to securing continuous improvement: progressively improving performance in relation to standards, or seeking planned year-on-year improvement over and above minimum standards already attained. In either case, improvements may need to be supported by the buying organisation: the process of supplier development.

Finally, we discuss what happens if agreed corrections and improvements are not achieved. We explore a number of constructive and responsible approaches to managing and escalating problems with non-compliant suppliers – including ethical approaches to terminating (or not renewing) supplier contracts where necessary.

1   Supplier relationship management

1.1   We gave an overview of the need for ongoing contract and relationship management at the end of Chapter 7, emphasising that developing contract terms, KPIs and standards is only the *beginning* of the management of supplier sustainability.

1.2   The benefits of effective contract management in general are as follows.

- Better control by the buyer over the execution of a contract (including performance to sustainability standards)
- Maintaining communication with the supplier during the course of the contract, and helping to achieve better performance of the contract by the supplier
- Promoting improvements in cost, quality and sustainability, thereby adding value
- The ability to anticipate and foresee sustainability problems early, and deal with them before they become serious

1.3   The syllabus places the management of compliance with sustainability standards – and, more particularly, the handling of performance gaps and standard infringements – within the broader context of supplier relationship management. This is a process which maintains continuity of relationship and development with suppliers *beyond* the demands of any individual procurement contract. Supplier compliance management may thus be seen in the context of a particular contract (contract management) – but may also be seen in the context of ongoing commercial relationships over time, across an aggregate of contracts (relationship management).

Prioritising relationship investment

1.4   As we saw in Chapter 8, not all purchase items or categories of spend will be worth investment in long-term relationship development or supplier development for sustainability. For some categories – such as leverage and routine items – the aims of the organisation may best be served by arm's length, transactional or even adversarial buying, aimed at securing best value and transaction efficiency. For bottleneck and strategic items, however, the aims of the organisation will best be served by securing long-term supply and developing collaborative value: in other words, by closer and longer-term supply relationships. (If these ideas don't ring a bell, recap our coverage of the Kraljic matrix in Chapter 8.)

1.5   A buying organisation may seek to develop closer, longer-term and more supportive relationships with:

- Suppliers who offer most potential for best-practice sharing, capacity-building, ongoing development and added value in the area of sustainability (and therefore offer a good return on relationship investment)
- Suppliers who present a potential risk to the organisation in the area of sustainability (which can be managed and minimised by closer relationship)
- Suppliers who require long-term business, support and development in order to make measurable improvements in their social and environmental performance, where this is a core goal of the buying organisation in relation to its supply chain.

The relationship spectrum

1.6   You should be familiar, from your studies in other units, with the fact that supplier relationships may vary widely in the extent of their intensity, mutuality, trust and commitment – in other words, their 'closeness'. This is often expressed as a relationship 'spectrum' extending from one-off arm's length transactions at one end to long-term collaborative partnerships at the other. Andrew Cox's 'stepladder of contractual relationships', for example, describes a spectrum including the following relationships (in order of increasing closeness and mutual dependency).

- *Adversarial leverage:* multi-sourcing and hard-negotiated short-term contracts for routine purchases, where no unique competence is required of suppliers. This may support the economic sustainability of the buyer, by maximising value and cost efficiency, but often comes at a cost to social and environmental sustainability, and the economic sustainability of smaller, vulnerable suppliers.
- *Preferred suppliers:* smaller list of potential suppliers on the basis of vendor rating and accreditation, for more important purchases where some special competence is required of suppliers. This may support sustainability via pre-qualification eg on environmental or labour management standards.
- *Single sourcing:* purchasing strategic supplies from a single quality supplier who can offer distinctive, important competencies. This may support sustainability by enhancing potential for capability-sharing and ongoing development.
- *Network sourcing and partnerships:* partnerships between the main buyer and a first-tier supplier, which develops partnerships with second-tier suppliers, to integrate and control the wider supply chain. This may support sustainability by enhancing potential for ongoing development and collaboration, and by managing sustainability risks throughout the supply chain.
- *Strategic supplier alliances or joint ventures:* formation of a jointly owned separate firm to produce the supplied product or service, where the buyer and supplier's competencies are complementary and of equal importance. This may support sustainability by leveraging both parties' sustainability capability and brand strength.

EXAMPLE: VOLKSWAGEN

'As a part of our supplier training courses, Volkswagen has been working with its business partners since the mid-nineties to optimise environmental protection in supply chains. The dialogue with our suppliers combines several elements: the exchange of environmental data, certificates and reports, seminars, workshops, symposiums and an award for green innovations in products and at plants. In recent years, solutions for new sustainability issues have been developed in collaboration with our partners. Environmental aspects like material recommendations and bans are incorporated in product-related specifications for components and modules, as quality standards for all parts. In addition, there are VW-specific and industry-specific environmental norms.

'Together with our partners, Volkswagen is taking another step towards sustainability with the introduction of global environmental and social standards. Using the concept "Sustainability in Supplier Relations", the group has set the aim of moving forward the process of the partnership development for production and plant-related environmental and social standards: an environmentally aware and socially engaged supplier is also an economically good and reliable partner. Methods for early recognition, and requirements for environmental and social standards, as well as intensive communication with suppliers, are important elements of this sustainability concept. In the future, a team effort in regard to sustainability is expected from everyone, without exceptions, along the whole supply chain.

'The production processes and working conditions at suppliers of Volkswagen should be oriented at global minimum standards. The standards which are used by Volkswagen itself also represent the measure for our suppliers.

'Volkswagen orients its requirements to first-tier suppliers with whom we have direct contractual relationships. Efficient sustainability management for a carmaker like Volkswagen demands that the requirements of the OEM (Original Equipment Manufacturer) are passed along the whole chain.'

1.7 The most appropriate relationship type for a given purchasing situation may therefore depend on factors such as the following.

- The nature, importance, risk and sustainability issues of the items purchased
- The competence, capability, co-operation and performance of the supplier
- Geographical distance: close trust-based relationships may be more difficult to establish and maintain with overseas suppliers
- The compatibility of the supply partners (eg in relation to sustainability values)

- Supply market conditions. If supply is subject to risk, the buyer may wish to multi-source; if prices are fluctuating, it may wish to use opportunistic spot-buying – or to lock in advantageous prices through fixed contracts. If the market is fast-changing and innovative, it may avoid being locked into long-term supply agreements. If there are few quality, capable, high profile, sustainable suppliers, it may wish to enter partnership with them – and so on.

1.8 The advantages and disadvantages of collaborative or partnership relationships for sustainable procurement are summarised in Table 10.1.

Table 10.1 *Advantages and disadvantages of partnering for sustainable procurement*

ADVANTAGES	DISADVANTAGES
Greater stability of supply and supply prices	Risk of supplier complacency over time
Greater buyer influence to drive sustainability improvements	Less flexibility to change suppliers at need
Better supplier motivation and responsiveness, arising from mutual commitment and reciprocity	May be locked into relationship with an incompatible, inflexible, under-performing or compliance-vulnerable supplier
Access to supplier's technology and expertise for sustainability	Costs of relationship management and supplier development
Information sharing, supporting capacity planning (which supports labour standards)	Loss of cost gains from opportunistic buying
Ability to plan and collaborate on long-term and continuous improvements	Reputational risk by close association with compliance-vulnerable suppliers
Reflects a non-exploitative, gain-sharing orientation to supply relationships	

1.9 So what is the 'best' or most strategically advantageous type of supply chain relationship for sustainable procurement? Essentially, there is no one answer. It all depends... In the end, an organisation may need to develop a portfolio of relationships, appropriate to each supply situation. An 'adversarial-collaborative' approach, for example, might allow a buyer to work co-operatively with a supplier on ethical and environmental monitoring, product development or continuous improvements – and to negotiate hard in order to secure the best possible share of the resulting value gains. In other words, collaboration 'enlarges the pie' – of which competition seeks to gain a bigger slice.

2 Corrective action planning

Gap analysis

2.1 Gap analysis involves identifying the difference between the current situation and the desired situation: between where we are now and where we would like to be in relation to sustainability objectives.

2.2 Lysons & Farrington argue that for the purposes of planning supplier and supply chain development, gaps should be considered from the supplier side, as well as from the buyer side.

- From the buyer's side, for example, there may be gaps between: suppliers' current environmental or CSR performance and the buyer's policy objectives (or the requirements of benchmark standards); suppliers' current capabilities and systems for innovation – and the buyer's future needs.
- From the supplier's side, there may be gaps between: the information required from buyers (eg re specifications or sustainability targets, or accurate forward volume requirements) and the information supplied; the level of profitability required from a contract (to maintain adequate wages, benefits etc) and the level of profitability allowed by the buyer.
- From either side, there may be gaps between the level of collaboration, gain-sharing or relationship development desired or expected by both parties, and what is actually being delivered.

2.3 Gap analysis involves a systematic process (discussed in Chapters 7 and 9) of: defining the critical success factors in sustainable performance; defining key performance indicators (KPIs) which define desired levels of performance in those factors; measuring current performance on those indicators; and comparing the current and desired measures. The 'difference' between the two is the 'gap' to be closed, ideally by collaborative improvement and development planning.

2.4 Undertaking a gap analysis is a key part of attaining environmental accreditations such as ISO 14001. It enables the organisation to work through a checklist of critical success factors such as: the existence of a clear environmental policy with top management support; adequate resources to implement and maintain an environmental management system; systems in place for compliance monitoring, identification of environmental impacts, identification of learning needs; and so on. Are these elements in place? If not, what needs to be done to put them in place?

2.5 Once gaps have been identified, targets and plans can be put in place to close them – whether in a single project or initiative, or in a series of incremental steps for continuous improvement.

EXAMPLE: EPSON

Imaging company Epson – along with Hewlett Packard (HP), L'Oréal, Volkswagen and Titan – is a contributor to the CSR Europe web portal, which aims to share experiences of responsible supply chain management.

It has also developed strong policies for helping suppliers to meet CSR standards.

'Our position is unique because we purchase a lot from our own Epson facilities in Asia. In Europe, we expect suppliers to meet our standards, not just on the environment, but in areas like social fairness and community involvement. We are also on the look-out for the use of cheap or illegal labour.'

On issues such as the use of chemicals, Epson goes beyond EU law on hazardous substances and bans over 30 more. Suppliers need to comply with this. 'Our scrutiny goes down to the level of a small carton to put a product in. A supplier gives it to us assembled, but we check the glue, paper and ink used to ensure their origins comply with our standards.

The company conducts periodic supply audits and asks for data specifications to ensure suppliers are conforming to requirements. The size of supplier does not affect Epson's expectations, but [the company] admits smaller ones may need more support. 'Sometimes they need our help because they do not have our clout. For example, we work with a small supplier of plastic strapping to tie products together, and we asked about the origins of the printing on the banding. We asked what the ink was made of, and they went to their ink supplier who said the information was confidential. So we went back with the small supplier, and the ink manufacturer was then willing to comply.'

If there are gaps in what suppliers can provide, in many cases Epson works with them, but not always. 'Sometimes we stop working with them if they are not willing to change. We have good stories of people willing to take time out and come back with better ideas.'

Adrienne Margolis, 'A Global Revolution', *Supply Management*, 27 August 2009

Creating corrective action plans

2.6 A corrective action plan (CAP), remediation plan or improvement may arise in various ways.

- As the output of, or response to, an audit process: setting out the specific areas in which improvements or corrections need to be made in order for a supplier or site to be fully compliant with a relevant standard or code of conduct (in response to specific adverse audit findings)
- As the output of gap analysis, risk analysis or other problem identification processes (such as investigation of an alleged infringement of the ETI Base Code): setting out step-by-step actions,

10

resources and timescales for resolving the problem or deficiency

- By incorporation in supply contracts and continuous improvement agreements: setting out agreed improvements to be made within the following contract period.

2.7 According to the ETI, a corrective action plan or remediation plan should contain the following elements.

- A description of each of the identified infringements or performance shortfalls being addressed
- The nature of the remedial or corrective action to be taken to address the problem
- The timescale for the corrective action to be taken
- The persons responsible for implementing the plan
- How the costs of corrective activities will be shared between the buyer and the supplier (according to existing contracts or specific agreements made between them)
- How the buyer (or third party) will monitor, measure and validate the supplier's compliance with the remediation plan
- Any changes in the buyer's trading practice, or other contributions by the buyer, necessary to support corrective action by the supplier

2.8 The Corrective Action Plan may be prepared collaboratively, as a joint problem-solving exercise. Alternatively, it may be prepared by the buyer, as a statement of improvements required – or by the supplier, as a statement of proposed response to audit findings. In either case, it will need to be shared and discussed with all relevant decision-makers and stakeholders, to reach joint agreement on the way forward. Consultation may include purchasers, the owners and managers of the supplier, the suppliers' site managers – and also workers' representatives.

2.9 The RPI *(Win-win)* argues that: 'Since it is workers' rights which are usually assessed through audits, sharing audit data with workers' organisations supports their capacity to negotiate fair conditions, which is the sustainable long-term solution. Workers can comment on the veracity of the audit, suggest improvements and highlight the highest-priority changes. Workers are the best monitors of whether changes have occurred at their workplace.'

2.10 The report goes on to argue that: 'Commercial audit companies may offer to monitor the implementation of the "corrective actions". However, the buyer's direct involvement in discussions with suppliers and worker representatives emphasises the purchasing organisation's desire for improvements to be made. For example, they could update the contract to make a commitment to the supplier for a fixed term, on the condition that improvements are satisfactorily implemented.'

2.11 The buyer (or third party) will monitor the progress of corrective action. Once the infringement has been remedied, or improvement target reached, a report should be issued stating that the CAP has been completed: again, stakeholders should be involved in validating that this is the case, from their point of view. Once an instance of non-compliance has been remedied, the issue should be kept under review by the company in its annual auditing programme.

EXAMPLE: AVON COSMETICS

'Auditing suppliers is a key element of managing the supply chain and working towards adherence to our standards. Avon collaborates with external compliance and auditing firms hired to provide expertise to the supplier auditing process, including communication with suppliers and the scheduling of audits and re-audits.

'If an audit reveals an instance of noncompliance, Avon works with the supplier to develop a corrective action plan, with key action points and deadlines.

'Suppliers are responsible for reviewing their corrective action reports and managing the improvement process under the guidance of Avon. In the event of noncompliance, re-audits are required to verify that corrective actions have been implemented accordingly. Avon prefers remediation rather than termination, which delivers improved conditions that offer a 'longer-term benefit to the supplier and the community. Avon will, however, discontinue a relationship with any supplier who fails to address critical issues, such as child labour, or fails to make the necessary corrections requested within a specified, reasonable time period.'

3 Continuous improvement planning

3.1 We have emphasised that sustainable procurement – like quality management and other process improvement techniques – ideally goes beyond mere auditing or compliance checking and corrective action planning to secure compliance with standards.

- In areas such as social sustainability, a compliance-based 'pass-fail' approach may only perpetuate the problem, if buying organisations withdraw from supply relationships and effectively 'abandon' workers to their fate.
- Compliance auditing may disguise underlying problems, such as suppliers' lack of awareness of standards requirements; lack of appreciation of the benefits and rewards of sustainable performance; or lack of resources for change and improvement.
- Compliance auditing may actively discourage transparency: concealing problems and issues (in order to appear 'compliant') rather than bringing them into the open where they can be dealt with.

3.2 Ideally, therefore, sustainable procurement involves:

- The application of progressive, improvement-based standards (or general agreement to pursue year-on-year improvements to current performance levels)
- The ongoing and continual examination and improvement of existing processes: 'getting it more right, next time'
- The willingness of both supplier and buyer to collaborate in improvement-seeking
- The active support and investment of the buyer in supplier education, development (capability building) and improvement – based on the business case for managing reputational risk.

3.3 The process of continuous improvement planning is sometimes referred to by its Japanese name of *kaizen*: 'a Japanese concept of quality management based on continual evolutionary change with considerable responsibility given to employees within certain fixed boundaries' (Laurie Mullins: *Management and Organisational Behaviour*). *Kaizen* looks for uninterrupted, ongoing incremental change: there is always room for improvement.

3.4 Planning for continuous improvement is one way of ensuring that there is continuing commitment to sustainable procurement principles, and progress towards consistent standards compliance. There are various ways in which this can be done in practice.

- Periodically benchmarking organisational, supplier or supply chain performance against peer organisations, industry or sector leaders, key competitors, national or international standards or (in the public sector) the flexible framework – as a way of identifying potential for improvement
- Best-practice sharing (eg through professional knowledge networks, supplier networks or trade and industry conferences) – as a way of identifying potential for improvement
- Gathering feedback from key stakeholders (including internal and external customers and suppliers, and NGO partners and consultants), highlighting risks and areas for improvement
- Implementing rolling performance reviews, objectives and targets, so that the 'bar' is continually set higher as each milestone is reached
- Negotiating continuous improvement agreements as part of supplier contracts – with incentives built in for progressive sustainability innovations and improvements. Incentives and rewards for improved performance may take the form of: price premiums or bonuses, higher volume orders, contract extensions or additional opportunities to tender for contracts through approved supplier status.
- Setting up staff and supplier suggestion schemes, with rewards for implemented suggestions for improvement (including small ones – to reinforce the perception that incremental change is valued)

10

- Making progress indicators and reports, and year on year improvements, highly visible (eg on the corporate website), to maintain accountability and motivation.

3.5 Long-term collaborative supplier relations may contribute to continuous improvement by virtue of increased mutual commitment, familiarity with each other's capabilities and requirements, and year-on-year learning and adaptation. However, it also lends itself to a more intentional, contracted commitment to continuous improvement targets. Contractual commitment may, in fact, be necessary in a long-term relationship, because of the potential for complacency.

Raising awareness of standards

3.6 One of the key elements in any sustainability improvement initiative is likely to be the raising of supplier awareness of standards. Buyers may need to take steps such as the following.

- To provide suppliers with guidance on good practice and/or national and international standards requirements
- To help suppliers to keep up to date with relevant economic, social and environmental legislation and industry standards
- To collaborate with local trade unions and other stakeholder advocacy organisations to inform and educate workers about their rights under relevant legislation and standards

3.7 A number of organisations publish awareness-raising tools and resources for workers and small producers, to inform them of international standards, good practice and worker rights. Here are some examples.

- The ETI's Sri Lanka Workers' Leaflet. 'Most workers in global garment factories aren't used to being asked what their issues and priorities are at work, and are unaware that many of the people who buy the clothes they make actually care about how they are treated at work. A group of ETI members organised training for over 5,000 Sri Lankan garment workers and the distribution of over 17,000 worker awareness-raising brochures. Workers were trained about their rights as workers and what to expect from workplace audits. Workers learned about ethical trade and gained confidence in speaking up about their issues.
- The ILO Better Factories Cambodia 'At the Factory Gates' booklets for Cambodian export garment factory workers
- The ETI's booklet 'Working for a Better Life: What smallholders need to know'.

Involving workers in workplace matters

3.8 We have already discussed (in Chapter 6) the importance of encouraging and supporting workers' rights to organisation and representation at supplier work sites. The RPI *(Win-Win)* emphasises that: 'Ultimately, the sustainability of supply chain code implementation rests with workers and suppliers.'

3.9 The presence of trade unions or independent workers' organisations on site can help to inform and educate workers about their rights, and to provide formal avenues for workers to discuss their priorities and grievances with management on an ongoing basis. This is generally regarded as a more cost-effective and sustainable approach to improving labour standards than a purely compliance-based approach, for the following reasons.

- It provides structures and processes for continuous problem-solving and improvement, based on workers' real needs and concerns, rather than periodic identification and rectification of generic infringements
- Workers are best placed to monitor standards compliance and the attainment of improvements in their workplace, and to suggest ways in which community benefits might be obtained
- The empowerment of workers by improving awareness of rights, and providing opportunities for dialogue and negotiation with management, potentially has a wider effect on labour conditions, beyond any single work site or employer.

3.10   The buying organisation may, for example, include in its improvement agreement provisions for the establishment of a workers' committee at a supplier factory or work site. Such a committee would be empowered for collective bargaining and consultation, and would also meet regularly with management to raise concerns and share ideas for performance improvements.

3.11   Similar arrangements may be made to empower smallholders in dealing with buyers, eg through the formation of co-operatives. Traidcraft *(CSR: Does it Make a Difference?)* argues that: 'Fair Trade ensures that workers or smallholders are able to influence how income from the sale of the Fair Trade product is spent, and this crucially empowers those producing products... Many companies do not recognise that an essential and sustainable way social rights can be realised will be if workers or smallholders are organised and have a credible mechanism of discussing their issues with managers or buyers, respectively.'

Multi-stakeholder collaboration

3.12   Collaboration with other stakeholders in sustainability performance (including NGOs, industry bodies, other buyers and suppliers) can be useful in continuous improvement initiatives, for:

- Reinforcing the buyer's influence or commercial leverage to drive sustainability improvement (eg by independent endorsement of standards, or consortium buying influence)
- Harnessing the expertise of organisations which are dedicated to understanding local issues and constraints in a particular industry or country, and have experience and network contacts for working with local stakeholders to bring about improvements
- Harnessing expertise and influence to seek collective, integrated solutions to compliance problems, at an industry or national level: eg tackling public policy obstacles and mobilising public support for better enforcement of regulations
- Resourcing supplier development, through the production of good practice guidance and the provision of advocacy, consultancy and training services.

Maintaining commitment to sustainable procurement principles

3.13   Maintaining long-term commitment to sustainable procurement principles will be difficult at the best of times. The aim is, after all, to ensure that sustainability eventually becomes part and parcel of 'business as usual', being thoroughly integrated into procurement and supply procedures and practices. However, this also means that it is no longer new, exciting or 'front of awareness' for participants and other stakeholders. Critical incidents recede into the past, issues 'go off the boil', risks fail to materialise, public and NGO attention moves elsewhere...

3.14   In the current economic climate, there is the further issue that, while social and environmental sustainability are widely recognised as necessary or desirable, they may cease to be the top priority in the face of recessionary pressure. Strategic priorities may switch to corporate survival, shorter time-frames for return on investment, the need for cost reductions and so on.

3.15   The following are some strategies for maintaining momentum and commitment to sustainable procurement principles.

- Keeping sustainability at 'front of awareness' through ongoing communication (eg via newsletters, bulletins, progress updates, agenda items for supplier reviews and staff meetings)
- Maintaining top-level championship, demonstrating the continuing importance of the issues and the seriousness with which they are regarded (eg in executive speeches, annual reports)
- Implementing rolling reviews and improvement targets, tied to accountabilities, so that participants cannot become complacent about performance
- Implementing periodic learning needs analysis, refresher training and so on, to continually upgrade skills and awareness
- Maintaining risk and environmental reporting, so that key issues and drivers are continually refreshed

10

- Setting targets for quick wins, to create the momentum of success and reported impacts and benefits
- Creating opportunities for symbolic action to re-energise the vision (eg staff involvement with charity fund-raisers, participation in 'Earth Hour')
- Offering incentives for improvements and initiative (eg supplier awards, employee suggestion schemes, performance-related rewards)
- Tying continuing improvement to staff and supplier performance appraisals
- Maintaining accountabilities, penalties and sanctions for non-compliance
- Continually documenting, disseminating and acknowledging sustainability results, impacts and benefits, to reinforce the sense of achievement, contribution, 'feel good factor' – and business case.

EXAMPLE: WAL-MART

'Self-reinforcing spirals [momentum for sustainability] are created when new business imperatives move through supply chains. There is no bigger example of this today than what's been happening at Wal-Mart, the world's largest retailer, which announced a new goal in 2008: to work with suppliers to make many of the products it sells 25% more energy-efficient within three years. Noah Horowitz, a senior scientist at the Natural Resources Defence Council, says: "When Wal-Mart asks, suppliers jump... There are positive ripple effects throughout the supply chain." As suppliers work to improve their products, a snowball effect occurs, and innovations will spread to other products, industries and customers.' (Senge, The Necessary Revolution)

Wal-Mart's CEO Lee Scott has openly admitted that the company's early conservation efforts were part of a campaign to clean up its sullied image – but it now has an integrated sustainability strategy.

'At Wal-Mart, we see sustainability as one of the most important opportunities for both the future of our business and the future of our world. Our opportunity is to become a better company by looking at every facet of our business – from the products we offer to the energy we use – through the lens of sustainability.'

Wal-Mart is introducing Fair Trade banana and coffee products; implementing sustainable seafood procurement, in partnership with conservation organisations; and developing 'high efficiency' pilot stores (sustainable building practices, energy-efficiency, use of geo-thermal energy etc).

Meanwhile, it has traditionally had a poor reputation for social sustainability, particularly in using its size and buying power to squeeze out small, local and specialist retailers. It has striven to counteract this perception, by emphasising 'economic opportunity' benefits:

'Wal-Mart's overall impact on the retail industry and beyond has changed the way business is conducted globally, and increased consumer benefits – regardless of where they shop. From raising tax revenues and lowering overall pricing on goods, to boosting customer traffic at surrounding stores and creating new jobs, Wal-Mart takes every opportunity to be a good neighbour and to provide economic advancements in communities it serves throughout the world.'

Benefits of a continuous improvement approach

3.16 The benefits of continuous improvement for the buying organisation should be obvious.

- It prevents supplier (and buyer) complacency, maintains competitiveness and ensures that year-on-year value gains can be demonstrated.
- Sustainable procurement and production may require substantial changes, so it will be a prudent (and sustainable) approach to set realistic incremental progress targets over time: avoiding unrealistic (unsustainable) demands on suppliers, and corporate 'indigestion' as a result of unconsolidated change.
- Continuous improvement enables emerging sustainability issues and priorities to be taken into account, because it sets up a framework for the re-negotiation of priorities and targets.
- Continuous improvements may be aimed at specific areas such as process efficiencies, standards accreditation, defect reduction or customer satisfaction, which would bring their own reputational, operational and commercial benefits.

3.17 For the supply chain, the benefits of continuous improvement may be as follows.

- Incentives for the development of sustainability performance, which may in turn improve suppliers' competitiveness and access to other contracts
- Co-investment by the buyer in supplier and supply chain development (which will be discussed in the next section of this chapter): resources, information and support for process or performance improvements
- Financial incentives, built into the contract, for attaining continuous improvement targets
- Opportunity for innovation: implementing or devising new solutions that may be commercially exploited with other customers, or may enhance the supplier's reputation
- Opportunity for accreditation (eg on quality, social or environmental management standards), enhancing suppliers' value, standing and opportunities.

4 Supplier development programmes

Supplier development

4.1 Supplier development may be defined as: 'Any activity that a buyer undertakes to improve a supplier's performance and/or capabilities to meet the buyer's short-term or long-term supply needs' (Handfield & Nichols)

4.2 JL Hartley & TY Choi identify two overall objectives for organisations engaging in supply development programmes.

- Raising supplier competence to a specified level (eg in terms of improved environmental or social performance). *Results-oriented* development programmes therefore focus on solving specific performance or sustainability issues: the buyer supports the supplier in making step-by-step technical changes, to achieve pre-determined improvements.
- Supporting suppliers in self-sustaining required performance standards, through a process of continuous improvement. *Process-oriented* development programmes therefore focus on increasing the supplier's ability to make their own process and performance improvements, without ongoing direct intervention by the buyer: the buyer supports the supplier in learning and using problem-solving and change management techniques. The process of continuous improvement (discussed earlier) is an important aspect of this kind of supplier development.

Structuring supplier development

4.3 Supplier development programmes will often involve cross-functional representatives from both buyer and supplier organisations, perhaps working in a project team or sustainability task force. In addition, there will probably be multiple contact points in both organisations, for ongoing monitoring and management. Another common practice is the temporary transfer of staff: supplier staff may be seconded to the buyer organisation to learn, or buyer staff may be seconded to the supplier to advise or train, say.

A supplier development programme

4.4 It will be an ongoing challenge for the buying organisation to educate, motivate and develop suppliers to buy into, comply with – and contribute proactively to – sustainability objectives. The challenge may be particularly acute in regard to particular suppliers.

- Small suppliers, who may lack the resources, capabilities and skills to implement sustainability standards, and may be unfairly discriminated against in access to contracts if sustainability criteria are too stringent
- Suppliers in developing countries, who may again lack the resources to implement sustainability standards, and may also lack supporting standards and legislative regimes, and awareness of international standards

10

- Powerful suppliers (eg large in size relative to the buying organisation, or suppliers on whom the organisation is dependent for supply of strategic items), who may lack incentives to achieve above-statutory levels of sustainability performance

4.5 The essential points in managing the challenge of raising supplier capability for and commitment to sustainability can be summarised as follows.

- The need to prioritise purchased items and suppliers for development, on the basis of sustainability-related and supply risks
- The need for a systematic approach to capability and performance appraisal and gap analysis, in order to focus management attention and resources on leverage areas (which should be matched to identified sustainable procurement issues, risks and priorities such as the reduction of energy consumption or GHG emissions, or the development of compliant labour management standards)
- The need for a jointly agreed development plan to 'close' identified gaps, which may involve a variety of collaborative measures (each of which should be subjected to cost/benefit analysis prior to commitment). Particular challenges may have to be met by different suppliers at different times. In the face of recession and credit restrictions, for example, development measures may focus on supplier resources and cashflow: supportive staged-payment terms, co-investment, the lending of plant and equipment, or help with low-cost procurement, say. For public sector suppliers, development plans may be driven by the need for Flexible Framework improvements.
- The need to build continuous improvement targets into supply contracts and partnership agreements where possible, in order to incorporate further and emerging sustainable issues and priorities progressively over the duration of the relationship.

4.6 A nine-stage approach to implementing a supplier development programme is suggested by Lysons & Farrington (*Purchasing and Supply Chain Management*): Figure 10.1.

Figure 10.1 *The stages in a supplier development programme*

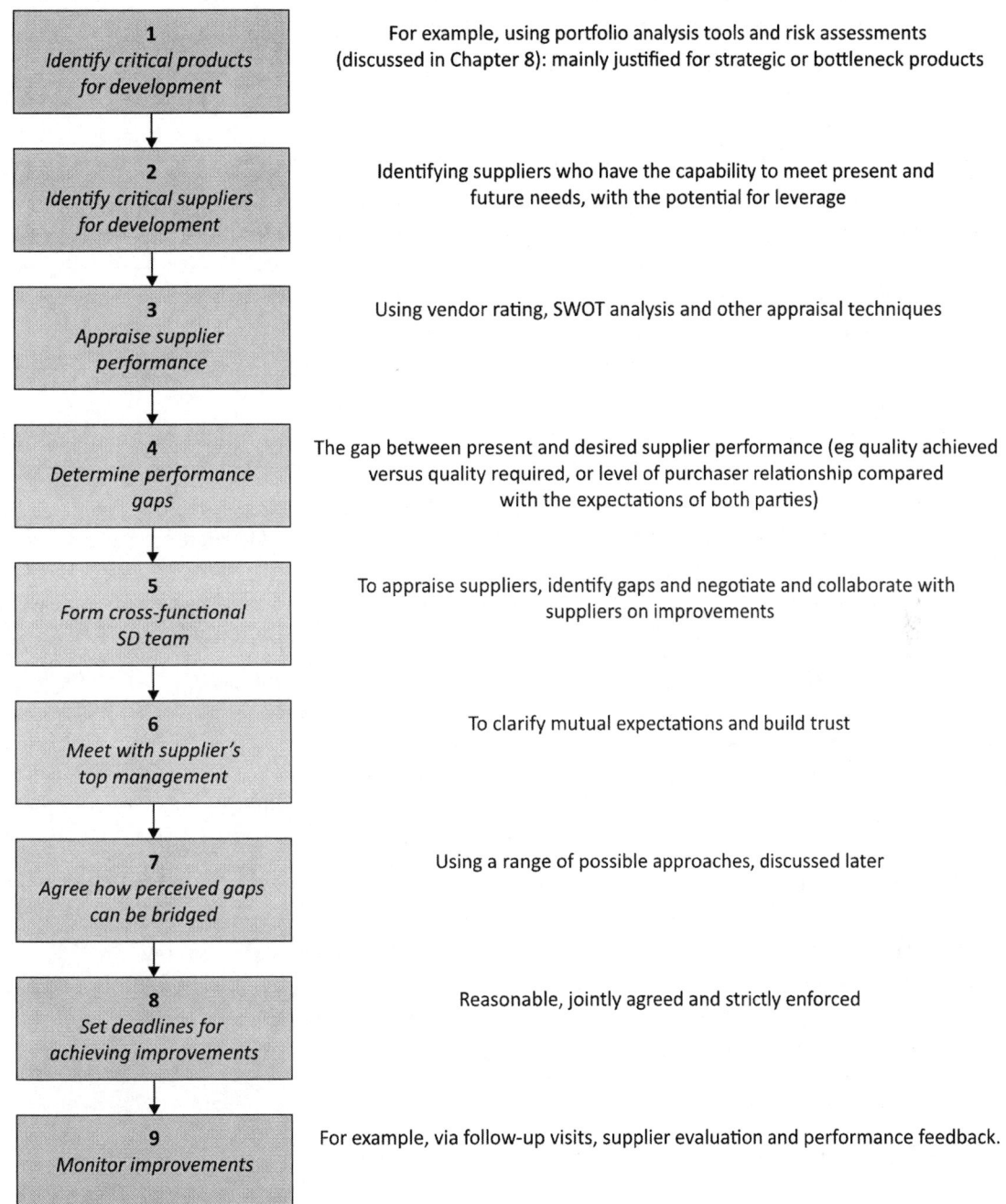

Approaches to supplier development

4.7 A wide variety of approaches may be used to support and develop suppliers in improving sustainability performance and standards compliance. Here are some examples.

- Enhancing working relationships (eg by improved communication systems) and changing procurement practices which contribute to supplier sustainability issues
- Clarifying or increasing performance goals and measures (eg KPIs for improvements in waste reduction or workforce welfare), and associated incentives and penalties to motivate improvements
- Seconding purchaser's staff to the supplier (or *vice versa*) for training, coaching, consultancy, support or liaison
- Using price premiums or direct co-investment to contribute to the costs of suppliers pursuing

10

social and environmental standards certification (in recognition of the value placed on improved performance and reduction of reputational risk)

- Providing capital (eg to help finance a new development project or the acquisition of greener, safer or more efficient plant and equipment)
- Providing progress payments during the development of a project or product, to support the supplier's cashflow
- Loaning machinery, equipment or IT hardware. (CIPS guidance cites some practical examples including: a buyer paying for a supplier's manufacturing processes to be updated, in return for discounted supplies in future; and a buyer giving an outsource supplier the machinery previously used to perform the activity in-house.)
- Granting suppliers access to IT and ICT systems and information (eg extranets and databases, computer aided design capability and so on)
- Offering training for the supplier's staff in relevant areas (eg technical aspects of requirements, best practice in environmental management, or worker rights)
- Empowering suppliers' workers (eg through education in worker rights and encouraging worker representation) and suppliers (eg through cascading of responsible purchasing codes through the supply chain) to support continuous improvement mechanisms
- Providing help or consultancy on value analysis (waste reduction) programmes, environmental procurement or other areas of expertise
- Encouraging the formation of supplier forums, smallholder consortia and other stakeholder networks which bring key suppliers together on a regular basis to share information, expertise and best practice, and to encourage joint problem-solving and improvement planning.

Supplier performance evaluation

4.8   Performance measurement is an important part of supplier development, because both parties will want to:

- Select the right partners to work with: buyers will undertake development activities only with suppliers capable of improvement and leverage
- Measure the 'gap' between current and desired performance and outcomes
- Measure the gains from the cost and effort put in. Both parties will want a 'before and after' picture of performance to reassure themselves that the activities were effective and justified.
- Plan escalation mechanisms and exit strategies, if agreed improvements do not occur despite all efforts to support the supplier.

Costs and benefits of supplier development for sustainability

4.9   Bearing in mind the expense and effort that may be involved in supplier development, buyers will expect to make significant gains from sharing in the specialist knowledge of the supplier and/or improving supplier and supply chain performance to achieve sustainability objectives (and their business benefits). As with other forms of collaborative relationship, however, the aim is for benefits to accrue to both sides: Table 10.2.

Table 10.2 *Costs and benefits of supplier development for sustainability*

BUYER'S PERSPECTIVE	
COSTS	BENEFITS
Cost of management time in researching, identifying and negotiating opportunities	Improved economic sustainability in the supply chain: reduced supply risk
Cost of development activities: risk of over-investment in a relationship which may not last or prove compatible	Improved sustainability performance by suppliers (and supply chains): reduced sustainability, compliance and reputational risk
Costs of ongoing relationship management (where required)	Streamlining systems and processes: reduced waste, process efficiencies, cost reduction
Risks of sharing information, intellectual property	Support for sustainable outsourcing
SUPPLIER'S PERSPECTIVE	
COSTS	BENEFITS
Cost of management time in researching, identifying and negotiating opportunities	Support for eco-efficiencies, leading to greater profitability
Risk of over-investment and over-dependence, if customer is demanding or unprofitable	Improvements in customer satisfaction, leading to retained or increased business
Costs of ongoing relationship management (where required)	Improved capability for sustainability, leading to additional sales to other customers
Risks of sharing information and intellectual property	Direct gains in knowledge and resources provided by the customer
Cost of discounts or exclusivity agreements given as *quid pro quo*	Enhanced learning and flexibility: skills for problem-solving and continuous improvement

Customer education and development

4.10   One of the key implications of sustainable 'end-to-end' supply chain management is the challenge to educate and develop downstream *customers* as well as suppliers. The purchasing profession can contribute to the development of 'sustainability-intelligent customers' by the following means.

- Challenging the unsustainable requirements, requisitions and specifications of internal customers
- Supporting the design, specification and production of innovative sustainable products (since supply is a driver of customer demand, as well as an effect of it)
- Educating customers in the sustainable storage, use and disposal of products (eg via packaging and labelling)
- Involving customers in sustainability and CSR objectives, eg through feedback and suggestion schemes, voluntary 'pledges' (as with the Marks & Spencer Plan A programme), or offering carbon off-setting options (as with purchase of tickets from some airlines).

5   Problem-solving and exit arrangements

Managing problems and disputes

5.1   It may be that despite the best efforts of the buying organisation in communicating sustainability standards and supporting supplier compliance, infringements of standards persist, and target improvements are not made. Steps will have to be taken:

- To confront the non-compliant supplier with evidence of infringement
- To confront the non-compliant supplier with the consequences of continuing failure to improve
- To diagnose (if this has not already been done) the root causes of non-compliance, and collaborate in problem-solving to remove barriers to improvement
- To set a time-table for implementation of corrective action plans or improvement plans, with clear

consequences for failure. Penalties may be applied on an escalating basis (eg with warnings, price penalties and the final threat of withdrawal of business).

5.2 Where handled responsibly, confrontation and escalation of problems can be constructive for supplier development and sustainability (including the sustainability of supply relationships), when its effect is to clarify performance problems, compliance issues and power relationships; focus attention on the need for improvement and problem-solving; avoid the risk of 'groupthink' and complacency by encouraging the testing and challenging of assumptions; highlight the need for better communication; and emphasise accountability for improvement.

5.3 There are many approaches to the management of conflict, and the suitability and sustainability of any given approach must be judged according to its relevance to a particular situation. There is no 'right way'. In some situations, the best outcome may be achieved by compromise; in others, the use of power or influence to impose a sustainable solution may be required; in others, the process of seeking a win-win solution, whatever the eventual outcome, may be helpful – particularly where the parties want to preserve ongoing working relations (a key sustainability issue).

5.4 There may be formal mechanisms for consultation and negotiation with suppliers to resolve problems or disputes around sustainability compliance.

- **Consultation** is a form of 'issues' management, in which potential causes of conflict are discussed, and both parties have an opportunity to give their input, before the problem arises (or as soon as possible, once it has arisen). Less formal consultation and problem-solving may take place in sustainability project teams, supplier conferences and regular contract management communication.
- **Negotiation** is a useful approach to conflict resolution at any level. As an official mechanism, it is often used in supplier relations, to formulate agreements on contract terms, supplier development and continuous improvement plans and so on. Informal negotiation may also be used as a communication and management style, to reach mutually acceptable solutions to problems.

Handling ETI Base Code violations

5.5 The Ethical Trading Initiative has issued guidelines for members on action to be taken where there is an alleged violation of the ETI Base Code at supplier production sites, including: investigation of the alleged violation, and remediation of confirmed violations. Here are some key principles of handling such problems.

- **Transparency:** the parties should be open with each other about all aspects of the allegation, its investigation and remediation
- **Co-operative approach:** the parties should adopt a co-operative approach to working with each other, investigating allegations and achieving code compliance where breaches have occurred
- **Respect for the facts:** an emphasis at all stages on establishing the facts as reliably as possible
- **Direct communication:** facilitating direct communication amongst those affected by the alleged code violation, so that the issues can be resolved as close as possible to their point of origin.
- **Promptness:** investigation and remediation to occur within the shortest period of time appropriate to the nature of the allegation or code breach
- **Finality:** finding out whether or not code breaches have occurred, and if they have, remedying them expeditiously, as far as possible in the circumstances, so that all parties are able to agree that as much as can be done has been done.

Escalating problems

5.6 The Responsible Purchasing Initiative *(Win-win)* emphasises that: 'Where a problem [of infringements of sustainability standards] is not being resolved, an effective escalation process should be used to ensure that threats to the development programme are being communicated, and that accountability for resolution of threats is correctly assigned.'

5.7 Supply contracts and performance agreements will often set out the methods that will be used to settle infringements of standards (and contract terms), and when and how they will be 'escalated' (taken further or to a higher level) if necessary. If suppliers persistently under-perform or fail to meet agreed standards or improvement targets, for example, the supplier development or sustainability team may refer the matter upwards to more senior management.

5.8 There may be mechanisms for escalating penalties to be applied (including, as a last resort, early termination of a contract or relationship), or for formal dispute resolution. In all cases, sustainability will be a key consideration: problems and disputes should be handled as ethically and constructively as possible, leaving the door open to future dealings where improvements are made.

Responsible handling of contractual disputes

5.9 Grievance mechanisms (or dispute mechanisms) are structured processes to address grievances, problems or disputes that arise between two or more parties engaged in contractual or commercial relationships. A range of grievance mechanisms is commonly provided for in contracts, in order to ensure that performance and relationship issues can be dealt with constructively.

5.10 In buyer-supplier relationships, supply contracts will often include clauses setting out the methods that will be used to settle contractual disputes between the parties, and how they will be 'escalated' (taken further or to a higher level) if necessary. As you will be aware from your earlier studies, these usually take the form of mediation and/or arbitration clauses, providing expressly that disputes must be referred to mediation or arbitration prior to litigation. They may also indicate which frameworks will be used for mediation or arbitration.

5.11 A responsible procurement policy would suggest the choice of neutral frameworks, so that overseas suppliers are not unfairly disadvantaged by the location of the proceedings, the language used or the procedures supplied. There are well established frameworks for international dispute arbitration, using the International Chamber of Commerce (ICC) court of arbitration, or the United Nations Commission on International Trade Law (UNCITRAL) arbitration code.

Responsible handling of stakeholder grievances

5.12 Grievance mechanisms may also be used as a tool for establishing open, transparent and equitable communication channels between business and communities, as part of a responsible organisation's approach to sustainable development and community relations.

5.13 They can offer a channel for local communities to voice and resolve concerns related to development projects (such as human rights, labour rights or environmental concerns), and a way for companies to address those concerns. At the same time, such mechanisms and forums support the company in systematically identifying emerging issues and trends which may create risks in international development projects, as the basis for proactive issues management and reputational defence.

5.14 The World Bank argues that: 'Locally-based grievance resolution mechanism(s) provide a promising avenue by offering a reliable structure and set of approaches where local people and the company can find effective solutions together'. Such grievance mechanisms would typically recognise a range of

10

internationally recognised human rights, labour and environmental standards, as the basis for desired outcomes and remedies.

Contract reviews

5.15 At the end of a contract period, or when deciding whether to exercise renewal or extension options, buyers should include sustainability performance as part of the contract review process. Before a contract is renewed or extended, buyers should:

- Review supplier performance against agreed sustainability KPIs and standards
- Assess whether desired sustainability objectives have been met
- Assess whether the supplier still represents best value for sustainability (eg whether there are new, more sustainable products or technologies available, or more innovative suppliers in the market)
- Document any lessons learned from the contract, for use when planning future contracts.

Exit arrangements

5.16 The RPI *(Win-Win)* argues that: 'In extreme cases, where required improvements have not been made, it may be necessary to exit a relationship with a supplier. This should be a last resort, after the purchasing organisation has made significant effort to support the supplier, but the supplier demonstrates no intention or activity to improve. To continue to source from such a supplier indicates to competitors and other suppliers that the purchasing organisation is not serious about working to a required standard.'

5.17 As part of the risk assessment of a contract, it is important to identify where early contract exit or termination may be required, and how this will be managed. This is an issue relevant to ethical contract management – and to economic sustainability, because the buying organisation cannot afford to get 'trapped' in contracts or long-term relationships with under-performing and non-compliant suppliers.

5.18 There should be a clear understanding of the circumstances in which a contract or relationship can be terminated (other than those mandated by contract law, such as breach or frustration of contract), what processes should be followed, and what notice given.

5.19 Ideally, there should also be provision for review, feedback and learning from the 'failure' of the contract – and for keeping the door open to future relations, where possible (with clear parameters for the changes and improvements required).

5.20 In a sustainable procurement context, particular consideration will have to be given to the social and economic impacts of termination of contract on dependent suppliers, and their workforces and communities. CSR policies may address areas such as the following.

- The discouragement of supplier dependency on any one buying organisation
- Phased withdrawal and performance management procedures and options to be explored prior to termination
- Assessment of reputational risk arising to the buying organisation from terminating the relationship with the supplier (eg from resulting loss of jobs)
- Ensuring that any workers laid off by the supplier as a result of termination have been and will be paid what they are owed (before final payments to the supplier are made) – and, where possible, that other safeguards are in place to protect employment and conditions.

Post-contract 'lessons' management

5.21 As we saw earlier, sustainable procurement programmes should contain provision for review and the planning of continuous improvement. There is an important opportunity for this activity in the immediate post-contract period, or post-completion review phase of a procurement project.

5.22 The contract management and/or sustainability team (or a multi-disciplinary review team comprising both) should intentionally review the contract's history and outcomes, and gather feedback from a range of contract and sustainability stakeholders on what went right and what went wrong in the life and performance of the contract; how things could have been done more effectively or efficiently; and what new knowledge or lessons have emerged from the contract and should be carried forward to future contracts and contracting processes.

5.23 A post-completion audit is often used as a formal review of a procurement, outsourcing or sustainability project, in order to assess its impact and ensure that any lessons arising from it are acknowledged and learned. Such an audit may be carried out using a survey questionnaire of all project team members and key stakeholders, or meetings to discuss what went well and what didn't. The focus will be on assessing:

- Whether and how far the project outcomes met the expectations of the sponsor and other stakeholders: were the deliverables up to standard, were sustainability objectives achieved, and were they on time and within budget?
- The effectiveness of the management of the process: the plans and structures set up for the project (eg sustainability improvement task forces); the performance of individuals and teams; what problems (communication lapses, conflicts etc) might affect similar projects in future – and how they can be avoided.
- What ongoing risks, challenges, conflicts, trade-offs and barriers to sustainable procurement emerged during the project, and what solutions, improvements, steps forward or potential future opportunities (if any) could be identified.

Chapter summary

- There is a spectrum of possible supply relationships and buyers should select the appropriate type with each supplier or category of suppliers. Modern thinking emphasises the advantages of collaborative relationships with critical suppliers.
- Corrective action planning begins with gap analysis: identifying the difference between the current situation and the desired situation. From there, buyers and suppliers can work collaboratively to bridge the gap.
- In some cases it is unrealistic to expect suppliers to match the highest sustainability standards right from the beginning. However, with all suppliers the buyer should aim for continuous improvement in this respect.
- Where the importance of the procurement merits the investment, buyers should consider systematic supplier development as a means of achieving sustainability objectives.
- In the last resort, suppliers may fail to meet the sustainability targets set by buyers. In such cases, buyers must have systematic procedures in place for escalating problems and responsibly handling disputes.

Self-test questions

Numbers in brackets refer to the paragraphs where you can check your answers.

1   List benefits of effective contract management. (1.2)

2   What factors are likely to determine the choice of supply relationship with a particular supplier? 1.7)

3   List advantages and disadvantages of partnering for sustainable procurement. (Table 10.1)

4   List the steps in a systematic process of gap analysis. (2.3)

5   List elements of a corrective action plan as identified by the ETI. (2.7)

6   Describe methods of planning for continuous improvement in achieving sustainability objectives. (3.4)

7   Describe strategies for maintaining commitment to sustainable procurement principles. (3.15)

8   List stages in a supplier development programme. (Figure 10.1)

9   List costs and benefits of supplier development for sustainability. (Table 10.2)

10   List principles to be adopted in handling violations of the ETI Base Code. (5.5)

Subject Index